RONALD K. SIEGEL, Ph.D., is an associate research professor at UCLA, and the author of *Intoxication*. He has served as consultant to two presidential commissions and the World Health Organization, and has been called as an expert in many criminal cases, including the Manson family trials and the death of John Belushi. His work has appeared in numerous journals, as well as in *Omni*, *Psychology Today*, and *Scientific American*. He lives in Los Angeles.

RONALD K. SIEGEL

FIRE IN THE BRAIN

CLINICAL TALES
OF HALLUCINATION

A PLUME BOOK

PLUME
Published by the Penguin Group
Penguin Books USA Inc., 375 Hudson Street, New York, New York 10014, U.S.A.
Penguin Books Ltd, 27 Wrights Lane, London W8 5TZ, England
Penguin Books Australia Ltd, Ringwood, Victoria, Australia
Penguin Books Canada Ltd, 10 Alcorn Avenue, Toronto, Ontario, Canada M4V 3B2
Penguin Books (N.Z.) Ltd, 182-190 Wairau Road, Auckland 10, New Zealand

Penguin Books Ltd, Registered Offices: Harmondsworth, Middlesex, England

Published by Plume, an imprint of New American Library, a division of Penguin Books USA Inc.
Previously published in a Dutton edition.

First Plume Printing, March, 1993
10 9 8 7 6 5 4 3 2 1

REGISTERED TRADEMARK—MARCA REGISTRADA

LIBRARY OF CONGRESS CATALOGING-IN-PUBLICATION DATA
Siegel, Ronald K.
    Fire in the brain : clinical tales of hallucination / Ronald K.
Siegel.
        p.   cm.
    ISBN 0-452-26953-9
    1. Hallucinations and illusions.   2. Hallucinations and illusions—
Case studies.   I. Title.
RC553.H3S54   1993
154.4—dc20   92-31497
                                                CIP

Printed in the United States of America
Original hardcover design by Steven N. Stathakis

For Jane, My Dream, My Love

CONTENTS

FIRE IN THE BRAIN

PREFACE

I never saw the sixties while I was a graduate student at Dalhousie University in Halifax. I spent my days inside a laboratory where I conducted experiments with animals. At night I placed a mattress on the lab floor and transformed the room into a private theater for my friends, who took turns as human guinea pigs. My subjects would take a drug such as marijuana or LSD, lie supine on the mattress, then describe the brightly colored hallucinations that appeared to them in the darkened lab.

First came simple geometric forms, flashing and dancing through the air. Despite individual differences, all my subjects reported the *same* basic geometric structures. These simple forms were followed by complex scenes: cartoons, pictures of familiar people and places, and images so fantastic that the subjects wept in awe.

When the hallucinations stopped, I walked the subjects home. The streets were as dark as the lab. But the windows in the houses we passed were often illuminated by the faint bluish glow of television sets. Sometimes, if we heard voices coming from the TV, we played a game of trying to guess the accompanying pictures on the screens. It would have been a simple matter to peek through the windows and see what was playing. But how could I see through the window of my subjects' eyes? How could I see their hallucinations? Their words described the images, but radio is a far cry from television.

I went to the library and wandered through the stacks looking for answers. I found a little red book, about the size of a cassette tape, buried between texts many times larger. The book, *Mescal: The 'Divine' Plant and Its Psychological Effects*, was written in 1928 by Heinrich Klüver, an experimental psychologist at the University of Chicago. Klüver studied the hallucinogenic peyote cactus, or mescal, and found that all mescal visions contained the *same* geometric forms. The forms consisted of tunnels, spirals, cobwebs, and checkerboard designs.

"I found the same geometric forms with marijuana and LSD," I wrote in a letter to Klüver. It was the first in a series of letters and telephone calls that was to extend over many years.

Klüver responded with a long, friendly letter and enclosed several reprints of his other work with hallucinations. He was not surprised to learn that marijuana and LSD produced identical geometric patterns. He suspected that many drugs would do the same thing. The forms might even be found in hallucinations produced by such conditions as paranoia or schizophrenia. Perhaps, he wrote, one would find them in states of fever delirium, hunger, thirst, fatigue, or other forms of trauma. Maybe they're also present in vivid dreams. He suggested that the study of these hallucinatory forms might provide a window to the hinterland of the mind itself. It was a suggestion that would guide my research for years to come.

But now I wanted to know how I could trust what my subjects were telling me. After all, if they were hallucinating—and therefore making errors in perception—how could I trust their descriptions of the hallucinations? Were the reports accurate? Were they complete? What did these tunnels and other structures really look like? And what about the other complex visions, the ones that hushed them or caused them to cry in awe and wonderment? Was there a common structure to these as well? If I could only find a way to put a camera behind their eyes and look out and see what they were seeing.

I wrote Klüver for help. I knew about a turn-of-the-century experiment in which the scientist tried to understand how a fly saw the world by looking through its disembodied eyes. How, I asked, could we see through the eyes of our human subjects.

Klüver's response was abrupt: "Become the fly!"

And so I became a subject in my own experiments. Taking the drugs myself, I was able to see the hallucinatory world first-hand, then design experiments to map and measure it. Later, when I studied hallucinations in the other conditions Klüver listed, I used the same method of self-experimentation as I joined my research patients and subjects on fasts, in grueling tests of physical endurance, inside sensory isolation chambers, or under the influence of any number of psychological and physical traumas.

As I jumped through the window into the world of halluci-nations, I kept one foot firmly grounded in reality with a series of controlled laboratory experiments and studies. The results helped to explain the mysterious and bewildering hallucinations I found in both my patients and myself. The cartography of that hallucinatory world, as revealed through the cases presented in this book, shows that even in our wildest and maddest hallucina-tions, the mental landscape is the same for all of us.

INTRODUCTION

I am waiting for *them* to carry me away. *Them,* of course, are the extraterrestrials, or E.T.'s. Ever since I was a little boy, I had watched the stars and dreamed of possible encounters. Now I was doing something about it: I was spending my Sunday inside a tank, floating to meet them.

The tank was the size and shape of a large coffin, and it was filled with ten inches of water. The water was heated to a soothing ninety-three degrees Fahrenheit and contained enough Epsom salts to keep my body bobbing near the surface. My mouth, nose, and eyes were above the water, and although it was pitch black, I could sense the ceiling of the tank only inches from my face. At first, thoughts of suffocation made me uneasy. But after many hours of floating I relaxed. I passed the time thinking about how I got here.

The day started many hours earlier when I left the UCLA campus, where I had a research laboratory in the Neuropsychiatric Institute, and drove north to a ranch in the remote hills of Malibu. The ranch belonged to Dr. John C. Lilly, the controversial scientist best known for his work with dolphins. One of Lilly's most publicized hobbies was using this sensory deprivation tank to see E.T.'s. Lilly insisted that while in the tank, he had communicated with beings from deep space who were sending messages directly into his brain. According to Lilly, I had only to float in the tank for a few hours—a boost from the hallucinogen ketamine might help—and I could tune in to this extraterrestrial network and hear the messages for myself.

So here I was in the tank. Warm and calm, I finally felt I was starting to separate from my body—I even sensed my "mind" hovering slightly above my physical self. It was in this disembodied state that Lilly had instructed me to await the E.T.'s. Indeed, nakedness was not enough. I had to shed my corporal form, freeing my mind from all bodily sensations, in order to receive the visitors. It might take most of a day, Lilly informed me. But what's a day, even a wet one, when you have wished for a close encounter all your life?

Inside the tank, small, odd-shaped objects with luminous borders started to fly in front of my eyes. Geometric forms, like skyscrapers sculpted from lights, filled my visual space with a futuristic architecture. A tunnel emitting a pulsating blue light appeared straight ahead. The camera of my mind's eye zoomed in and emerged on the next stage, a mental landscape where my thoughts and memories were displayed like a slide show.

I brushed aside images of the scenic drive to Malibu along the Pacific Coast Highway and flashes of people I had met at the ranch. I was waiting for something more . . . alien.

Then, a surge of power, like afterburners igniting on my tank, boosted me into a sea of nothingness. This was the stage, Lilly had told me, at which he encountered the beings. And I could see that I would have an encounter as well. In the distance a tiny pink pearl materialized. As I got closer I saw that the pearl was a miniature Buddha—not the sacred Buddha of Hindus but an animated cartoon version that looked more like the Pillsbury Dough Boy. The Buddha was naked except for an oversize pair of Mickey Mouse ears. He was holding a pink balloon that read *"I am them."* The Buddha started laughing at me, holding his sides as they expanded with each new chortle and gasp. Then, with a magician's flip of the hand, he produced a shiny golden needle from behind his ear and poked himself in the navel, exploding in a burst of thunderous white light.

I coughed and vomited salt water. With a quick thrust of my arms I pushed the escape hatch open and climbed out of the tank into the cool evening air. Apparently I had rotated onto my side during the float, and my face had slipped beneath the surface. I returned to the ranch house, showered, and then looked for Lilly. We compared our experiences. Lilly's E.T.'s were certainly different from my Buddhist prankster. But *I* knew that both were the products of the same brain mechanisms. Very simply, they were stored visual images comprising elements from memories and fantasies now projected onto the mind's eye. The isolation tank had enabled me to see these images.

My Buddha appeared vivid and solid enough to touch, but I recognized it as a false perception or hallucination. When hallucinations fail to fool people, they are called *pseudo*hallucinations. Lilly, on the other hand, would not accept this analysis. His belief in the reality of his E.T.'s was unshakable. He not only believed in the existence of the beings, he also allowed them to control a good deal of his everyday thinking outside the tank. Lilly's E.T.'s apparently fooled him—they were *true* hallucinations.

Throughout history many people have been influenced by such strong hallucinatory events. Socrates, Joan of Arc, and Saint Theresa, among others, have been moved to act on the basis of hallucinatory voices or visions. In many of these cases, as with Lilly's, the hallucinations assumed such startling intensity that the person could easily mistake vividness for veridicality. Questions of sanity and scientific naiveté aside, if the hallucination appears real enough, anyone could be fooled. After all, some hallucinations have all the sensory qualities of real perceptions including sights, sounds, tastes, and smells. They appear just as concrete and "out there" as real events. When these hallucinations are coupled with a will to believe in them, then people start acting as if they are, in fact, real. Lilly was prompted to talk with his beings just as Saint Joan listened to her voices.

These were not necessarily the productions of brains seething with drugs or sliced apart by schizophrenia. One does not need sainthood or scientific wizardry to experience them. Perceptions like these can occur when even ordinary people are subjected to extraordinary conditions. In addition to the sensory isolation of the tank, such conditions include hunger, thirst, loss of sleep, life-threatening danger, and even loneliness. Explorers alone in caves, lost in the polar night, or cast adrift on the open seas have often encountered such projected images. People bombarded by the sensory overload of strobe lights have seen them. And so have monks sequestered in meditation, children who can't stop hyperventilating, and the victims of near-fatal accidents.

Hallucinations can also occur in more familiar environments, even your bedroom. Fever delirium caused by influenza, tonsillitis, or malaria can generate images so compelling that patients will rise out of their beds to walk and talk with hallucinatory visitors. Terminal patients, alone on their deathbeds, often speak with hallucinations of long-forgotten childhood friends. And most of us have experienced vivid images during that semiconscious period immediately prior to sleep (the hypnagogic state) or just before awakening (the hypnopompic state), images that can be accompanied by hallucinations.

There have been a number of surveys indicating that not only are hallucinations common in the normal population, but the number of people reporting them is increasing. In a census taken in 1894, approximately 10 percent of the population reported hallucinatory experiences of one type or another. A 1957 study of normal people by famed British psychologist Peter McKellar found that 25 percent of the people questioned had had at least one hallucinatory experience. My own international questionnaire, distributed by *Omni* in 1988, revealed a startling escalation. Fully 79 percent of the respondents reported hallucinations. Furthermore, more than a third said that they had been fooled by their hallucinations into thinking they were real events. The average age of these respondents, representing equal numbers of men and women, was thirty-three years, and most were well-educated with more than four years of college. While all of these surveys varied in methods and populations sampled, a 1990 census, using methods and samples similar to the 1894 census, found a 50-percent increase in the incidence of hallucinations.

I have always been fascinated by hallucinations. As an undergraduate student at Brandeis University I started reading the philosophical and psychological literature on the subject and spent my spare time observing hallucinating patients at various hospitals affiliated with Harvard Medical School. At Dalhousie University and Albert Einstein College of Medicine, where I received formal training in experimental psychology and psycho-pharmacology, I began my first studies. I developed methods of training laboratory pigeons and monkeys, who have visual systems similar to our own, to "tell" us what they saw while hallucinating under the influence of various drugs. Looking inside the "mind" of another creature was fascinating but frustrating work because the animals, of course, could not speak (they could only press response keys that displayed a limited number of images). When I started collecting accounts from friends who took the same drugs, I knew there was much more to hallucinations than the colored geometric forms the animals were able to report. I began human studies to learn more.

From my base at the UCLA School of Medicine, where I became an associate research professor in the Department of Psychiatry and Biobehavioral Sciences, I conducted extensive clinical research using drugs, sensory isolation rooms, and other methods to induce hallucinations in volunteers. I co-edited a medical text on hallucinations, then wrote a series of articles in several popular magazines. Soon people were flocking to my lab to report their hallucinatory experiences. I devoted many years to collecting their reports and studying them under controlled conditions. I traveled around the world examining rare cases of hallucinations in high altitude climbers, religious mystics, and even hostage victims. At UCLA I worked with psychiatric patients but found many others who experienced hallucinations, including a surgical patient who got up off the table to chase a ghost, a famous Hollywood actress who saw voodoo people throwing darts at her whenever camera lights were turned on, and a departmental colleague who confessed that for twenty-five years she had been working with two imaginary research assistants. And in my private forensic practice, where I was called upon as an expert witness in criminal trials around the world, I was able to study people who experienced hallucinations in situations of kidnapping, rape, and torture.

I always began by asking people to describe their experiences, to share the sensory impressions as recorded by the camera of their mind's eye, ears, and other senses. In other words, I asked them to take me on their trip.

The cases collected in this book examine these hallucinatory worlds through the eyes and senses of those who have taken the trips. But the cases I have selected are more than mere descriptions; they are illustrative of the underlying causes and mechanisms for these amazing perceptions. In order to further understand how the hallucinating brain can control behavior, I gave everyone complete batteries of psychological and physical tests, interviewed friends and family members, and observed the individual for weeks or months. Sometimes it was necessary to actually live with the patients in their homes or hospital rooms, or take my portable equipment and accompany them on dangerous outings in order to catch them in the act of hallucinating.

In most cases I could relate the experiences to the vast body of medical literature describing hallucinations. But sometimes the experiences were so unique that I had to use unusual diagnostic approaches and take the trip myself in order to understand it. For example, when an ex-POW told me about some particularly strange visions he had had while locked inside a tiger cage in Vietnam, I had myself locked inside a similar cage for several days in order to understand just what happened to him.

A common theme in all these cases is the perceived *reality* of the hallucination, which allows it to influence the lives of the individual patients and subjects. Unlike others who may have similar experiences but judge them to be unreal, the people portrayed here all believed what they saw and heard. Their behavior changed as they struggled to cope with the strange perceptions. The hallucinations may have been born out of their brains, but once released they caused the people to act as if such things actually existed in the world outside. They walked, talked, played, and even made love with their hallucinations. In a sense, the hallucinations became alive, they became waking dreams. By examining their descriptions and behavior we, too, can see and hear them. And what they show and tell us is that under the right conditions anyone can hallucinate. In the province of the mind, the border between hallucinations and reality is easy to cross.

We begin our journey in Part I with visionary drugs, the most common tickets to the land of hallucinations. Inside my lab we find a group of experienced voyagers (psychonauts) who all report the same disturbing marijuana vision of a black curtain covered with disembodied eyes. The curtain falls in front of their eyes even when they are sober. This unbidden vision is suddenly reported by other subjects from India, Japan, and England. Did my laboratory experiments somehow unleash this nightmarish hallucination? Were millions of recreational marijuana users now in danger? With the help of a Mexican Indian shaman, I take a trip to penetrate the curtain, reveal its true nature, then destroy it forever. In other chapters we meet a music teacher who, under the influence, hears the voice of God; two women who are actually raped during their hallucination; and a pool hustler who is haunted by a flashback from a previous LSD trip.

The most common nondrug gateways to hallucinations are dreams, as explored in Part II. But for some people the gate stays open when they awaken. Many people have been awakened from a deep sleep only to find an incubus, an old hag, or other night terror sitting on their beds. Sometimes it is the middle of a sunny day and the people are wide awake when they are confronted by a terrifying vision, as happens to a young student in "Daymare." When it happened to a father and son in "UFO," they claimed that they were abducted by the image and taken for a wild ride on the spacecraft. Yet the scenery they rode through was the same hallucinatory landscape seen by earthbound dreamers. And when Sheila, a night-duty nurse, kept the gate closed by depriving herself of sleep, her brain started dreaming while she was awake. Her waking dream: swastikas on the bedsheets of her patients.

In childhood, the hallucinations of imaginary companions, discussed in Part III, are not only common but normal. Thirty-one percent of the respondents in my questionnaire study had imaginary playmates as children, although other researchers report between one-half and two-thirds of all children have them. Children need only a fertile imagination to enter this hallucinatory world wherein fantasies are mingled with reality. However, there are children who never let go of their imaginary friends, and as grown-ups live in a world of giant dragons and invisible rabbits. Even if an adult never had an imaginary friend during childhood, extraordinary situations can conjure one. We watch as these "solid ghosts" appear to a father who longs for a daughter and to a lonely sailor who is caught in a storm in the Bermuda Triangle. In "Take a Picture," a lovesick young man is so haunted by the face of his first girlfriend that he cannot control when and where she will appear to him. But Henry, a bored student who takes an invisible assassin to school with him, is only waiting for the substitute teacher so that he can unleash his deadly companion "Sergeant Tommy" for all to see.

Whereas imaginary companions may arise in the absence of sufficient stimulation, too much of the wrong stimulation will also cause the brain to hallucinate. This happens in Part IV, where ordinary people are subjected to life-threatening danger. Here we meet a POW held in severe conditions of physical and psychological abuse; a kindly grandmother kept locked in her closet by a burglar who constantly threatens to kill her; and a torture victim who learned to scream a secret word that admitted him to a paradise in the antipodes of his mind where no pain existed. While the predictable pattern of geometric and complex images is found throughout all of these hallucinations, it is clearest in the visions of the afterlife as reported by an elderly professor who survives "Death."

In the past, hallucinations were often regarded as the exclusive domain of the insane. Through the research and cases in this book, we begin to understand that anyone can have them. They arise from common structures in the brain and nervous system, common biological experiences, and common reactions of the brain to stimulation or deprivation. The resultant images may be bizarre, but they are not necessarily crazy. They are simply based on stored images in our own brains. Like a mirage that shows a magnificent city on a desolate expanse of ocean or desert, the images of hallucinations are actually reflected images of real objects located elsewhere. The city is no less real and no less worthy of study because it is not where we think it is. This book is a visit to those captivating cities of the mind.

PART ONE

VISIONARY
DRUGS

1

THE PSYCHONAUT
AND THE
SHAMAN

William Shakespeare winked at me. I moved closer. He growled like a bulldog. His face changed into the face of an Indian. The Indian winked at me. Then he was Shakespeare again. Then the Indian. The figures kept flashing back and forth across a black stage, couplets dancing on my intoxicated brain.

The stage exploded with a burst of golden light. A gigantic scaffolding of fluorescent girders stood in its place. The girders twisted themselves into a long spiralling tunnel filled with polygons and other geometric shapes. The mouth of the tunnel turned toward me as it writhed and pulsated, a Euclidian snake pregnant with light and form. Suddenly it disgorged a storm of images: stars, pinwheels, snowflakes, mosaics, and fans. The fans rotated, then changed into records spinning on a turntable. The records changed into a tire that became a Ferris wheel with twinkling colored lights on the spokes. The lights melted into a rainbow. The rainbow fell across a blue sky. Below there were pyramids, sphinxes, even an improbable city skyline. Moses rode by on a bicycle, waved, then exited stage left. He was followed by a pack of ninety-nine little Moseses on tricycles trimmed with twinkling lights.

In a few moments the tunnel belched again. And again. Eventually the forms and pictures faded. In a final eruption, a mountain sprung up from the stage and Porky Pig burst forth from the top stuttering "That's all, folks!" A black curtain fell. It was a curtain with dozens of eyes staring at me!

I gasped and sat up on the lab mattress, straining to see more of the curtain. After all, this was the precise hallucination I wanted to capture. I scrutinized the dark room. But all that was left was a vague afterimage. As it faded away, I was overcome with a profound sense of loss. The description of the apparition in *Macbeth* came to mind: "Show his eyes, and grieve his heart; Come like shadows, so depart."

While I hadn't taken the witches' brew with eye of newt and toe of frog, the heavy dose of marijuana I had smoked was sufficient to cause these visions. I was following the same experimental protocol I used with my research subjects. These subjects, called psychonauts, were experienced drug users who had logged many hours describing their hallucinations. They were trained to make precise psychophysical judgments about the forms, colors, and movements. For example, they learned to classify forms by breaking them down into simple structures such as tunnels or spirals. They could identify the exact spectral wavelength of light. And familiar people, places, and things were labeled with a convenient verbal shorthand. Furthermore, in order to keep up with the rapidly changing images, they were trained to detect and describe an image even if it lasted for only a fraction of a second.

The reports enabled me to make a map of the world of drug-induced hallucinations, a world divided into simple and complex forms. The simple forms consist of tunnels, lattices, and other geometric shapes. These forms arise from unseen structures within the visual system that become illuminated by the action of the drugs. For example, dancing spots are created when red blood cells float through retinal capillaries, casting a shadow on the underlying rods and cones. Other forms are produced when the drugs cause neurons to discharge in the retina and visual cortex. This creates a series of bright lights known as phosphenes. Phosphenes can take the shape of spots, concentric circles, spirals, tunnels, grids, even checkerboard patterns. Still other forms are generated from the visual cortex of the brain where excitation of organized groups of cells produces repeating polygons, mosaics, and symmetrical arrays.

The complex forms are constructed from images stored in memory, "the warder of the brain" as Shakespeare put it. Sometimes these remembered images are projected against the simple geometric arrays, thus appearing in unique combinations and arrangements. Although many complex images are recognizable, many are not. Complex images can be more than pictorial representations of items stored in the brain. Like dreams, images of hallucinations are often elaborated and embellished into fantastic scenes. They can become highly creative and imaginative variations of retrieved memory images, so transformed as to appear unrecognizable.

All hallucinations encountered by the psychonauts were variations on these two basic themes. The geometric forms might be combined in unique ways, but the constructions were always composed of common elements. Scenes from one's memory might contain highly personal pictures, such as a particular Ferris wheel or face, yet these would behave with fixed actions and patterns. While I might have been the only one in the world to see Moses and his little clones ride cycles across the stage, the animated sequence was not unlike the novel combinations and duplications of images reported by all the psychonauts. The drama of their hallucinations may have had different actors and props, but everyone was reading from the same basic script.

How, then, could we—the psychonauts and myself—see the *exact* same scene of a curtain with dozens of eyes? In any given intoxication, there were hundreds of thousands of images. The chances must have been infinitesimally small that we would experience the identical hallucination. Yet every psychonaut described the same image: a black gauzy curtain with a large human eye in the center surrounded by a symmetrical arrangement of smaller eyes. The eyes were alive, leering. I asked the psychonauts to count them. Each time the count came back the same: thirty, plus or minus one or two.

Terry was the first to see the curtain. Under the influence of a hallucinogenic dose of marijuana, he reported intensely illuminated and brilliantly colored geometrics. After a time they took on the appearance of richly patterned carpets or mosaics. These soon gave way to recognizable scenes: a chipmunk here, a dandelion there, all playfully displayed. They appeared like a slide show flashing about two feet in front of his eyes, but solid and three-dimensional, almost vivacious. Terry laughed, "I'm very high. My imagery is fantastic. . . . I'm really getting involved in it."

The tunnel belched and heaved its images, then inhaled and sucked Terry into its very center of light. He was now entering the stage Aldous Huxley called the "Other World"—that remote region of the mind inhabited by the raw materials of our perceptions. Terry flew through an aurora borealis, under mandalas, over buildings, mountains, and giant lollipops. He saw many images repeating and multiplying, a feast of identical lollipops marching in columns across the black tablecloth of his visual field. "Oh my God," exclaimed Terry, "there's a bunch of eyeballs watching me!" The image was quickly replaced by others. Several minutes later, as the effects of the drug peaked in Terry's brain, the imagery intensified.

"There's a realistic tunnel becoming an alley. The alley is turning into a street. One I've never seen before. At the end of the street, it's very dark. There's something there." Terry's voice sounded frightened, distant. "If I try I might be able to make it go away," he whimpered.

"Let it flow," I whispered through the lab intercom. "Trust your nervous system."

"Oh! Those eyeballs again . . . maybe . . . maybe . . . thirty of them. There's a large one glaring at me from the center surrounded by smaller ones. They almost form a spiral . . ."

There was a long pause. "Report," I demanded. I would say this whenever more than one minute of silence elapsed. Terry resumed his commentary on a rush of new images.

I didn't think about the eyeballs again until several weeks later when Anne, the first female psychonaut, smoked one of our government marijuana cigarettes and reported the same image. Anne saw the eyeballs, all thirty of them, on a black field. When Jim, a graduate student in literature, saw the image, he named it the Demon, after the vision described in Edgar Allan Poe's "The Pit and the Pendulum":

Demon eyes, of a wild and ghastly vivacity, glared upon me in a thousand directions where none had been visible before, and gleamed with the lurid lustre of a fire that I could not force my imagination to regard as unreal.

Everyone was disturbed by the vision. Terry saw it on almost every trip, even with other drugs such as psilocybin, a hallucinogen found in "magic mushrooms." Anne saw it once while walking across the UCLA campus after an all-night session in the lab. Jim went under the influence of LSD and tried to open the curtain. He was seized with profound nausea and vomiting and couldn't remember anything about the experience.

Terry, Anne, and Jim were all members of the first psychonaut team I had trained. I was testing the procedures with them before beginning a series of formal studies with a new group of subjects. When the eyeballs kept reappearing, I decided to postpone the training of the second team until I could understand the basis for this unbidden image.

I considered several explanations. Perhaps the image was an artifact of a prior cultural experience. After all, the psychonauts were all white, middle class, North American college students who had lived through many common experiences with drugs during the 1960s. Maybe it came from something they had read or heard or seen before. Perhaps the curtain with eyes appeared on a record album, poster, or in a movie. I rejected this notion when Rajiv, an exchange student from a remote village in India, and Hiroshi, a visiting physician from Japan, volunteered for a pilot study and saw the curtain with thirty *Caucasian* eyes. Now I was puzzled.

Puzzlement turned to terror when Nick, who had been smoking marijuana all his life in England and never had a hallucination, saw the Demon during his very first marijuana trip in my lab. I allowed my paranoia to run wild. Did my drug experiments somehow unleash this nightmarish hallucination? Was the image now floating in the ether around my lab where it could be picked up by any subject in an altered state? Could the lab be haunted? In the movie *Close Encounters* an alien intelligence zaps people with the mental image of a rock formation known as Devil's Tower. Could a fiendish force be zapping my subjects with these evil eyes?

There is a belief held by some parapsychologists that marijuana and other psychedelic drugs open the doors of perception to forms of ESP such as telepathy. According to this view, people under the influence are more receptive to the projected thoughts and mental images of others. Investigators report that after ingesting mescaline, for example, research subjects are able to "see" a particular picture or painting being "transmitted" by a person who is staring at it in another room. In order to enhance the emotional strength of such transmissions, the "senders" often look at photos of Nazi concentration camp victims and other gruesome pictures while simultaneously listening to sorrowful music. I was stunned to discover that these experiments in emotional telepathy were actually taking place in a laboratory adjacent to mine at UCLA's Neuropsychiatric Institute (NPI)!

Dr. Thelma Moss, parapsychologist, former actress, author of a book on LSD, and friend of Uri Geller, occupied the lab next to mine. Inside her lab was a soundproof and lightproof isolation chamber where her subjects—the transmitters—watched emotion-laden slides and listened to musical accompaniments through headphones. The transmitter tried to send the images to a receiver subject located in another room down the hall. Midway between transmitter and receiver was my lab with an identical isolation chamber wherein the psychonauts were tripping out on drugs. They were in a direct line with the so-called telepathic transmissions! I was so angry and frustrated about having to stop my experiments that I was ready to believe that Dr. Moss's lab was responsible for the Demon.

I ran next door to confront Thelma. Her research assistant, a greasy little man who claimed to be a psychic, didn't know who I was or why I was there. I made him guess. He couldn't. I quickly explained my interest in the telepathy experiments and asked to see the slides used as visual targets. He directed me to boxes filled with hundreds of slides.

I spent days poring over the slides, examining each one in a hand-held viewer. The assistant kept me amused with a recitation of his psychic abilities. I tried not to giggle when he told me that photographs of his fingers did not come out unless he was in a trance and that every watch he had ever owned gained ten minutes each day. He claimed that his mere presence could kill a houseplant at five yards, the only claim I was willing to accept at face value. But he was correct when he said there were no Demons in the slides. I didn't find a single eyeball in the bunch, let alone anything resembling a curtain with thirty eyes. I had wasted the better part of a week and now felt very foolish.

The brief interlude in Dr. Moss's lab gave me another idea. Many parapsychologists hypothesize that people with true mystic visions can tap into parts of the brain that psychoanalyst Carl Jung called the collective unconscious. Therein rest archetypes, primordial mental images that seem to be innate and universal. One such Jungian archetype is the mandala, an image reported by every psychonaut. "As psychological phenomena," Jung wrote, "[mandalas] appear spontaneously in dreams, in certain states of conflict, and in cases of schizophrenia." His followers added states of intoxication to this list.

Typically, mandalas are circular patterns that contain symmetrical squares, crosses, stars, or other geometric shapes. The view through a child's kaleidoscope provides a classic example of a symmetrical mandala pattern. Mandalas may also contain symmetrical arrangements of complex figures such as deities, people, or animals. Some arrangements may take on a spiral shape. Jungian analysts believe that specific mandalas represent the archetypal motifs of birth and death, heaven and hell, good and evil. They are an inherent part of our history, our mythology, our soul.

While I was inclined to believe that mandalas were simple geometric forms, derived from structures in the visual system and then filled in with memory images, I was at a loss to explain the specific Demon mandala with thirty eyes. Could the Demon be an archetypal image? If so, it should have appeared before. I decided to go on an eye hunt.

I started with Jung's collection of mandalas painted by his patients. Several showed a single eye consisting of a simple circle or oval with a dot in the center. None contained the eyeballs, lids, or lashes that characterized the Demon. After searching through these drawings, I directed my staff to gather further examples of eyes in art and architecture. I was still hopeful I might find the original source of the psychonauts' hallucination. "Bring me eyes," I roared in mock madness.

The eyes began multiplying on my desk. A painting by the Swiss artist Peter Birkhauser depicted four terrifying eyes looking through a dark, gauzy background. I counted fourteen vacant eyes in a nightmarish lithograph by British artist John Spencer. There were similar eyes with lids and lashes on ancient Egyptian and Etruscan amulets used as representations of the evil eye. While elements of the psychonauts' vision could be found in all of these artworks, none displayed the fixed symmetrical arrangement of the Demon's thirty eyes. Since symmetrical patterns appear as constant features of drug-induced hallucinations, perhaps the Demon was an archetypal mental image available only to those in an altered state of consciousness. If it was an ancient symbol, long-buried in the unconscious, and now unearthed by my team of psychonauts, perhaps members of other hallucinogen-using cultures saw it.

My suspicions were strengthened when the poet Allen Ginsberg visited my office after a speaking engagement on campus. He saw the pile of eyes of my desk and told me that he had once seen something similar in Peru after taking *yaje*, a hallucinogen used by Tukano Indians in the Amazon. Ginsberg reported seeing a "Great Being," a mysterious black hole with a large eye in the center. This grand master of verbal imagery was at a loss to describe the Being. Instead, he sketched the vision. The picture showed a large eye surrounded by a perfectly symmetrical arrangement of smaller eyes! While there were only twenty eyes in the drawing, together with numerous snakes and other creatures, my psychonauts agreed this was very close to their image of the Demon.

Are eyes seen by others who use hallucinogens? I asked the late R. Gordon Wasson, a researcher who is best remembered for his work on hallucinogenic mushrooms. Wasson, the first outsider to participate in a Mexican mushroom ritual, was intrigued by my story of the curtain with thirty eyes. During his own intoxication he saw a vision of himself as "a disembodied eye." While he could not explain the psychonauts' specific hallucination of thirty disembodied eyes, it was obvious to Wasson that such visions came from within. "Somewhere within us," he explained, "there must lie a repository where these visions sleep until they are called forth." But whether such hallucinations as the Demon are transmutations of things read and seen and imagined, so changed as to be unrecognizable, or visions stirred from greater unknown depths, Wasson could not guess. He encouraged me to take my questions to the most experienced seers he knew—the shamans of Mexico.

I took my next vacation in Mexico. When I failed to locate a shaman, I spent the remaining days searching through libraries and museums for more eyes. They were there, all right, but, for some inexplicable reason, I could not see them. In the National Museum of Anthropology in Mexico City I apparently walked right by several murals with motifs of disembodied eyes. On a sight-seeing excursion to the ruins of Teotihuacan I brushed against magnificent sixth-century columns but never knew that carved into the columns, and watching me, were rows of disembodied eyes inlaid with obsidian pupils. Was I caught in some B-grade horror movie, literally brushing shoulders with the Demon and not knowing it? It would take a second trip to Mexico and a one-hundred-year-old shaman in order for me "to see."

I joined an expedition organized by Oscar Janiger, a research psychiatrist who was studying the effects of hallucinogens on human chromosomes. There was a fear in the early 1970s (now disproved) that long-term use of hallucinogenic drugs might damage people by causing genetic defects. The team would take blood samples from a group of Huichol Indians in Mexico. If anyone was likely to show chromosomal damage and have a record of genetic abnormalities it would be the Huichols, who had been using peyote since Aztec times. Peyote contains the hallucinogen mescaline, which has stronger and more toxic effects than even LSD.

The Huichols devoted their lives to exploring peyote visions in the isolation of the Sierra Madre Occidental. In such an environment they were untouched by the cultural images and specific experiences of the psychonauts. If they saw the Demon under the influence of peyote, it *had* to be an archetypal image. I wanted to sample their imagery as much as Janiger wanted their blood.

Our team arrived in Tepic, a small town that was the jumping-off point for all expeditions to the Sierras. I spent some time browsing in local shops where Huichol artists traded their yarn paintings for pesos. Yarn paintings are flat pieces of wood covered with beeswax and inlaid with striking designs made with colored yarn. The paintings, which illustrated peyote visions, depicted the same polygons, tunnels, and geometric shapes reported by the psychonauts, further evidence of the universal nature of these hallucinations as dictated by the brain. The complex imagery in the paintings consisted of mountains, clouds, deer, snakes, scorpions, and other familiar objects taken from the Indians' environment.

I asked a shopkeeper about eyes, using the Huichol word *tsikuri*. He showed me a cross of bamboo splints interwoven with colored yarn in the form of a diamond. The central part of the diamond was white and the surrounding sections were blue and red. "It's a God's eye," he announced. "The Huichols offer them to the gods so that they will hear their prayers. God's eyes are symbols of the power of seeing and understanding unknown things." I purchased a small one and put it in my pocket.

The following day the team flew into the forbidding Sierras. Our map had a chilling footnote: "Vertical errors in excess of 2000 feet have been reported by users. Relief information should be used with caution." The pilot barely managed to land the two-engine Beechcraft on a tiny mesa outside the village of San Juan Peyotan. After we unloaded the gear, I stood on the hot surface of the mesa and started filming. As the camera panned across barren rocks and yellow stalks of grass shimmering in the midday heat, the wreckage of a small plane came into view. Squatting in the shade of its only remaining wing was our Huichol guide. The telephoto lens zoomed in on his youthful face. He didn't move, not even to blink in the gusts of raw wind that blew across the mesa. There was nothing, absolutely nothing else even remotely alive to see. Suddenly, a roaring cloud of dust covered my view, and I turned the camera around to catch our plane taking off. It was scheduled to return in several weeks. I touched the God's eye in my pocket.

We hiked to a more remote village, which was the geographic center for a group of Huichol farmers living in ranchos scattered around the mountains. It was dusk when we arrived, and the village appeared to be cast in shades of gray. A small dog, with bulging eyes and ribs, barked a few times at our approach and then returned to eating stones. Here and there a vampire bat flapped through the air. Somewhere a donkey brayed with an eerie cry. A few Huichol males helped with the gear, then escorted us to our hut. They watched as we unpacked. Women and children were nowhere to be seen, but I was certain that they, too, were observing us. I collapsed on top of my sleeping bag, too exhausted to care if the Demon was also watching.

At daybreak, everything was still gray. The gray spilled out of shadows from the surrounding mountains and from the smoke of cooking fires. It swept over stone fences and around thatched huts. It lived in the swirling dust and in the somberness of the Indians' movements. As Janiger's people set up a field clinic for the examinations and blood collections, I wandered through this bleak scene.

The only touch of color was in the men's clothing: white muslin pants and shirts trimmed with embroidered geometric designs. The embroidery was done with a variation of the cross-stitch, a technique that enhanced the details of the patterns and their saturated colors. There were many colors here but blue and red seemed dominant. The designs were repeated on their woven cloth belts and shoulder bags. Since most of these designs were copied from peyote visions, it was not surprising to find symmetrical mandalalike forms, including lattices, tunnels, and polygons.

My interviews with the Indians revealed that there was much more to their peyote visions than these simple designs. I asked about recognizable images; the answers, filtered through separate Huichol and Spanish translators, came back as chopped words: the moon, the stars, the sun, rainbows, eagles, deer, cattle, snakes. I asked about eyes. The only eyes they ever saw were the ones on the animals. How many? Two, they would answer, then giggle at the stupidity of my question. I struggled to make sure my question had been translated correctly. I pointed to my own eyes. Did you ever see more than two in a peyote vision? Many eyes all over? I gestured to my eyes and to other spots on my face. You have only two eyes, the Indians answered politely. It was obvious they were holding back their laughter. Did you ever see eyes without animal or human bodies? The Indians burst out laughing. I was totally frustrated and pulled out a U.S. dollar bill. I pointed to the great seal on the back. "*Tsikuri*," I yelled as I pointed to the disembodied eye set in a triangle surrounded by the sun's ray. I pulled out several other dollars and passed them around. The Indians kept laughing as they walked away with my money.

I decided to climb down to the river, some two hundred and

fifty feet below the village, and cool off. After a refreshing swim, I hiked along the riverbank to a sacred cave. Huichols have a great many sacred caves where they leave idols and other offerings to various gods. If the caves also contain a spring or pool, the water is used for religious purposes. But nothing else is to be removed from the caves. I found such a cave within a few miles of the village. I knew I was not supposed to enter, let alone disturb any of the artifacts, but I felt I had paid the price of admission.

The cave was a small one and I had to crawl on my stomach to get in. I had seen a rattlesnake sunbathing on the river rocks below the cave. Did snakes nest here? I suppressed the thought and pushed ahead. Once inside the cave, I turned on my flashlight and surveyed the contents. There were several God's eyes, numerous prayer arrows with hawk feathers tied to them, and a stack of candles covered with animal blood. I noticed several dark, round disks resting on the candles. The disks had been cut from the tops of gourds. I directed the beam of my flashlight at one of them. A thousand eyes lit up!

The "eyes" were actually tiny white glass beads. The beads had been pressed into beeswax, which covered the disk. These disks, called *nearikas*, were left as prayer offerings. Despite my desire to see the beads as eyes, no particular design was being portrayed. Rather, the beads were intended to make the disk more attractive to the gods. Leaving a *nearika* as a gift is said to symbolize a pact between a particular person and a specific deity. I took the miniature God's eye from my pocket and placed it next to the *nearikas* on the stack of candles. As I left the cave I scraped against the rocks, tore my jeans, bumped my head, and scratched my glasses. I cursed back at the darkness.

Several nights later there was a peyote ceremony in the village. It started early in the day with the grinding of dry peyote cactus into a fine beige powder. The powder was mixed with a sweet corn beer and slices of fresh green peyote to make a thick gruel. Everyone was expected to drink the gruel that night, but only those whom the gods deemed worthy would be given the gift of peyote visions.

The shaman, or *mara'akame*, would lead the ceremony. He arrived in the village that afternoon after walking for several days from his isolated rancho in the mountains. I was told he was over one hundred years old, and the lines on his face seemed to say the same. From the mud-caked sandals on his feet to the torn gray blanket draped over his shoulders, the shaman was without color. He didn't even have the traditional embroidered designs on his clothes. But his black eyes had the sparkle one acquires after seeing all the peyote visions there are to see.

Generally, *mara'akames* are reluctant to discuss their visions with outsiders. But this shaman had never seen a tape recorder before and I used it to my advantage. He was fascinated by the machine. Each time he said something, I immediately played it back to him. He loved it! I would ask a question; he would answer, then sit in stoic resolve until I played his response. It took forever, but I got my interview. He said that when he closed his eyes he saw many colors and patterns like those on the embroidery or yarn paintings. If he opened his eyes he could see these designs projected against the night sky and all that he looked at. The visions started off in black and white, then turned blue, then red as the experience peaked. This progression seemed to account for the two dominant colors used in Huichol embroidery.

He saw sequences of complex images that animated important "stories." The stories were familiar to all *mara'akames*: the birth of the world, the sacred peyote hunt, among others. He echoed the belief that these peyote visions were gifts from the gods, but he was honest enough to admit that he never saw a particular element that was totally new. All the complex images were recognizable to him, although they may have been put together in unusual ways. Sometimes they were downright bizarre, as when he saw an ox on a mountain change into a god. But he had heard about this particular god before and immediately knew who it was. And every self-respecting Huichol knew what an ox looked like, even one painted with geometric patterns.

I was just about to ask him about the Demon when he walked to the edge of the ceremonial grounds. He lit a hand-rolled cigarette and started the chants and songs that began the festivities. Musicians started playing homemade violins and guitars. People danced up and down on a log, stamping their sandals to attract the attention of the gods. I turned on my camera and tape recorder. After a few hours the shaman sat down in front of the campfire. I positioned myself next to him as other Huichols joined in a circle around the fire. I would remain there for the next twelve hours. I was hesitant to distract him and decided to put away my tape recorder and movie camera, although I had permission to use them. Instead, I would rely on a Minox spy camera without a flash. Hopefully, the light from the campfire would be sufficient to catch the events.

The shaman took a few swigs from a bottle of a potent liquor made from the agave plant, then passed it to me. I matched him swig for swig. Then he picked up the bowl of peyote gruel and took a long drink. I counted the gulps and took the same amount. This continued throughout the night.

The night sky was clear. Every constellation was visible. Our campfire was small, but viewed through my dilated pupils it seemed bright enough to cloak the mountains around the mesa with fiery auras. We were sitting in a cathedral of light. The gods could not miss us.

Waves of nausea caused me to close my eyes. The nausea passed and I opened my eyes. The sky was much closer to the earth. Then the stars came down. They darted about the mesa, leaving tracer patterns in the air. I reached up to grab one but missed, creating a rainbow of afterimages in the wake of my moving hand. I closed my eyes again.

More patterns. Yarn paintings, embroidered clothing, woven bags, and trinkets paraded across my eyelids. Hours of this stuff went by, pulsating so hard and so brilliantly that it turned into a pounding headache. *I don't want this tourist junk.* I opened my eyes and looked at the shaman. He was speckled with color and patterns. He was also very drunk. When he put his arm around me and started singing, I decided to pop the Demon question.

"Has anyone ever had a peyote dream of eyes, many eyes floating in the air?" I asked. The shaman listened quietly to the translation, then shook his head. He didn't speak. He didn't laugh. He just gave this gesture signifying an absolute, final no. *What am I doing here?*

Another wave of nausea and I turned around and vomited. A lizard crept out of the vomit, followed by thousands of army ants wearing party hats. *Stop it! I want answers, not cartoons!*

The shaman stared through me. "*Mara'akame,*" I pleaded, "my friends all see the same hallucination of *treinta tsikuri.*" I purposely used the Spanish and Huichol for emphasis. "Why?"

He took a small mirror from his shoulder bag and held it

in his hand in front of the fire. He stared at the mirror. "There are no hallucinations with peyote. There are only truths." Then the great *mara'akame* got up to vomit. It seemed to go on forever. And so did my visions of Huichol patterns and paintings that had been the focus of my attention for so many days. I saw other recent memories including images of the airplane, the trek to the village, the sacred cave, and the slaughtering of the bull we had had for supper.

After twelve hours I was actually bored with my hallucinations. The shaman was catatonic, a sitting statue with open eyes. The few Huichols still remaining around the fire had the same blank staring expression, faces frozen in the dreams of a timeless ritual. I left the circle and returned to the hut. There I stretched out on the floor, turned on my tape recorder, and tried to describe the images that still flashed in front of my open eyes.

In this position, separated from the festivities, and with a lapel microphone clipped to my shirt, I felt I was back in the comfort of the lab. I started reporting: "Rotating kaleidoscopes . . . kaleidoscopes moving horizontally . . . weeds, lots of yellow weeds multiplying, embellished with colors . . ." I was really enjoying being a psychonaut again. "There's a beautiful campfire, very beautiful . . . red lattices . . . reddish mountains . . ."

The air shuddered with a sharp "Ping!" The world went silent. I looked up at the roof of the hut and there, floating near the bamboo rafters, was the *mara'akame*! At least it looked like the *mara'akame*. But his clothes were covered with the most elaborate embroidery, the colors fluorescing like a Day-Glo poster. And there, where his sandals used to be, was a new pair of hiking boots. He was smiling but his eyes, his two black eyes, had become a mass of eyes swimming over his face.

Another "Ping!" My skin prickled with electricity. A seizure lifted my body off the floor. I saw the *mara'akame* again. His entire face was a black hole and in its place was the Demon! There it was: the black curtain, the large eye, and the thirty smaller ones! I didn't move or say a word for fear that it would disappear. It didn't. The near-toxic dose of mescaline I had ingested by drinking peyote all night kept the Demon alive for many seconds, long enough "to see." The eyes looked like pictures that had been cut out of magazines and pasted together in a collage conceived by a deranged artist. In the lower right-hand corner I saw the letters *ES* followed by a series of numbers. The Demon faded away before I could read them.

But I had seen enough. The letters and numbers were part of a code I put on the borders of the slides used in the psychonaut training course. The subjects never saw the code numbers, but I used them for identifying the contents of each slide. These slides were projected on a piece of black cardboard (the black curtain) tacked to the laboratory wall. The training slides were all black-and-white drawings of simple geometric forms such as tunnels or lattices.

The *ES* series was very different. It consisted of dramatically colored "psychedelic" scenes created by artists for light shows, Hollywood films, and other commercial productions. I had obtained a collection of these slides from *E*dmund *S*cientific, a mail-order supply house in New Jersey. But I had not used the *ES* series in training. I was saving them to show the psychonauts *after* the experiments were completed so that they might be able to select images that were similar to their own hallucinations. Somehow, one of the *ES* slides must have slipped into the batch of training slides and imbedded itself in the psychonauts' memories. I was certain that when I returned to the lab I would find it.

The Demon was nothing more than the surprise of a disturbing image spontaneously retrieved from memory. Rather than feeling disappointed that a "real" Demon did not exist, I was surprised and humbled to discover that internal images can be powerful enough to be mistaken for external ones. Disturbing images have a way of burrowing their way into our memories, even after a single exposure. In Luis Buñuel's 1928 surrealist film *Un Chien Andalou*, a man slowly and carefully sharpens a straight razor. As he works, he looks at the moon just as a sliver of cloud is about to cross it. He then slices the eye of a young girl. At the moment of cutting the eyeball, the film shows a cloud slicing across the moon's circle. Immediately, we see the razor finishing its work and the interior of the eye pouring out. It is the eye, not the moon we remember. This nightmarish image appears only briefly in the movie, yet it still disturbs and shocks people who saw the film more than a generation ago. These images can be evoked by simply remembering, or they may erupt in spite of conscious efforts to avoid them. Such eruptions are common in hallucinations, especially in those induced by drugs. They form a type of involuntary reminiscence, complete with many of the feelings and emotions that were present when the image was first recorded.

My own peyote hallucinations illustrated this process. Not only was the long forgotten Demon slide evoked by the visionary drug, but recent memories of Huichol artwork kept dominating my imagery despite my deliberate attempts to dispel them. The mescaline generated spreading waves of cortical excitement throughout my brain, randomly activating old and new memories.

The morning after, I awoke soaked in sweat. My clothes were soiled with vomit and pieces of peyote. I hurried down to the river for a bath. The *mara'akame* was standing naked in the shallows. He looked very ordinary.

"Que pitu hay nu?" I asked. Even without my translator I knew the words. It was the same question I had asked every Huichol about their peyote visions: What did you dream?

He laughed and gestured wildly with his entire body. His fingers traced the outlines of rectangular boxes. He leaned into the imaginary boxes, then opened and closed his mouth rapidly. He cupped his ears, then pointed every which way. *Tape recorders! He saw a bunch of little tape recorders multiplying all over the place!* I laughed with him.

"Que pitu hay nu?" asked the naked man.

How do you tell a shaman that you traveled to a forgotten corner of the earth in search of your personal Demon, only to find it was a cheap picture available by mail-order? How do you tell this holy man who believes he has the power to see the gods that there are no more gods or Demons than there are images of those things in the brain? How do you tell a poor naked farmer who has only his peyote dreams that the world of our dreams is all inside our minds?

"There are no hallucinations. There are only truths," I said in a mixture of broken Huichol and Spanish. But he understood. After all, it was something he had said only yesterday.

Weeks later I was back in my lab. I found the Demon. It was a slide, all right. It had accidentally fallen into a slide tray of training slides. Never again! I removed the slide, made a print, and mailed it to a friend in Mexico to give to the shaman. "Tell the *mara'akame*," I wrote, "that it's a picture of my dream." I enclosed a picture I had taken with my Minox of the shaman gulping down the peyote. It was a bad picture: the shaman's face was entirely black.

2

CONVERSATIONS WITH GOD IN C-SHARP MINOR

I never heard a cactus sing. Yet many Indians claim that peyote provides them with their songs. I never found the cactus to be a particularly "noisy" plant. Yet some Indians complain that they can't sleep near peyote because the sounds keep them awake. I never spoke with my deceased cousin Harvey, yet Indians often talk with their departed ancestors through the magic of peyote.

My hearing was excellent before I took peyote. While I was under the influence it seemed even better. Whispers from across the mesa were understandable. The sounds of a woman making tortillas in a distant rancho slapped against my ears. The faint droning of an unseen plane rocked the sky. These and similar perceptions were typical of the auditory changes induced by peyote as well as other hallucinogens.

The sounds I heard seemed louder than they really were, but hallucinogens can also make them seem softer, closer, farther away, or distorted in any number of ways. And sometimes people hear things that they normally ignore. For example, the psychonauts became aware of background noises from the lab ventilation system, the sound of air rushing through their nostrils, even the telltale thumping of their own hearts!

Noises that are normally undetectable can also be heard with the drugs. These noises—the auditory equivalent of phosphenes and other unseen structures in the visual system—arise from movements of the muscles governing middle-ear function. Vibrations of these muscles, or attached structures like the eustachian tubes, are heard as clicking or crackling noises. Fluttering and popping noises can be produced when the muscles that alter the tension of the tympanic membrane contract, thereby altering the timbre and volume of hearing. Minor contractions generate fading noises like blowing or rushing wind. Sudden reflex contractions produce loud noises like shots or knocks.

You don't have to be under the influence to perceive these noises. Millions of people who suffer from tinnitus hear them. The most common perception is a ringing in the ears that can vary in pitch from a low roar to a high squeal or whine. If a person other than the patient hears the noise, the tinnitus is called "objective" because the sound can be confirmed. Most cases of objective tinnitus are caused by muscle spasms, but abnormalities in blood vessels around the outside of the ear can also produce them. Conversely, "subjective" tinnitus can only be heard by the patient, but there is still a real physical cause for the sound. In addition to drug intoxications, subjective tinnitus can be produced by allergies, high or low blood pressure, a tumor, diabetes, thyroid problems, or a variety of other causes.

These noises form a class of acoustic phenomena known as elementary or unformed hallucinations. Hallucinogens do much more than permit detection of these basic sounds. The drugs promote their mishearing and misinterpretation. The noises become templates upon which the mind builds more recognizable sounds. Clicking noises become "someone tapping on a tin can," "a woman walking in spiked heels," or "water dripping." Fluttering turns into "people murmuring" or "a pneumatic drill." The fading noises are the "whoooosh" and "ziiiiig" of passing trucks and cars. Finally, the startling loud shots can be heard as "a door slamming" or "an object falling on the floor."

Elementary hallucinations are very different from "voices," which are complex, or formed auditory hallucinations such as spoken words, laughter, and singing. These voices evolve from normal verbal thought, a type of thinking in words that is best understood as "inner speech." There is convincing experimental evidence that verbal thought in some people is accompanied by genuine changes in the speech muscles. In schizophrenic disorders or psychoses, this pattern of subvocalization can be mistaken for voices originating from an external source. It is not uncommon to see actual lip and throat movements in patients when they claim their voices are speaking to them. The voices are frequently of an offending or threatening nature, but they may offer advice or instructions as well. Luther was reproached by the voice of the Devil. Socrates was guided by a monitory voice— his "Demon"—as was Joan of Arc, who listened to voices from a more heavenly realm. All three either spoke with the voices or mouthed their words.

Of course, not everybody moves their lips or subvocalizes when they engage in thought. Most people think in terms of mental images. Mental imagery allows us to perceive images in any sensory modality, although visual images are generally more dominant than auditory ones. For example, when we think of a white cat we can usually see a distinct mental image of a white cat in our mind's eye. If we try to hear the cat's meow, however, we might be able to hear the image in our mind's ear but it won't be as clear.

Hallucinogens tend to intensify auditory mental images as well as visual images. Under the influence a person loses volitional control of what is seen and heard as the imagery takes on a life of its own. Words and sentences, like visual images, are retrieved from memory and cognitively transformed into elaborate productions. For auditory images, these constructions can result in voices with as much to say as their corresponding pictorial constructions have to show. The more vivid and concrete the imagery, and the stronger the drug intoxication, the more it is "out there." The gods were already inside the *mara'akame*'s head when he took peyote, but the drug made their voices seem to sing from heaven itself. Yet only he could hear. When God spoke with Mrs. Constance Temple, she figured out a way we could all listen to the conversation.

It was Saturday and there was no school. Constance Temple, an attractive, middle-aged grade-school music teacher, could relax.

Saturday was a time for practicing on her Steinway piano and seeing private students. She didn't like giving piano lessons to a bunch of kids who wouldn't practice, but she owed money on the Steinway and the extra income helped. The piano was the only item she had ever purchased on credit besides her VW Bug, which she had bought in 1964. That's when she painted a flower on the front hood. Only part of the flower was still visible, but a larger part of Mrs. Temple was back in the sixties.

The VW smelled brand-new when Connie drove it to Millbrook, the infamous estate in Dutchess County, New York, where Timothy Leary and his followers were experimenting with hallucinogens. It was there that she was introduced to DMT (dimethyltryptamine), a legal short-acting psychedelic known as "the businessman's high" because you went up and down in a half hour and could take it on your lunch hour. Government officials who eventually outlawed the drug gave it the nickname "terror drug."

DMT trips are among the most intense drug experiences in the world, and only their brevity makes them bearable. The drug is found in several mind-altering plants used by South American Indians to transport themselves to "distant places" where they communicate with spirit forces. DMT also occurs normally in everyone's brain. Why? What is this powerful drug doing there? Why does stress increase the amount of DMT released into cerebrospinal fluid? Do schizophrenics, who are locked in some "distant place" inside their minds, have an excess of DMT as some researchers believe? The questions are intriguing but must remain unanswered until more is known. However, it was enough for Connie to experience thirty minutes of pure ecstasy to know that DMT was the drug for her. She left Millbrook with a lifetime supply hidden in the trunk under the flower.

Connie finished high school, married, attended music school, then started teaching and playing the piano semi-professionally as Constance Temple. Although she was now divorced, she kept the "Mrs." for her pupils, saying that it inspired respect. Her career hadn't left time for DMT, and she was missing her Millbrook trips on this particular Saturday.

After her last student left, Mrs. Temple settled down on a huge pile of overstuffed velvet pillows. Except for the black Steinway, her entire living room was done in white. The white

Victorian furniture, marble table, and Italian silk drapes gave the room a religious tone, a most fitting atmosphere for her choice of a background tape, Beethoven's *Missa solemnis,* which was now playing through a pair of gigantic Yamaha speakers.

She opened a Ziploc bag containing DMT powder mixed with parsley, sprinkled a few crumbs of the mixture into a glass pipe, and lit it. There was a smell like burning plastic. She smoked quickly. Her blood pressure increased. Her pupils dilated. Then she heard a faint, almost imperceptible whistling noise.

The living room turned into an elevator whisking her to the top of a skyscraper. There was a rushing of wind, like a vacuum seal being broken. The elevator soared through the roof. She ignored the "retinal circus," Timothy Leary's phrase for the swirling and tumbling visual images, and tilted her head up to watch the silk-draped elevator merge with the white light of the Creator. Constance's joy was incomprehensible.

The whistling turned into harmonic overtones, similar to the sounds of distant wind chimes. Constance listened to the sequence and pitch of the tones, storing them in her musical memory. Then from the other side of the chimes came the voice of Almighty God. As God spoke, the chimes vibrated in resonance with his voice. Constance trembled. God talked to her about the nature of love, beauty, and immortality. The chimes sang. Constance's eyes filled with tears as she listened.

The elevator became a roller coaster hurtling down from the top of the building. It plunged back to the living room before Constance had time to say amen. She went to the piano and tapped out the harmonics of the chimes. *Interesting,* she thought, *like delicate grace notes.*

Constance took many more rides on the elevator, and each time she heard new arrangements of the tones. The sounds were glorious. But a problem developed when she began hearing the chimes at times when she was sober. It happened often enough to frighten her. She couldn't play with God talking in her ear—it was too distracting. She stopped playing. Then she stopped teaching. When her Steinway was repossessed, she came to my office for help.

Mrs. Temple was dressed in a white dress of antique lace. I learned later that she had made it herself by stitching together dozens of linen handkerchiefs, the kind that schoolteachers are always receiving as gifts from their pupils. Her blond hair was pulled back into a long ponytail that almost touched her waist. She wore black horn-rims, a beautiful smile, and no bra. I asked what I could do for her.

"Just tell me, Doctor, will I ever play the piano again?" she quipped with a nervous stutter. I liked her right away.

Constance told me about how DMT had allowed her to hear the voice of God. Although she had stopped smoking months ago, she still heard the voice. She was curious to learn more about it and volunteered to be a research patient. I assumed that she wanted me to stop this divine intrusion in her life.

"How do you know it's really the voice of God?" I asked. Who was I to tell God to be quiet?

"Well, he doesn't sound like Charlton Heston playing Moses in *The Ten Commandments*," she said. "He sings in high-pitched tones, like the angels, I suppose. It sounds like wind chimes. I tingle all over and my heart tells me it's God."

She described the chimes as pure harmonics, taking time to explain that harmonics are secondary tones that form a component of every musical sound, although they are not heard distinctly. Since I had studied the violin for many years—until I discovered I was playing out of tune—I knew something about these sounds. By lightly touching one of my violin strings at a certain point instead of pressing it down firmly against the fingerboard, I could produce a flutelike sound with a high pitch. I always enjoyed producing these harmonics, and I remembered there was a mild "tingle" associated with them. Constance maintained that God spoke to her with such sounds.

Just then God chimed in. Constance cocked her head to the left and put a finger to her thin lips. I remained silent as I studied her face. She didn't have the blank stare expression of a drugged catatonic or the glazed look of a hallucinating schizophrenic. Rather, Constance was acting as if she was *actually* listening to something! "C sharp ... A ... E ... F sharp," she whispered for my benefit. "If I pay close attention, I can hear him almost all the time."

"What is he saying?" I asked, pushing the tape recorder closer to her chair.

"He's telling me about the nature of reality, the ultimate nature of all things in the universe," she said with a straight face.

"He says all this in only four notes?" I sounded incredulous. I had to get Constance to realize that the chimes were only noises in her head and nothing more. I had to expose her God for the whistling in the ear that I knew he was. I had to confront her hallucinations and stop them from becoming a full-blown psychosis.

She ignored my question. "The mind of God is the only reality. All else exists in his mind as an idea," she said.

"How does this explain the chimes or the voice?"

"You probably think they're simply hallucinations in my head. I admit they're mental phenomena, but reality is essentially mental or spiritual," she said. "Therefore the chimes and the voice of God are real."

This metaphysical discussion was bothering me. But I decided to play along. Besides, I had studied philosophy at Brandeis and I felt I could keep up with her. I pointed out that her reasoning was outdated solipsism and no philosopher adopts this position. She replied that God can adopt any position he wants. I countered with the argument of materialism: all things are forms or functions of physical matter; all science is ultimately reducible to physics. Her chimes were based on physical not spiritual events. I quoted Lucretius. Constance countered with Kant, Leibnitz, and Hegel. She was good. We got carried away in a scene that could have come from a Woody Allen movie, and we broke up in hysterical laughter.

After we caught our breath and wiped the tears from our eyes, Constance admitted she was putting me on, performing for the tape recorder. Halfway through the discussion I knew it too, but it was fun. Constance was bright, witty, and a good witness to her experiences. She didn't hear philosophical dissertations, she confessed. All she heard were the chimes, but she *really* heard them. She was as eager as I was to find their source.

Before I went any further, I arranged for Constance to have a complete examination. An initial urine screen showed no evidence of recent exposure to drugs. However, there was no test available for DMT. I had to rely on her statement that she had quit. There was no history of antibiotics or other medications that could cause hearing problems. The neurological and physical examinations, including the ear, nose, and throat, showed no relevant abnormalities. The findings from routine laboratory tests were normal. Physically, she was in good health. The results of audiometric testing were mixed. If Constance was tested on a day when the chimes were not around, there was no loss of hearing. However, if the chimes were present she was so distracted that there was an apparent hearing loss, primarily in the left ear.

Constance clearly had musical hallucinations, but there was no detectable physical cause. There have been cases in the medical literature showing that musical hallucinations were caused by brain tumors or neural diseases, and these were usually treatable. But Constance showed no signs of such pathology.

"There's no physical problem," I told her in our next meeting. "So I would like you to take a few psychometric tests, an electroencephalogram (EEG), and talk to one of the staff psychiatrists. Then we can decide on what treatment to use." She refused, stating that you can't find evidence of God in an EEG tracing and she didn't need a shrink who didn't believe in God telling her that God didn't talk to people. Chimes in the key of C-sharp minor were all the proof she needed.

"I . . . am . . . not . . . hallucinating," insisted Constance as she paused to emphasize each word. "The chimes are truly there." She didn't sound crazy. After all, the *mara'akame* had said there are no hallucinations, only truths. The truth for Constance was that she heard these chimes, somewhere and somehow, and that experience was intense enough to be perceived as real.

I knew that the chimes were originally acoustical noises produced by the DMT. Other users have described similar sounds. One woman heard a voice that sounded like a rising, metallic whine. One heard a high-pitched staccato tinkling, like the sound produced by rubbing your finger around the rim of a champagne glass. Another heard "an extremely faint sound on the very edge of audibility, rather akin to the sound that might proceed from distant wind chimes."

These sounds were coupled with powerful emotional feelings generated by the drug. Constance felt ecstasy as did her friends at Millbrook, who even wanted to call the drug "ecstasy" to denote the feeling of being transported to a divine place.

Some trippers saw the face of God, walked in his garden, or participated in a divine sexual union.

But everybody came down from their trips. Well, almost everybody. If Constance had a borderline personality, it was possible that DMT had pushed her over the border, thereby stranding her in some remote place. Musical hallucinations abound inside these mental closets. Patients report hearing everything from Bach chorales to Beatles songs. One young man heard Gabriel's trumpets and was afraid to move for fear they would stop playing. Over the years his legs atrophied, turning into useless sticks. However, I saw no evidence of such psychosis or schizophrenia in Constance. And when she finally consented to an EEG, I saw no evidence of temporal lobe seizures or other neurological disorders that could explain the hallucinations.

What I saw was an extremely talented musician with perfect pitch and vivid auditory imagery. When I asked her to think of sounds such as a honk of an automobile or the clapping of hands in applause, she rated the image aroused as perfectly clear and as vivid as the actual experience. She also demonstrated remarkable control over her imagery. Asked to think of the mewing of a cat and then manipulate the image, Constance turned it into a nerve-piercing mental screech that made her wince. Perhaps Constance's chimes were caused by a vivid auditory image still reverberating in her memory. If so, they should be controllable. I tried to get her to manipulate the auditory image of the chimes, but she failed at every attempt. When the chimes sounded, all she could do was stop and listen to them.

The prognosis was not encouraging. Auditory hallucinations from physical, neurological, or mental disorders could be treated to some extent. Cases of benign musical hallucinations like Constance's were highly resistant to treatment. When there is no obvious cause to treat, some clinicians simply minimize the phenomena for patients by labeling it "musical reminiscences." Unbidden songs by any other name are still a nuisance.

It was possible that Constance would have to learn to live with her chimes just as some patients have had to endure an assortment of lullabys, Irish jigs, and advertising jingles for decades. One eighty-year-old nun with progressive deafness heard ringing, buzzing, and someone singing "Jingle Bells" for over eleven years. While the nun adjusted to her hallucinations, could Constance ever adjust to the loss of her career? Psychotropic drugs can sometimes shut off hallucinations, but the medications have nasty side effects and often create additional problems. I remembered the case of an eighty-nine-year-old woman with a longstanding hearing problem. She was kept awake by gospel hymns coming from inside her head. Medication allowed her to sleep at night, but the gospel music continued during the day with the addition of a strange male voice that hummed along, and not always in tune.

I had a fleeting image of Constance in old age, lying in a nursing home, too drugged to complain that neither time nor medicine had ever stopped the chimes. The voice of God and the music he created were still alive inside her arthritic body, but the hands were too gnarled to express it. Someone was playing "Happy Birthday" on a piano in the day room. The body that was once Constance Temple did not even recognize the instrument.

The image illustrated my despair over this case. There was no treatment in sight. Everything pointed to a lingering DMT effect. Although the drug is short-acting, one possibility was that Constance was just not metabolizing it correctly. In fact, only small fractions of the DMT or its metabolites are recovered from blood or urine, and no one knows exactly where they go. Perhaps her body didn't produce enough of the enzymes needed to dispose of the drug. Or maybe there was an idiosyncratic disturbance in her brain chemistry and an unknown DMT by-product was floating around in her cerebral cortex. Another possible explanation was that the stress of dealing with the chimes only generated more endogenous DMT in Constance's brain, thereby keeping the chimes going. If such metabolic pathways existed, they could explain how some DMT users never fully recover and descend along the road to schizophrenia.

While these metabolic effects might correct themselves over time, how long should I wait? Constance was not getting worse, but there was no indication she was getting better. She had equal numbers of good days when the chimes were absent and bad days when they were always present. If I waited for the chimes to disappear on their own, I ran the risk of her developing more serious emotional problems, even schizophrenia. I was reminded of tragedies caused by hearing problems in the lives of other musicians. Deafness caused Beethoven to become more isolated, exaggerated his personality problems, and rendered his work increasingly introspective. The Czech composer Smetana fought against tinnitus and progressive deafness for years, forcing himself to work. He finally went insane and died in an asylum. Constance's career was already shattered. Would her window to reality be the next to go?

Constance felt the despair as well. She was unwilling to wait any longer. That's when she took matters into her own hands. She reported her efforts to me in our next meeting.

"I've got something to show you," she announced with a coquettish smile. She hurried over to the chair and put her left foot up on the seat. Then she hiked up her skirt, revealing her bare thigh. There were a couple of tiny puncture marks. One looked fresh.

She explained that she had injected DMT a few times to see if she could work with the intoxication and turn off the chimes. Intramuscular injections have a slower onset than smoking but the effects last longer, the ultimate elevator ride to the sky. Constance would have been able to experience the intense effects for most of an hour, long enough, she thought, to do some psychedelic psychotherapy on herself. It didn't work. She was undaunted. She wanted to try it again, this time combining the DMT with amphetamine for good measure.

I was downhearted. Not because it didn't work but because transference was now working on both sides of the clinical relationship. I knew Constance had become dependent on me. The little gifts she brought to the office and the telephone calls in the middle of the night made it very clear. And I was starting to care deeply about this woman. Now she was descending into a reckless and desperate panic with the same drug that caused the problem in the first place. The image of Constance in the nursing home seemed closer.

Her desperation was understandable. Constance felt alone with her chimes. Despite the transference, there is a distance between patient and doctor, a gulf that cannot be charted. I tried to bridge the gap by sharing the knowledge I had acquired as a psychonaut. We walked into Westwood Village, adjacent to UCLA, and had lunch at a sidewalk cafe. I spoke of Demon visions, the "ping" I heard on the mesa, and of mandalas and *mara'akames*. But Constance knew I did not hear the chimes.

"Let me hear them," I asked. "Play for me."

"I can't."

"I don't mean play a full piece," I explained. "Just try to make the same sounds you hear. You said you did it once. Remember Tartini's 'Devil Trill,'" I said in reference to the composer's sonata based on music the devil played for him in a dream.

Constance agreed and before she could change her mind, I escorted her to a piano practice room in the music department. I stopped at a drugstore on the way and made a small purchase.

She approached the piano and let her hands glide over several arpeggios. They were cut short by the chimes. In the acoustical isolation of the practice room, the chimes seemed louder than ever. I encouraged her to echo them on the keyboard. She hit a high C and put a trill on it. Another trill. A trill on C sharp, followed by C. A turn on E, then trills on C. *Fine.* She could not go on.

I opened the bag from the drugstore and removed a small box. The box contained several pink wax earplugs. I placed one of the plugs in her left ear, the ear favored by the chimes. *"Spiel! Spiel!"* I yelled in memory of my old German violin teacher. Constance felt the plug with her finger and looked around the cramped practice room. It was a quizzical look. I removed her glasses and placed them on the piano. *"Spiel!"*

She skimmed over a few arpeggios again, pounded a couple of chords, then dove into a passage I did not recognize. It sounded a bit rusty, but she kept playing. Then, a most delicate Chopin nocturne. The tempo was rushed, the notes slightly uncertain, but she played for several miraculous minutes. There were many moonstruck colors, a sensuous rubato, and subtle nuances.

When she finished, neither one of us said a word. Eventually she explained that the plug caused an immediate cessation of the chimes. She removed the plug, waited a few moments, then said she could hear the chimes again. I leaned over and closed her hand around the box of earplugs, kissed her softly, and left.

The earplug was not the spontaneous idea it appeared to be. I had spent weeks checking with colleagues on the latest gimmicks used in management of both tinnitus and auditory hallucinations. Tinnitus patients are often helped by devices that mask the ringing in their ears with electronic noise or static. There is even a commercial tinnitus masker: a small electronic noise generator built into a hearing aid. However, such gadgets also mask many of the delicate sounds essential to a musician. Another technique is to distract the patients by having them wear headphones connected to a portable cassette player or radio. One patient listened to heavy rock tapes and reported a reduction in his hallucinations. I couldn't imagine Constance playing Chopin while listening to Pink Floyd.

The most dramatic success has been achieved through occlusion of monaural auditory input—a single earplug stuck in one ear. Nobody knows why this works, but earplugs have proven to be an immediate cure for many schizophrenics suffering from auditory hallucinations. When all else fails, when patients are unresponsive to intensive pharmacotherapy and/or psychotherapy, psychiatrists stick it in their ears. I saw no reason not to try it with Constance.

I didn't see much of Constance after that day in the music department. We did keep in touch by telephone. The earplug continued to work, she said many times with many thanks. Then she started working again, teaching school part-time. I loaned her the money to get the Steinway back, and soon she had her private pupils returning. She joked that they still didn't prepare for their lessons, but now she could tolerate their playing by using two earplugs. Her own playing took a unique turn. She called it a new interpretation. She claimed she was playing better than ever. I suspected it was nothing more than the "halo effect" that patients often feel after they conquer a particularly difficult disease or addiction.

Months later Constance invited me to a recital. She would be playing an all-Beethoven program including the "Moonlight Sonata." It's in C-sharp minor, she reminded me. I would be there.

She wore the same white dress she had worn to my office. Her hair cascaded loosely over her shoulders, obscuring her ears, so I couldn't tell if she was wearing the earplug. Once she started playing it didn't matter. She opened with the "Moonlight." The program notes emphasized that Beethoven called this work a

Sonata quasi una fantasia, a sonata in the manner of a fantasy. Ms. Temple would be offering an original interpretation.

The first movement, the adagio, began with such delicate notes that one could see a boat floating in the moonlight on Lake Lucerne. Her tempo was liquid, and everywhere the lightest touches on the pedals, like oars skimming the water. Then, in the moonlight, a grace note appeared. Then another. Moon drops of grace notes falling on the lake, then evaporating in an instant. This was a Beethoven I had never heard. I recognized why: it was graced with the beauty of divine chimes. I tingled and recalled the line from *Amadeus* where Salieri, upon hearing the music of Mozart, remarked, "It seemed to me I was hearing the voice of God."

The allegretto began with a trill here, a turn there. Constance sweetened it with the faintest hint of a chime on the final D flat. The trio was crisp, flawless. Now the presto. Bold, triumphant, pure Beethoven. There, on the G-sharp trill, the echo of a chime. It seemed to hang there for several glorious beats. It made you long for more. Then an accelerating crescendo, the pressing on to the finish. Salieri spoke: "It was beyond belief."

The audience loved it and rewarded Constance with a warm, sustained applause. I noticed I was the only person standing. Perhaps only I knew that God was speaking through this woman for all the world.

3

RAPE
IN A DALI
LANDSCAPE

The artist aimed the gun and fired. A volley of paint-filled darts splattered against the canvas. The weapon, a Cap-Chur Projector, was better known for its use in capturing wild animals with drug-filled darts. The artist, Salvador Dali, who was using the gun to create an abstract painting, was better known for his surreal paintings of a real world transformed into melting watches and other dreamlike images.

Visionary drugs do more than bombard the eyes and ears with things that do not exist; they transform the real world of sights and sounds into a surrealist landscape. Under the influence of hallucinogens, the psychonauts could close their eyes and see dancing demons. With open eyes it was the furniture that danced while the walls breathed and the clock melted. DMT rang the hallucinatory chimes for Constance Temple, but the drug also caused real voices to sound distorted. Distorted sights and sounds are examples of illusions, misperceptions of real external stimuli. They can occur in any of the senses.

The most dramatic illusory effect reported by the hallucinogenic drug user is that things look different. There is a different perspective, a new interpretation. Dali provided an example of this in *The Great Paranoiac*, a 1936 painting with a single ambiguous image that can be viewed in two entirely different ways. One can see either a large troubled face or a collection of tormented figures. The effect is startling. Initially the psychonauts were confused by such startling changes in their visual field, but they adjusted and soon were able to describe the illusions.

Colors appear brighter and more deeply saturated than normal. Contrast is enhanced and the contours of objects become sharply defined. The result is a more three-dimensional view that adds hyperrealism: objects "pop out" of the visual field. They begin to oscillate and undulate. In a sense, inanimate objects become alive and appear to "breathe." Then they start changing in size and number, turning into a wonderland of Lilliputian creatures and gigantic doors with keyholes big enough to crawl through. Your own body can shrink to the size of a mouse or stretch to the roof. Look in the mirror and you can watch as your facial features turn into grotesque caricatures.

Afterimages abound as people move about in stroboscopic fashion, vanishing from over there, then materializing right here—all in the blink of an eye. Now there are two images. Suddenly there are dozens. In the flickering light of the campfire, when peyote kindled my brain, I saw the *mara'akame* divide into two, then four, then sixteen identical *mara'akames*, all intent on stealing my tape recorder.

There are striking parallels between changes in real stimuli seen with open eyes and those reported for mental images seen with closed eyes. Probably the same mechanisms in the brain are responsible for duplicating images of polygons or *mara'akame*s. These processes can just as easily scramble mental images or structures of the real world into random and sometimes nightmarish arrangements, like pieces of a picture puzzle thrown on the floor. The floor becomes a Daliesque landscape of floating body parts, a head without a face, and incomplete trees.

This madcap universe is in constant motion. For reasons that are still not understood by psychologists, heavy objects do not appear to move as much as lighter ones. Mountains will hardly shimmer, but matchsticks jump about. A bowl of spaghetti may look like a churning knot of worms while the table it sits on remains motionless. Perception is further confounded by staccatolike cuts of images taken from memory and superimposed on real visual targets. Dali, who collaborated with Luis Buñuel on *Un Chien Andalou*, used the film to illustrate the illogical nature of these abrupt transformations. A woman in the film sees ants crawling out of her hand. The ants dissolve into a woman's armpit, which in turn becomes a sea urchin, then the top of an androgynous head.

Sounds are amplified, but they are not always clear. A simple swallow, for example, might sound like the crashing surf, but where is it coming from? Since *Un Chien Andalou* was a silent film, one can't help but wonder about the soundtrack Dali and Buñuel would have chosen to convey these auditory illusions. What is the sound of a razor slicing an eye? Since reverberating echoes are as frequent as visual afterimages, how many times would we endure the razor's cutting sounds? It is easy to imagine how the psychedelic heaven visited by Aldous Huxley can change so quickly into a surrealistic hell.

This hell even has a strange smell because the sense of olfaction is more acute, although the recognition of particular odors may be impaired. The faint odor of soap, for example, may still be detected on one's body for hours after a morning shower, but *what* is that smell? Tastes are also difficult to decipher, and sometimes the taste of a food will be entirely blunted. Experienced users may nibble fruit or sip bland teas on long trips, but there is danger in sampling exotic cuisines. Persistent aftertastes from spices, like recurrent afterimages of razors, may ruin the rest of the perceptual feast.

To touch objects is to experience sensations that are at once both strange and familiar. The specks of dirt and grime on your skin make it feel like sandpaper. You run your fingers along the surface of your woven clothing only to get lost in the hills and valleys of each weave. If the ground feels like cotton candy, it is because the laws of gravity have been suspended. How else can you explain why you are floating? French writer and mescaline user Henri Michaux described the user as being in a "sensory Tower of Babel" wherein thousands of items of information arrived in a constant untranslatable bombardment.

The senses fuse. Colors have sounds, and sounds have physical shapes. The autumn leaves fall to the ground in a rain of distinctive chimes. A telephone rings and tiny fluorescent bands ripple through the air. Each beat of the Huichol drum splashes color onto the nocturnal rituals. These synesthesias are not always the funhouses they appear to be. The television screen casts a bone-chilling blue beam on the room. Radio is no better as the disembodied voices generate a spectrum of ghostly images and paranoid feelings. Then, a plumber's nightmare: you flush the toilet and lights go on!

The reason for all this sensory chaos is electrical confusion in the brain itself. Hallucinogens generate a continuum of electrical activity in the central nervous system that progresses from mild excitation to seizures. It begins with irregular waves of high-frequency, low-voltage activity in the brain. People experience excitement and euphoria during this initial stage. As the process continues, the brain activity is characterized by intermittent bursts of synchronous waves, the signpost of hallucinations. This increased excitation starts to overload the part of the brain that regulates incoming stimuli. The result is a failure in the brain's ability to modulate incoming signals, thus permitting all signals to enter with full power. The gates of the brain's sensory systems swing open, so to speak, and we are given access to many more inputs than we are able to sort through. This creates the sensory confusion. As the electrical waves surge through the brain's circuits, users will fluctuate between states of relatively clear perception and ones marked by hallucinations and illusions.

LSD is typical of hallucinogens that produce intermittent changes in perception. But some hallucinogens, such as mescaline, cause continuous synchronized waves in the brain, thus generating longer-lasting hallucinations. One hallucinogen, ketamine, drives the electrical activity in the brain to such extreme levels of arousal that it's in a class by itself. In addition to hallucinations, the trip is full of sensory distortions. But ketamine also renders users cataleptic and unable to move. The brain is alive and awake, but it seems oddly disconnected from the body. There is no sense of touch, no pain, and no way to resist. People become so tractable that anything can be done to them, even surgery. This is the stuff of which waking nightmares are made.

Zelda paced. She sensed something was about to happen. I filled the dart with Vetalar, chambered it in the Cap-Chur rifle, aimed and fired. The dart stuck in her thigh for a second, then bounced out. Zelda the lion roared.

Vetalar, a trade name for ketamine, started to work immediately. The drug was recommended to veterinarians for use as an immobilization agent in cats and subhuman primates. I was using it to capture Zelda, one of the many lions I studied on a game preserve, so that I could give her a routine physical. In five minutes Zelda started to sway. I approached her and started my examination. At one point I propped up her hindquarters and inserted a rectal thermometer. Zelda didn't seem to mind. Straddling her back, I lifted up her head and opened her mouth so the vet could check her teeth. Fifteen minutes after Zelda was darted she growled and made several attempts to rise and crawl away. I kept pulling her back by her tail. Finally, I had to administer a booster dose of ketamine in order to complete my work.

Far away, in the jungle of New York City singles bars, a subhuman primate by the name of Richard Esposito stalked his prey. His bait was a large plastic bag filled with so-called pharmaceutical cocaine—actually a harmless white powder adulterated with ketamine. He told the young women who flocked to the sparkling crystals that they had never tried anything like it. Then he took the hollow tube of a Bic pen and pushed it into the bag until it was jammed full with powder. Grabbing each woman by the chin, he took the pen and inserted it into each of their nostrils, then blew. The women remembered starting to sway, then nothing.

One of Esposito's male friends, Angelo, described what typically happened to the women after they were blasted with the Bic pen. Since the women had difficulty moving about, Richie would have to carry them to the car or a motel room. Once inside, he removed their clothing, usually just from the waist down, then raped and sodomized them. "Come on, join in on the fun," Richie would say to Angelo and other friends. The assaults turned into gang rapes. Throughout it all the victims did as they were told. If necessary they were given additional doses of ketamine, then literally molded into postures for oral or anal sex. Afterward, when the women came to, they would find themselves sitting on a bed next to Richie with no memory of what had happened.

Richie bragged that the ketamine was the best thing he ever

discovered, a real marvel. He started carrying a small bag of the powder in his wallet, the way some men carry condoms. The chemical rapes took place at least once or twice every day. This went on for three years. There were over a thousand victims out there and they didn't even know it. The super doses of ketamine had rendered them totally amnesic. Richie couldn't stop laughing.

On a July night in 1984 he was still laughing and having a good time at Valentine's, a disco in the Sheraton Hotel at New York's LaGuardia Airport. When Donna and Barbara, two young, attractive, well-dressed women, stopped for a drink, Richie couldn't take his eyes off them. Donna described him as a shark because he kept circling the girls' table, then finally invited himself over. Angelo and another male friend, Patsy, followed. Richie offered cocaine but the women refused. This necessitated a change in tactics. How about a drink? The women said no but Richie persisted: "Come on girls, have a drink, just one." Eventually Barbara agreed and Richie ordered a screwdriver for her. The women got up to dance.

Donna was the first to return to the table. Barbara's drink was sitting there, invisibly laced with ketamine. Donna was thirsty so she gulped down half the glass. Richie and the sharks stared. They stared and waited. Donna was beginning to feel nervous. The alcohol was quickening the absorption of ketamine into her bloodstream. Within minutes the nervousness turned into queasiness. Afraid that she might become sick, Donna said she had to go to the restroom. As she stood she felt that her body would keep rising until she hit the ceiling. Then she started to sway.

"You're sick," Richie told her. He offered to escort her to the restroom. In Donna's ketamine eyes, the hallway leading to the restroom looked like a tunnel stretching for miles. To make matters more difficult, Donna felt she was only two feet tall and the trip through the tunnel was going to take forever.

"It got to the point," Donna explained later, "where I couldn't feel the ground. I mean, I knew I was stepping, because I could see through peripheral vision that I was moving, but I couldn't feel the ground, and I actually had to hold the wall . . . hold myself up by using it. . . . And I was so scared. I was so scared."

Richie guided her past the restroom, out the building, and

across the parking lot. She leaned over a planter and began to vomit. Richie grabbed her arm and led her away. Donna could no longer feel her feet on the pavement. She was walking on a cloud. "Oh, my God. What's happening?" cried Donna over and over again. Richie put her in his car, then locked the doors. *I have to get out*, thought Donna. But she was helpless. Her hands wouldn't respond to commands from her brain to open the door locks. It seemed as if a wax had been poured over her entire body and was slowly hardening. She was trapped.

Back in the club, Barbara finished dancing. She returned to the table and drank the rest of the screwdriver. Richie came over to tell her that Donna had become sick and was waiting for her out by the car. Barbara stood up. Dizziness seized her. Her breathing became labored. As she walked to the parking lot she grew more and more anxious with each step. Richie pushed her into her car. His moves were well-practiced. He grabbed her chin, pulled out the Bic pen, then blew a full load of ketamine into each nostril. Barbara remembered a sharp, burning sensation in her nose and the back of her throat. Then she blacked out.

Richie returned to his car and found Donna still struggling. He gave her the Bic treatment. Donna saw what was coming and tried to lift her arms but they wouldn't work. She managed to move her head as Richie blew and the first load of ketamine fell on her face. "You stupid bitch," snarled Richie as he reloaded.

"Oh, my God," cried Donna. *Pick up your arms. Hit him*, she kept telling herself, but her body wasn't obeying her brain. *Get out of the car*. The ketamine stung as it finally shot into her, Donna said, causing her to gag and cough. But she didn't black out. Instead, her head flew off her body. There, in some disembodied place, she watched what happened. She noticed the Hertz emblem on the dashboard, a flash of Richie's face, then the Bic pen again. "Oh my God. Oh my God. What's happening?"

Donna was viewing the world through the wrong end of a telescope. It was a world governed by micropsia, or Lilliputian vision. Everything seemed small and far away. There was no perception of time. People were talking, but there were no clear sounds other than a strange humming in her ears. Streamers of colored lights filled the car. The air outside was filled with confetti. Geometric forms were superimposed on real objects. Everything moved with afterimages. Richie's laughing face kept popping out of the telescope, like some sadistic jack-in-the-box.

In silent terror Donna watched herself being raped. It seemed as if it was happening to someone else. Richie and the sharks kept running back and forth to the other car where Barbara awaited a similar fate. At one point Barbara managed to open the door of her car and fell out on the parking lot. She saw a tunnel and tried to run away. But since she was only two inches tall, she couldn't cover much ground. Besides, the tunnel was a maze of geometric puzzles and cracks. Then Patsy told her to get back in the car. "I did what he said," she later reported to me. "Why did I do that?"

The reason is that ketamine is a powerful abreactive agent—it breaks down the will to resist. In 1973 a team of Iranian psychiatrists was the first to exploit this effect, and, since that time, ketamine has been used to abduct unwilling victims of hostage and terrorist operations. At certain doses, people can be persuaded to stop resisting because they realize they are powerless. This is not quite brainwashing, but using ketamine to tame unruly behavior can accomplish similar goals. It has even been used to manage kidnapping victims as fictionalized by the late Alfred Hitchcock in his 1976 film *Family Plot*.

Barbara was easy to manage. She would remember virtually nothing of the following events. One of the sharks, the skinny one, told her to get in the back seat. She crawled between the front bucket seats and into the back. Something was very wrong. She didn't know that the skinny guy was behind her, raping her. *I have to get out of the back seat*, she thought. She crawled into the front seat and huddled on the floor. Skinny was laughing: "Where are you going, Barbara? What are you doing?"

She crawled into the back again. Skinny was gone but a muscular guy was there. He raped her savagely. She felt strong pelvic thrusts and saw her own face crying in pain. She was screaming, but nothing was coming out of her mouth. *God, I'm dead. This is it, I'm dead*, she thought. Then she blacked out again.

Angelo drove her home as Richie followed in the other car with Donna and Patsy. Richie noticed that Donna was still struggling. At the next red light, Richie leaned over and gave her the Bic treatment again. He fondled her thighs and breast, kissed her arm and hand, and told her how pretty she was. He couldn't wait to have some more fun with her.

The two cars arrived at Barbara's house. Richie and Angelo carried Barbara inside to her bedroom. Barbara's mother woke up, opened her bedroom door, and saw two men in the kitchen. "What's going on?" she asked. Richie replied that Barbara was sick and they were taking her home. The mother ran to Barbara's room.

Meanwhile Patsy was guarding Donna in the other car. *God, I got to get out of this car*, thought Donna. *Barbara's mom is inside the house. I'll be safe there. Got to get out.* But she couldn't move. In addition to the chemical restraints, Patsy had wrapped his arms across Donna's chest for good measure. In a few minutes Richie and Angelo returned with a bracelet, several rings, and a watch. "We got a lot of good shit here," announced Richie. Donna recognized Barbara's jewelry.

Donna was helpless as they took her own silver rings, antique gold watch, and necklace. Then they drove her to a local motel. For Donna, the car became a spaceship, and the ride to the motel turned into a trip through a Dali painting. Fragments of road signs hung at impossible angles. Traffic lights were bleeding yellow and red trails in the air. The Triboro Bridge was floating in a sea of flashing white lights. Lilliputian vision alternated with Brobdignagian vision, or macropsia, whereby there is an apparent enlargement in the size of objects. Everything was zooming in and out of focus. The spaceship zipped through a white tunnel. Donna could still see but she couldn't feel. Parts of her body were disconnected and floating in space. She put her fingers in her mouth but still couldn't feel them. A strange "woo woo" sound filled her head. Then an ominous feeling as pieces of her past life flashed before her eyes. The images formed a mosaic of colored crystals, then fractured and fell apart.

The spaceship parked outside a motel. Angelo opened the door to a room while Richie and Patsy dragged Donna inside. The ketamine was still keeping Donna down. The boys began using cocaine to keep themselves up. Richie got between her legs while Patsy and Angelo worked on her mouth. Donna remembered penises slapping against her face. Everyone switched positions. The group raped her over and over again. Patsy turned

Donna over and sodomized her. She fainted. After two hours, the boys dragged Donna back to the rental car and placed her in the passenger seat. Richie drove to the Bronx, where he dropped Angelo and Patsy off at their homes. Inside her paralyzed body, Donna's wide-awake brain saw enough signs and landmarks to know where they were. When they dumped her on the front lawn of a house, she knew she was home.

"I fell on my knees and hands," Donna said. "The car took off, and then, looking at my house, I swear, it was like looking at a temple. I thought . . . I would never see that house again, and then, I was crawling up the stairs. I couldn't walk, so I was crawling. And I remember seeing my mother open the door. She looked like a saint. . . ."

"Oh, my God, Mother. . . . Oh my God. It's over. . . . I'm home," cried Donna. As her mother reached down to pick her up, she noticed a strange white powder on her face. Then Donna vomited in her mother's hands.

A few hours later Donna and Barbara were brought to the police station by their families. Donna's memory was much clearer than Barbara's, but both women agreed that they became ill from the drink and were robbed of their jewelry. They gave a description of the jewelry to the police, and Donna described the suspects, the blue rental car, even the first three letters of the license. Neither Donna nor Barbara mentioned a sexual assault. The police logged the complaint as grand larceny.

Recurrent images of the rape continued to nag Donna. They were too vivid to be remnants from a dream. Like the post-traumatic flashbacks experienced by combat veterans, the memories of the rape actually grew more intense and detailed with time. Richie's jack-in-the-box face was now popping up in Donna's brain all the time and she couldn't stop it. She and Barbara went to a local hospital for a physical examination.

The examinations revealed the unmistakable signs of vaginal and rectal penetration: inflamed tissues and white liquid discharges. Barbara also had bruises and scratches on both knees as well as a ghastly tear in her rectum. Donna's thighs were bruised and a fissure had opened in her vagina. The penetrations had been brutal. The women returned to the police and the case was refiled as rape and sodomy. The hunt for Richie and the sharks intensified.

Many weeks later Richie was stopped for speeding in Yonkers, New York. In his wallet was a small plastic bag containing a white powder. The officer thought it was heroin. Richie told him it was a veterinary drug called ketamine. It was not a controlled substance, and possession of it wasn't a crime. The police couldn't hold him for that, but they arrested him for possession of a .357 magnum pistol. Inside the Yonkers jail Richie still believed that the magic of ketamine would protect him from more serious charges.

The New York detectives working the rape case were checking local jails when they discovered that Richie had been arrested in Yonkers. They brought him back to New York for questioning. Richie was laughing. He knew that ketamine erased memories, and it would be impossible for victims to identify him. "Prove it," he barked at the detectives. "Do you think you have me? Do you think you have two other guys? Prove it."

Proving it was exactly what the detectives had in mind. A line-up was arranged. There were five other men standing next to Richie, each wearing a numbered card. Richie elected to wear number 4.

"Oh, my God," cried Barbara when she viewed the line-up. "Number four. He's the guy." She hurried out of the room.

Another line-up was formed and Richie changed his number to 6. Barbara's mother was brought in. "Oh God," she gasped. "Number six. He was in my kitchen."

A slightly nervous Richie decided to change positions for the final line-up. He picked number 2. It didn't matter. Donna had lived with his face for weeks. She literally knew it in her sleep. Her reaction was almost clinical.

"Do you recognize anyone?" asked the police.

"Number two."

"Where do you know that person from?"

"He assaulted me."

Although everyone identified Richie, almost anyone who sees this man agrees that his dark—almost simian—features make him stand out in any crowd. Some say he looks mean. According to one witness who saw Richie at Valentine's that night, he even moves like "a creepy kind of guy." Did everyone simply pick the meanest looking suspect in the line-up? Did the police really have a case?

Richie didn't think so, even when he was ordered to stand trial for the rapes. Of course they recognized him. They remembered him from Valentine's. That memory was formed before they got the drug, and it would have remained relatively intact. The memories of him as the rapist should have been confused if not erased entirely by the ketamine. Indeed, Barbara recognized him but couldn't place him as the rapist with absolute certainty. She couldn't even remember the details of what Richie's attorney called "the alleged rape." But Richie must have been worried that something had gone wrong with Donna's ketamine treatment. It was doubtful whether he would have been caught in the first place had it not been for the details supplied by Donna. Her memory showed few signs of the amnesia Richie had come to expect from ketamine. Why?

That was the first question I was asked by Ann Marie Rost, the assistant district attorney who was prosecuting the case. Her office had hired me as a consultant and possible expert witness. I didn't have an immediate answer for what I considered an academic question. But I had several more pressing questions of my own. If the dose of ketamine was sufficient for sedation, then it had to cause hallucinations and illusions. How much of their report was hallucinatory and how much was real? How could we tell? Never mind the fact that Donna remembered more than Barbara. If a crafty defense attorney discovered that ketamine was a super hallucinogen, he might be able to cast serious doubt on the testimony of either victim under the influence. And if the jury learned that rape fantasies are sometimes reported by surgical patients recovering from ketamine anesthesia, the prosecution's case might be lost. The only credible eyewitness left, Barbara's mother, could only testify that she had seen Richie in her kitchen. How much time could you possibly get for creeping through a kitchen? I could almost hear Richie laughing. I flew to New York in order to get my own answers.

Detectives Thomas Sullivan and Joseph Sofia met me in New York and briefed me on the investigation. Did they find Richie's drug source? Sullivan handed me a vial of Vetalar obtained from the same local veterinarian who supplied the vials to Richie. It was ketamine, all right, enough in each vial for a dozen rapes. But, incredible as it sounds, there was no physical proof Richie used this ketamine on the women! No one had

bothered to analyze the bag of powder in his wallet. No toxicological tests had been performed on the victims. No one thought
of saving the white powder on Donna's face. I could hear Richie
again: "Prove it. Prove it."

I could also hear a classic defense argument—the so-called
coke whore defense—that had been raised successfully in many
rape cases. According to this argument the white powder was
exactly what Richie said it was: pharmaceutical cocaine. He
offered it to the women. They accepted. Everyone partied. Barbara and Donna were not rape victims but cocaine whores who
engaged in consensual sex in exchange for free cocaine. Neither
the police nor the prosecutor could prove that the powder *was
not* cocaine. In order to counter this defense the DA said it would
be up to me to establish that the drug was ketamine. I rattled
off a list of examinations and tests I wanted to conduct. No time,
the DA told me. I was scheduled to testify in less than twenty-
four hours!

There was still time for interviews with the victims. Barbara
arrived first, and I was immediately attracted to her long hair.
Traces of drugs and their metabolites are permanently embedded in the hair each day as it grows. Barbara's hair was long
enough to hold a drug history going back over twenty-five
months. I took a few samples for later analysis. Although the lab
work would take several weeks—too long for use at trial—and
there was no existing test for ketamine in hair, I was confident
the hair analysis would confirm my clinical opinion that Barbara
was not a drug user. (It did.) Aside from the occasional social
drink, the closest Barbara had been to cocaine or any other drug
was getting Novocain from her dentist.

Barbara gave me a detailed account of her food and liquid
intake on the night she visited Valentine's. I calculated that any
drug she consumed in the screwdriver would have been effective
within minutes. Cocaine, for example, would have given her an
immediate rush of euphoria and stimulation. But Barbara
reported sudden dizziness and difficulty in breathing, the classic
initial signs of an anesthetic drug. While she remembered very
little of the subsequent experiences, she recalled enough to sat-
isfy the diagnostic criteria for ketamine intoxication. These experiences included changes in body imagery (she felt two inches

tall); an out-of-body experience (she saw her own face); and, thankfully, loss of pain and memory.

The changes in body imagery were drug-induced distortions of real things, not hallucinations of things not present. Her descriptions of the three men at Valentine's, the walk to her car, even the ketamine trip itself, all matched their real counterparts. The rape did not have the characteristics of a hallucinatory story full of imaginary people and objects. Rather, her account described an experience full of illusions. Barbara's report was no different from a sober person's description of an ordinary perceptual illusion. Consider a car shimmering on the road in the heat of a summer day. The shape of the car may change slightly; the colors may bleed together; it may even move strangely. But it is, undeniably, still a car. The road is still a road. Barbara's body was under the influence of ketamine, and the heat of its electrical excitation caused visual targets to change in size, to shift perspective, even to vanish from her memory. The little she remembered could not be discounted. Rape in a Dali landscape was still a rape.

Donna's experience was more difficult to explain. She received many more doses but remembered almost everything. There didn't seem to be a physical reason for the difference: both women were close in age, height, and weight. Perhaps Donna was an experienced psychedelic drug user accustomed to functioning in an altered state, hence the good memory. However, her history revealed that other than a social drink, she used no drugs. (Subsequent hair analysis confirmed no drug use for at least the past thirty months.)

There had to be another explanation for Donna's unusual reaction to ketamine. Otherwise the prosecution's case was incomplete. There was always the outside possibility that the jury might believe that Donna, unlike Barbara, who was technically unconscious for much of the rape, was not subjected to drugging or physical force. Richie might be found innocent of some charges against Donna.

I inquired into Donna's other habits. She was vegetarian, took vitamins, drank herbal teas, and worked out daily. Before going to Valentine's, she and Barbara had shared the same pasta dinner. I asked if she had anything else to eat or drink that night. "Cranberry juice," she answered matter-of-factly. She downed a giant glass of it before dinner.

I jumped to my feet. "I can't believe you said that! I can't believe you said cranberry juice!" I kept repeating myself as I paced around the room. "I can't believe you said that!" Donna had just said the secret word, and I could almost see the duck drop from the ceiling in the old Groucho Marx TV quiz show. Instead of surprising the guest who said the secret word with a fifty-dollar bill, the duck in my fantasy had a card with the verdict GUILTY printed in bold letters.

The reason for my childish excitement was that cranberry juice is a partial antidote to ketamine. The juice rapidly acidifies the urine and helps "pull" the ketamine out of the system. This reduces the severity of the psychological reactions and speeds recovery. And Donna was a virtual reservoir of the juice. She had been on a cranberry juice diet for weeks, drinking gallons of it. This explained why she remembered so much despite the repeated Bic treatments.

Donna was paralyzed but able to observe and record events. When she tried to struggle, the drug pinned her down like a frog on a dissecting tray. "Anything they wanted, they did to me," Donna recounted between tears and chokes. "And I couldn't do anything about it, absolutely nothing, because, God damn it, if I could, I would've."

She experienced the same classic ketamine symptoms reported by Barbara, but without the amnesia. For Donna the ordeal was outside the boundaries of time, leaving her with no sense of the passing minutes or hours. It was an eternity. Occasionally there were garbled voices, but she remembered only what was said directly to her. This was similar to my own experiences when I was given nitrous oxide (a dissociative anesthetic like ketamine) by my dentist. I could never make out the conversations between the dentist and his assistant yet I heard clearly his instructions to "open wide" or "spit." While I didn't feel pain I knew what was happening as I watched the drill enter my mouth. It always made me feel a little anxious. I shuddered trying to imagine what Donna felt.

After the interview with Donna, I met with the DA and informed her of my opinion: the drug was ketamine, not cocaine. I was equally certain that the rapes were not hallucinations. The DA told me to get some sleep and be ready to testify in the morning.

I couldn't sleep. I tossed and turned as my mind replayed the interview with Donna. I kept thinking about what it must have been like for her to be assaulted in the midst of a drug trip. Perhaps it was similar to the scene in the 1968 film *Rosemary's Baby*, where Mia Farrow, after being drugged, hallucinates she is being raped by the devil. The dreamy sequence is shattered when Farrow, realizing that the rape is real, screams in horror, "This is no dream! This is really happening!"

The thought prompted me to leap out of bed, get dressed, and leave the hotel. I hired a taxi to drive me to Valentine's and from there to the Andrea Motel, where Donna had been taken. Richie and his friends took girls there so often they referred to the motel as a member of the family—Cousin Andrea's. Along the way I saw the lights and bridges described so well by Donna. But she saw the world through the blurred vision of ketamine. I took off my glasses (I'm nearsighted) and watched the lights bleed and form trails in the air. Then I tried lying down on the back seat to see how it felt. I must have fallen asleep for a moment because the next thing I knew the taxi driver's face popped up in front of my own. He was in clear focus just as Richie's jack-in-the-box face had been for Donna. "Andrea Motel," the driver announced. After a quick look around I went back to my hotel and got a few hours sleep before court.

I thought my testimony went well. The jury seemed attentive and, surprisingly, so did the defense attorney. Everyone seemed eager to learn about ketamine. Richie smirked. He knew it all. He was the real expert. I was happy no one asked me about flashbacks to ketamine. People may have spontaneous recurrences of their ketamine trips years later, and I didn't want to alarm the victims. I also didn't want to give Richie another reason to smirk.

After court I said goodbye to everyone. Privately I told the DA that the victims would eventually recover from all flashbacks. For myself, I was uncertain if I would ever be free of Barbara and Donna's haunting cries of "Oh my God." When I went to shake hands with Detective Sofia he took off his lapel pin and pressed it into my hand. The pin consisted of a red enamel apple inset with a gold detective shield. He knew how much I admired it. I was hushed with gratitude.

I was wearing the lapel pin when I went to the airport. Police and security people seemed to recognize it and one even gave me a professional nod. I went to the airport bar to wait for my flight. Somehow the pin made me feel safe. Still, I ordered what has become my favorite drink in New York bars: a cranberry juice cocktail.

POSTSCRIPT

Richie was convicted of both rapes. Angelo and Patsy pled guilty. All three were sentenced to prison. Richie would have to stay there for one hundred and forty years.

A test for ketamine in hair was finally developed in 1990. Traces of the drug were detected in the July 1984 sections of Donna and Barbara's hair.

Zelda the lion gave birth to four healthy cubs.

Dali's dart gun painting sold for thirty-five thousand dollars.

4

FLASHBACK AND DEADBALL

Two winos sitting in a puddle of urine marked the narrow entrance to the hotel. "Welcome to Skid Row's finest," I said under my breath as I stepped over the pair. Just a few miles away in Hollywood there were stars on the sidewalks. Here, in the grim reality of downtown Los Angeles, the only stars were the ones the winos saw before passing out on the streets.

It was a late afternoon in October, when the sky is already dark and flashing neon lights from bars and cheap hotels beckon those still able to walk. I opened the door to the hotel and started climbing the stairs. The staircase was as dark as the streets. At the top of the first flight I noticed the reason why: someone was trying to save money by putting a tiny refrigerator lightbulb in a fixture that called for two floodlights. The bulb on the second flight seemed even smaller. On the third flight the hotel had apparently run out of bulbs. I stumbled upward.

Doughnuts! A sweet aroma, with just a hint of yeast, filled my lungs. The smell was unmistakable. Someone was making doughnuts! As a child I smelled doughnuts every Saturday when I climbed the endless dark stairs to Professor Edgar Alderwick's violin studio. The studio was located on the top floor of an old brick building on Columbus Avenue in Utica, New York. The wood and glass door to the building was always so dirty I had to open it with a handkerchief in order to avoid getting my fingers soiled before the lesson. The professor admired clean hands and nails almost as much as he liked perfect intonation. I was clean but not perfect. The first flight of stairs was filthy, and I had to avoid contact with the bannisters. On the second floor there was a single door. It was kept closed but one day someone left it ajar. That was when I peeked inside and saw people making doughnuts for the bakery next door. By the time I got halfway to the third floor the escaping smells would finally catch me. I would pause for several intoxicating moments, then go on to the top floor.

I was always early and unprepared for my lessons. The early arrival allowed me to go to the bathroom and relieve some of my nervousness. The bathroom was in a cavernous storage room adjacent to the studio. With the squeaks from one of the professor's pupils drifting through the walls and covering my movements, I tiptoed into the bathroom, lifted the seat, and turned on the light. Zillions of cockroaches scattered in all directions. I saw my first cockroach there in that bathroom. I never saw them anywhere else, and as far as I knew Alderwick's bathroom was the breeding ground for the entire species. After they ran to wherever cockroaches go, I quickly finished my business and returned to the studio waiting room. By this time the earlier pupil had usually left. I got nervous again. Even after eleven years of lessons with the professor, I was still nervous. *I am so unprepared for this. Why didn't I practice more?* Instead of doughnuts it was the smell of fear in the air. Yet, as in some bad dream, I could not stop myself from knocking on the door.

Rudy opened the door. "What the hell took you so long?" he yelled. He was flushed and covered with sweat.

"Rush-hour traffic," I explained. "And I had to park about a half mile away." It was true but Rudy wasn't listening. He was pacing around the room, preoccupied with his own problems.

"Doc, I know something's gonna happen." There was panic

in his voice. He lit a cigarette. I noticed one was still burning in an ashtray overflowing with butts. "Maybe you should get me to the hospital tonight?" he asked. He puffed a few times, then stuck the cigarette into the mound of butts.

"Tell me what is going to happen," I asked with all the clinical calm I could muster. It was difficult because I was so excited. I knew from Rudy's previous telephone call that he had used LSD many years ago but was still bothered by occasional flashbacks. When he whispered that he felt one was coming, I dropped the phone and rushed here. I didn't want to miss an opportunity to witness an actual flashback. *What should I do if he has one? I am so unprepared for this.*

Rudy said that a black hole was going to get him. The hole was the most feared of all his LSD flashbacks. The other flashbacks, he explained, were relatively benign. Sometimes he saw tiny dots of colored lights pulsating about two feet in front of his face. The dots would stay there for several minutes despite his efforts to blink them away. Or sometimes little orange amoebalike blobs rushed at him from the corners, then just as quickly disappeared. The dots and blobs made him anxious. The black hole had him terrified.

The black hole appeared once or twice a month in the most unexpected places: on the street, in the park, once even popping out of a newspaper. I knew how unpredictable and strong these experiences could be. My own flashback of climbing to Alderwick's violin studio came when I was innocently climbing similar stairs to Rudy's room. It was so vivid that I even smelled doughnuts, although I was certain that the smell was only in my mind, not my nose. While I could choose to indulge in this pleasant reminiscence or to ignore it, Rudy had no such choice. Unlike my doughnuts and their sweet-smelling memories, Rudy's black hole, once released, needed no personal invitation to stay around. Instead, it literally rolled down the street after him, a giant doughnut hole from the twilight zone. And Rudy would run to the nearest police station or hospital for help. The police laughed, and the doctors gave him tranquilizers.

"I took some of the pills tonight before you got here," Rudy said.

"What did you take?" I asked. Rudy handed me a bottle of one hundred Valium tablets, the five-milligram size. The bottle was empty. "Exactly how many did you take and when?" I demanded to know. I looked around for the telephone and saw it on the floor next to the bed. If necessary I could call the paramedics, but I didn't know what their response time was in this part of the city. "How many?" I insisted.

"Four, about twenty minutes ago," Rudy confessed sheepishly. "The rest are in the toilet."

I ran to the bathroom. Dozens of yellow Valium tablets were bobbing in the toilet bowl. I spotted a rainbow of other pills spread across the water: red and white Nembutals, orange Thorazines, green Libriums, blue Stelazines, and a pretty violet capsule I didn't recognize. I flushed them down the drain.

Rudy explained that the pills confused him and slowed his movements. He was literally sick and tired of them and vowed never to take another again. Besides, he had faith that I would cure him. *How? I've never done this before!* Rudy claimed that he was already feeling better since I arrived.

I knew that his relief was due to the Valium, which was just starting to kick in. At least he had stopped pacing. Twenty milligrams would probably lull him to sleep, but they would not kill him. I relaxed and decided to obtain some background information while he was still awake. I sat down on a desk chair near the telephone. Rudy sat on the edge of the bed, folding his hands and fingers together like a dutiful pupil. He was trying to sit still, but his huge frame caused the bed to jiggle constantly. Rudy had been obese since childhood and never shed the weight or the boyish appearance. His wavy red hair, freckles, cowboy shirt, and boots made him look like a fat Howdy Doody.

In high school Rudy took approximately a dozen LSD trips. He described the typical experiences, including geometric images and distortions in the visual field. These trips were always pleasant and entertaining. His last trip, however, was frightening. A new type of LSD, White Lightning, was moving through his school. Unknown to Rudy, a single dose of White Lightning contained more LSD than he had taken in all his previous trips combined.

Rudy knew it was strong almost immediately after he swallowed it in algebra class. The school seemed the wrong place to be and Rudy went outside. He felt he was entering a whole new world. He stretched out on the grass and felt green waves rippling through his body. The waves buoyed him into the sky, then higher and higher. Too high, Rudy thought, much too high. He thought he might die. He ran to his car and tried lying down on the seat. Suddenly, he saw a hand reach in through the window and turn on the ignition. The car jerked into gear and quickly accelerated. Rudy watched in terror as the speedometer needle went all the way around the dial and stayed there. He grabbed the steering wheel. It felt like hitting a brick wall.

The car *did* hit a brick wall, but Rudy walked away. He found some friends and told them he was loaded on acid, really freaking out. "Get me to a hospital," he stuttered and pleaded.

"You're stoned," someone observed just as Rudy slipped on the ground. Everyone laughed at Howdy Doody on LSD.

"I'm afraid I'll never come down," cried Rudy.

"Never come down. Never come down," taunted his friends.

The waves of White Lightning cresting in his body were carrying him to the edge of the void. Rudy fought desperately to stay anchored in reality, to stay alive. He thrashed about, flailing his arms and kicking his legs like a swimmer on the edge of a whirlpool. Eventually the police arrived and took Rudy to a hospital where he was treated for LSD poisoning, then released. It was the first of many visits to hospital emergency rooms.

While Rudy never took LSD or any other hallucinogen again, he was plagued by flashbacks from this last trip. He told me that the flashbacks would usually start with the same feelings of nausea he experienced after swallowing the White Lightning. Whenever he felt a flashback coming on, he would set out for the nearest hospital. The visual images would soon follow. But, since they never lasted more than fifteen minutes, by the time he got to the hospital lobby they were gone. Rudy described how he would sit in the lobby until the panic and feelings of impending doom also disappeared—usually within another thirty minutes. If the panic did not stop, he would seek admission. *So the visuals trigger the panic! What could trigger the visuals? It can't be something as simple as acid stomach.*

Lately the black hole was showing up almost every night. *Why does it come only at night?* This was causing Rudy to be in a state of anticipatory fear throughout most of the day. "At night I'm flashing," he said. I asked him if there were any times at night when the flashbacks did not occur. "Only two times," he said with a yawn, "when I'm sleeping or when I'm out shooting pool."

It was getting late, and Rudy's eyelids were starting to sag. Since it didn't seem likely that they would be open long enough to see a flashback, I told him to get some sleep. Tomorrow we would shoot some pool. My pool game was much better than my violin playing.

I spent the next day reviewing the scientific literature on flashbacks. The predominant view was that flashbacks are spontaneous memories. Most of the contents from a LSD trip are forgotten except for fragmentary memories. However, sometimes people have spontaneous returns of those memories complete with images, feelings, or sensations that were first experienced during the drug state. The memories might return as single fleeting images, like snapshots from a holiday trip, or they might appear as a rerun or flood of images depicting an entire sequence of events. The snapshots are almost always brief flashes lasting one or two seconds. Reruns have been known to go on for as long as one hour. As time passes, the flashbacks decrease in duration and frequency, eventually disappearing altogether. They tend to occur within the first few days after a trip, although flashbacks persisting for weeks or months after a particularly intense drug experience have been reported.

Rudy's flashbacks lasting for minutes and persisting for more than five years were unprecedented in the volumes of medical reports I searched. Yet his flashbacks had the same classic features as all the others: they were primarily visual, frightening, and unstoppable. The dots and blobs often formed simple geometric arrays that were identical to the hallucinogenic form constants described by Klüver. I suspected that even the black hole was a variation of the basic tunnel form.

The recurrent imagery of flashbacks is unrelated to the pharmacological action of the drug. There are no residual metabolites floating around in the brain, especially after years of abstinence. And no one has found any drug-related brain damage or neurological dysfunction that could account for such images. The literature was clear that flashbacks were not pathological but psychological in nature. They are best understood as vicariously experienced remembrances of things past, of literally unforgettable trips.

The flashbacks repeatedly coerced their way into Rudy's life, demanding attention and resisting all efforts to dispel them. Imagine someone sneaking up on you, grabbing your head, then forcing you to look at some old home movies over and over again. You can't turn away, and you can't turn the projector off. You are compelled to watch, listen, and relive the events until the movie is over. I knew that such recurrent unbidden images could evoke anxiety, neurotic hysteria, or even psychotic reactions in susceptible individuals. It was no wonder that flashbackers tended to abuse alcohol and other sedative drugs in an effort to turn off the projector. Rudy's abuse of prescription drugs was no different. But rather than stop the projector, the pills only clouded his perception and kindled his anxiety. I also noticed signs of psychotic thinking: he told me that the black hole had a will of its own.

The black hole was threatening to engulf Rudy. If that happened, Rudy explained, he would really be in the tapioca, a pool player's slang expression for a lonely and hideous place. Once you're in the tapioca, you're history. I feared that he could be lost forever unless these flashbacks were eliminated. In order to destroy them it would be necessary to identify the stimuli that triggered them. Some triggers are easy to find, and patients are quick to point out which music, pictures, or other stimuli remind them of their trips and spark the flashbacks. One patient couldn't listen to a particular Beatles record without re-experiencing the depersonalization he felt while listening to the same record under the influence of LSD. By avoiding such triggers, patients can exercise almost complete control over the flashbacks. For example, one patient found that getting high on marijuana triggered an LSD flashback. After he stopped smoking marijuana, the flashbacks ceased.

Neither Rudy nor I had any clue as to what triggered his flashbacks. He didn't use marijuana, and he was about as far removed from the physical and cultural environment of his high school LSD days as one could be. Perhaps the trigger was subjective rather than objective. It might be a particular feeling that prevailed during his initial drug trip. Sometimes a specific level of arousal, such as a stressful situation or an anxiety-provoking thought, is enough to trigger a flashback. The trigger—or triggers—could be virtually anything in Rudy's daily life. Since his flashbacks occurred only at night, the best chance I had to find Rudy's trigger was to become part of his night life.

That night I took Rudy to dinner. While I ate a salad, Rudy put away two steaks and a pack of cigarettes. He told me about his childhood, his boredom with school, the odd jobs, and how he got the nickname Deadball. In shooting pool the deadball shot is one in which the cue ball stops or rolls "dead" upon contact with an object ball. British snooker players call it the stun shot. To execute the deadball shot, a player must hit the cue ball so that it slides into the object ball without backspin or forward roll. Hitting deadballs is a powerful weapon for gaining position on the table, and Rudy's mastery of the technique earned him the nickname. He offered to teach me.

At a local poolroom, Rudy placed the eight ball on the edge of a corner pocket and took the cue ball to the other end of the table. When he hit the cue ball it knocked the eight ball into the pocket, then stopped dead in its tracks on the very edge. Flawless. He set up the same shot for me. I thought I was a good player, but I surprised myself by hitting the best deadball in my life. Rudy glared at me. "Rack 'em up," he said.

Rudy sunk a ball on the break, and I never got a chance to play that game. He cleaned the table without missing. His style was fast and self-assured. I sunk a few balls in the next game, and by the fourth game I was on a run of eleven balls. But I was taking my time stalking around the table and studying the physics of each shot. I was totally absorbed in this green felt world. Rudy must have given up with my plodding pace because I no longer heard him offering tips on which shot to take. When I missed a complicated bank shot I turned to him.

The first thing I noticed was his cigarette. It was still in his mouth—at least the filter was there—but the rest had burned down to ash while still holding its shape. I had seen this happen to Professor Alderwick when he took my violin to demonstrate how a particular piece should be played. Lost in the reverie of the music, the professor would ignore the ever-present cigarette he kept dangling from his lips until he finished playing. I was always afraid that it would fall and burn my violin. But it never did. Alderwick's statuesque posture, with almost no body movement except for his fingers and bow arm, kept the cigarette as secure as if it had been placed in an ashtray. It could be held equally immobile in a flashbacker's mouth.

While I was having one of my luckiest runs at the pool table, Rudy was having a flashback. He was rigid and didn't move until I went up to him and called his name. Then he told me that several of the orange blobs had hit him in the face. As he watched their attack, a tingling sensation moved up his back. He was too afraid to move, the result of a classic stun shot to the mind's eye.

I took his pulse and it was racing. Beads of sweat dotted his forehead. I didn't know what to do. Rudy ordered two beers and drank both of them. *The flashback happened while I was playing, but Rudy said they never happen when he's shooting pool. Maybe he just needs to keep busy.* I tried to distract Rudy by encouraging him to play some more. Show me your stuff, I suggested. "Get me to the hospital," he replied. It was too late, I said, then took him back to the hotel and told him to be at my hospital office first thing in the morning.

As I drove home I thought about what tests to run on Rudy at the hospital. His flashback in the pool hall was suggestive of certain seizure disorders that can have apparent catatonia, visual components, even kinesthetic sensations such as tingling. I made a mental note to schedule a complete neurological evaluation, including EEG. However, I had seen many seizures caused by epilepsy and drug overdoses. Somehow Rudy's experience *seemed* different. He remained conscious and fully aware of everything that was happening. In fact, he insisted he could move but was just too afraid. It was fear that caused the tingling sensation to creep up his spine, then hold him as still as a deadball. This was no seizure. Rudy's experience was more reminiscent of my own encounter with *The Tingler*.

In 1959 I saw the opening of William Castle's horror film *The Tingler*. I never missed a Castle film. He was always trying to scare the pants off his audience with some new gimmick. Before the ending of *Homicidal*, the projectionist stopped the film. Then an announcer invited the audience to step into "Coward's Corner" and receive a full refund if they were too afraid to see the rest of the movie. A uniformed nurse was there to offer free blood pressure tests to those who were uncertain if they could survive.

The gimmick in *The Tingler* was even better. In the movie, Vincent Price plays a mad scientist who tries to capture a tingler, a lobsterlike creature that grows along the spines of people when they are frightened. The only way to stop the tingler is to scream. He administers LSD to a mute woman. She becomes frightened but, of course, cannot scream. As her trip goes from bad to worse, the tingler grows strong enough to hold her spine in a paralytic death grip. After the scientist removes the tingler from her body, it escapes from his lab. At that precise moment, the movie screen goes dark and the projectionist pushes a special "Percepto" switch. The switch activates motors under selected seats in the theater, causing the audience to feel tingling shocks.

I remember sitting there in electrified silence, then screaming with the rest of the audience. Everybody loved the movie, and I went back to see it several more times over the years. The Percepto gimmicks had been removed after the first showings, but it didn't matter. Each time the screen went dark I started tingling. The tingling had become a conditioned response to the dark screen.

I suspected that Rudy's flashback was based on a similar mechanism. He had experienced a profound panic during his last LSD trip. Any visual imagery associated with that trip would now elicit the fear and panic. The usual treatment for such a panic reaction was to desensitize the person. This could be accomplished by gradually exposing them to the visual stimuli while teaching them how to relax. But Rudy seemed too impatient for such a slow approach. Besides, the only realistic way to present the blobs and other images was to turn him on again. Although I was licensed to give him LSD, I thought it would be too risky. I would do this only as a last resort. A safer approach would be to isolate and destroy the trigger. I still didn't know what it was.

When Rudy showed up at my office at the Neuropsychiatric Institute (NPI), he was shaking. The hole, he cried, was waiting for him just outside the front door. We sneaked out a side door and I drove him home. It turned out that he didn't actually see the black hole; he only sensed its presence. I managed to calm him down and convince him to return with me for a series of physical and psychological examinations over the next several days. The results of the tests were all within normal limits. And there was no evidence of an acid stomach. Even the neurological work-up failed to detect any dysfunction. I asked one of my colleagues, Dr. Frank Ervin, who literally wrote the book on seizure disorders, to evaluate Rudy. His opinion: Rudy was having "honest-to-goodness flashbacks." Another colleague, the late Dr. Sidney Cohen, who had written several books on LSD, agreed. Sid called it the most unusual case of flashbacks he ever saw.

Having satisfied myself that Rudy's flashbacks were genuine, I admitted him to the NPI as a research patient. He would be housed in a private room on a locked ward adjacent to my lab. The goal was to monitor and document all of his activities until he had several flashbacks. Then it should be possible to sift through a list of behaviors preceding each attack and find the common trigger. If he had one of his longer flashbacks, he could be rushed to the lab for on-line physiological and neurological measurements, including an EEG. No one had ever caught a flashback in a lab before, and I felt a strange fellowship with Vincent Price and his pursuit of the tingler. I ignored the fact that the tingler escaped from the lab and claimed the scientist as its first victim.

I briefed the ward staff on Rudy. They were instructed to keep a record of *everything* he did and call me at the first sign of a flashback. "My apartment is only a few blocks from the NPI, so call me any time," I told them.

The telephone rang as soon as I got home that night. Rudy was having an anxiety attack. I rushed to the ward, where I found Rudy pacing in his room. He had been watching TV when he started seeing dots. "The dots," he explained, "were two feet in front of my face, between me and the floor." The flashback lasted for ten minutes, but it had taken me at least that long to run to the NPI. All that was left of Rudy's experience was anxiety. I ordered a placebo injection for Rudy and waited around until he was quiet. Before I left the ward I checked the dayroom where Rudy had been watching TV. None of the patients noticed anything unusual about Rudy while he was having his flashback. As I left I saw that the vertical hold on the TV was not working, causing the picture to race up and down. The patients didn't seem to mind.

I slept on a bed in the lab for the next several nights. It was unnecessary. Rudy didn't report any more flashbacks. He seemed happy with all the attention, as well as the free room and board. The staff, however, was bothered by his disruptive behavior. He refused to participate in the afternoon group therapy sessions, calling the other patients a bunch of stiffs and deadballs. He folded his hands and sat in stoic resolve, occasionally chuckling as someone was spilling their guts to group. The psychiatrist running the group told Rudy that he must try to confront his problems and let the group help him. "You're not getting along because you refuse to connect with us," said the psychiatrist. He continued to blast away at Rudy's behavior. Rudy heard his high school friends taunting him.

"You're putting too much chalk on your dick," Rudy finally screamed at the flabbergasted doctor. The psychiatrist immediately called me to complain about Rudy's impertinence. I explained that Rudy was always speaking in pool hall slang and his remark was in reference to the chalk a pool player puts on his stick to increase the friction between the tip and the cue ball. I suggested that Rudy said "stick" while the psychiatrist heard "dick." The psychiatrist was not amused. He ordered me to remove Rudy from the ward during group meetings. Rudy was right—this was one overly chalked-up psychiatrist.

So every afternoon I took Rudy to the poolroom at the UCLA Student Union building, where he finally showed me his stuff. He was not only a national class tournament player but a master of trick shots. He set up a series of demonstrations, and I watched in awe as the cue ball zigzagged, bounced, jumped, stopped, and moved backward. In one shot Rudy hit a cluster of five balls and pocketed all of them. The shots seemed so natural to him that I could almost believe his patter about how his mother delivered him on a pool table. He also claimed that she named him after the daddy of pool sharks, Minnesota Fats, whose real name was Rudolph Wanderone.

Rudy showed me a few shots he liked to bet on. He placed two balls side by side against the foot rail. Then he placed the eight ball on top of the foot rail so that it leaned on the two balls below. The cue ball was placed at the far end of the table. "I bet you I can make the cue ball hit the eight ball first," said Rudy.

"Betcha," I challenged. The shot looked impossible.

Rudy shot the cue ball right in between the two lower balls; at the same time he discreetly bumped the table with his huge belly. The two balls moved out of the way, and the eight ball fell to the table just in time to be hit by the cue ball!

For his next trick, Rudy placed the eight ball on the foot spot, the spot in the lower middle of the table where balls are racked at the beginning of a game. He covered the eight ball with a handkerchief and placed the cue ball at the opposite end of the table. "Eight ball in the corner pocket," announced Rudy as he used a moderate stroke to hit the cue ball dead center. The cue ball rolled into the handkerchief and the eight ball rolled out, dropping in the corner pocket at the foot of the table. "Nothing to sneeze at," deadpanned Rudy.

Those afternoon pool sessions provided the only real excitement in the weeks that followed. My game improved and I even managed to beat Rudy on a couple of occasions. That only happened because he wasn't playing up to his normal speed. He didn't care about winning unless there was some money on the table; and I refused to bet him.

Rudy grew to like the arrangements at the NPI. He even found a girlfriend on the ward. But when the staff caught them in a compromising position, I knew it was time for Rudy to go home. Besides, there had been no more flashbacks since the first night, and Deadball was anxious to return to the betting world.

He liked to work the pool tables in bars or small poolrooms near the bus station. Rudy's style was to play deliberately below his level but slightly above the level of his opponent. He would exaggerate the difference with grandiose and irritating statements about his superiority, making sure to miss some very easy shots. When Rudy threw a five or ten on the table, the suckers couldn't resist a chance to shut him up. I spent many nights watching Rudy hustle a hundred dollars or more in this way.

One night I took him to a classy pool club on the west side that catered to the wealthier crowd. I thought I should dress up so I put on a slightly tight suit and my favorite paisley bow tie. Rudy had never seen me wear anything other than jeans and blue workshirts. He said I looked like a clown. Perhaps I did, but as soon as I stepped inside I was glad I had left my jeans at home. I recognized several colleagues as well as a dean from the university.

Rudy and I practiced on one of the tables while he sized up the other players. Nobody was very good but we saw lots of big bills changing hands. Rudy challenged a decent player on the adjacent table to a game of one-pocket. Hustlers can win in one-pocket without making a single outstanding shot. The suckers never realize what they are up against because strategy is more important than shot-making ability. The game is played with the usual fifteen balls racked in a triangle. Before the break each player chooses one of the two corner pockets at the foot of the table. The first player to make eight balls in his pocket wins. Inexperienced players tend to herd balls around their pocket, forcing the other player to spend time knocking them away. Experts like Rudy are not afraid to sink a ball or two for the opponent in order to gain position and continue running balls into their own pocket. Deadball always won. But the suckers always felt good because, thanks to Rudy, the score was always close. This only encouraged them to try again. I watched Rudy play for over seven straight hours and win every game.

It was 1:00 A.M. when we left the club and started walking outside. I wanted to go home and get out of my clown suit. Rudy also wanted to go home because his pockets were bulging with cash. A light rain was falling. He had trouble lighting his cigarette, his tenth one in the last thirty minutes. Since I never let him smoke in my car, I suggested we walk around the block until he finished his cigarette. After a few minutes we heard a crackling sound coming from above our heads. We both looked up and saw a neon sign shorting out in the rain. It was flickering like a strobe. I kept walking. Then I heard Rudy gasp and turned to see his face freeze in horror.

"It's here!" he whispered and bolted down the street. A contagious bolt of adrenalin shot through my own body, and I ran with him. There we were: Howdy Doody and Clarabell running for cover in Coward's Corner. After about a block I decided to look over my shoulder, half expecting to see a mugger after Rudy's cash. The street was deserted.

I grabbed Rudy. "Rudy! Stop and look at it." I forced him to turn around.

He became catatonic, stiffening like a statue. I kept yelling his name and asking him to describe what he was seeing. After five minutes he could talk again. The black hole was now gone, he panted, but he had seen it clearly for the first time: a giant funnel about sixteen feet in diameter. The outside of the funnel was covered with a black lacework, while the inside was lined with geometrically arranged girders. There was a bright light in the very center of the hole.

When Rudy said "light," I came to attention. I finally had an idea about the trigger's identity! Rudy had been staring at the flickering neon sign just before the flashback. And the TV in the dayroom was flickering just before his flashback. *Flickering light could be the trigger!*

But what caused the first attack, the one when I caught Rudy holding the cigarette in his frozen lips? Rudy smoked cigarettes all the time. That's nicotine! And that means central nervous system stimulation! The stimulation would not be critical unless consumption was excessive or it was coupled with flicker. There were no flickering lights in that first attack, but Rudy had been chain-smoking just like tonight. I had a hunch that nicotine was another trigger.

If flicker and nicotine were triggers, what kept Rudy from having flashbacks all the time? After all, he was always surrounded by pulsating neon lights and cigarettes. I knew that under the right conditions, flicker or nicotine could excite the electrical activity in his brain just as LSD had done years before. What were those conditions? Rudy was obviously uncomfortable in each situation leading to a flashback. In the first attack, it was a long ride in traffic ending at an unfamiliar pool hall that caused the discomfort. The next flashback occurred during his first night on a mental ward, an anxious situation for almost anyone. Tonight's flashback followed a nervous walk in the rain down a deserted street in the middle of the night with a bundle of cash. I had to admit that I was nervous, too. Even when Rudy first came to my office, terrified by the black hole, he had to ride a series of buses for almost two hours through unfamiliar areas of the city. I got nervous just thinking about riding a bus through some sections of Los Angeles. For Rudy it was more than nervousness; new or threatening situations probably created the necessary stressful conditions for the triggers to operate.

The following day I took Rudy back to the lab to test my

ideas. First, he was wired to an EEG machine that would constantly monitor his brain waves. Next, I asked him to sit on a chair in front of a translucent screen. Behind the screen was a photic stimulator, a type of adjustable strobe light. It was really no different from the flickering neon lights except the device allowed me to vary the frequency, intensity, and duration of the flicker. When people look at the screen, they do not see a simple flashing light. Rather, they tend to see specific geometric forms such as stars, snowflakes, crosses, spirals, even tunnels. Since these forms closely resemble those produced by LSD, I suspected that they might cause Rudy to have a flashback.

I explained the procedure to Rudy and asked him if he had ever done anything like this before. No, he replied, and he didn't like it. He said his hands were wet, and I could see that he kept rubbing them together.

"There's something about this . . . I don't know . . . being here, waiting, I can feel the tension building," Rudy said. The unfamiliar test situation was making him nervous. I told him to relax. *I hope he doesn't.*

I asked Rudy to look at the screen and tell me what he saw. "Nothing," he said. The EEG readings were normal.

Now I turned on the light and slowly varied the frequency of the flicker.

"It starts in one spot and goes in, around and around," he said. "The center . . . is . . . dark . . . rotating." His voice was trailing off, but there was no panic.

Rudy was looking directly into a black hole. Looking at the EEG readouts, I could see the same pattern of excitation that was associated with LSD intoxication. I knew that if the photic stimulation continued, Rudy might have a seizure. So I immediately stopped the test.

I should have been thrilled, yet the flashback I triggered in the lab was disappointing. It was far different from the ones Rudy experienced on the street. It took over seven minutes of photic stimulation, far longer than the few seconds Rudy was exposed to the neon lights. While Rudy eventually saw a black hole, it wasn't *the* black hole with girders and white light and runaway fear. Something was missing. What?

I realized it was still early in the morning. Rudy had been up for only a few hours, and, at my request, had had nothing to eat or drink. Photic stimulation sometimes produces nausea, and I didn't want Rudy vomiting all over the lab. I had not said anything about cigarettes, but Rudy avoided them the best he could—he only smoked two! That was far less than his normal load of nicotine. By the time it was dark, Rudy would have smoked over forty cigarettes. *That's why his attacks only take place at night!* Tonight I would repeat the photic stimulation.

Rudy moaned when I told him he had to continue his fast until dinner. However, I allowed him to drink noncaffeinated beverages and smoke all the cigarettes he wanted. We spent the rest of the day shooting pool at the Student Union. I kept a hand counter in my pocket and clicked it each time Rudy lit a cigarette. At 5:30 P.M. the counter was at sixty-one, and I took Rudy back to the lab. I adjusted the dials on the stimulator to produce the same rhythmic flash that triggered the previous flashback. Rudy's eyes sprang open.

"It's here," he shouted. "The hole, the hole."

The tingler crept along Rudy's spine. In a few seconds he was catatonic. He either could not or would not speak. I turned off the stimulator. Rudy refused to budge. I shook him hard, probably too hard. Rudy's fist connected with my shoulder. It stung. He pushed me away, kicked over the chair, and rushed out of the lab.

I caught up with him outside the NPI. Rudy said that the black hole he saw in the lab was *exactly* like the one he saw on LSD. "I felt the panic build and build and build," he explained. He was afraid he might react in the same violent way he did when the police took him to the hospital five years ago. Inside the police car Rudy had thrown punches and kicked out two windows. Rudy didn't want to hurt me.

He also didn't want to be a research patient anymore. I tried to explain that now that we knew what the triggers were, all he had to do was avoid them. That meant no bright lights, big cities, or cigarettes. To Rudy that meant no more hustling. He didn't think he could do that. He thanked me for my time and disappeared into the night.

A few weeks later Rudy called me. He had moved to another city and was finding new suckers to take. He was determined to keep moving around, never to find himself behind the eight ball or in front of the black hole again.

But the black hole eventually caught up with Rudy. He gave up running and called me for help, resigned to do whatever had to be done. I arranged for him to work with a behavior therapist whom I knew. Together we got Rudy to kick the nicotine habit and control his anxiety through relaxation therapy. There were a few minor flashbacks after that, but the black hole never found him again.

Later I visited Rudy's old ward at the NPI. I wanted to thank the staff for their cooperation and help. Jerry, one of the ward patients, cornered me in the dayroom. He was a likable young man who called himself an artist. The psychiatrists called him schizophrenic.

"There's been a terrible mistake," he whispered. "I don't belong here. Nobody believes me. But it's real."

"What is real?" I asked. I really didn't want to get into a metaphysical discussion with him.

"It follows me around all day long."

"What are you talking about?" I was annoyed.

Jerry handed me a fingerpainting of the black hole.

PART TWO

DREAMS

5

THE
SUCCUBUS

I was awakened by the sound of my bedroom door opening. I was on my side and able to see the luminescent dial of the alarm clock. It was 4:20 A.M. I heard footsteps approaching my bed, then heavy breathing. There seemed to be a murky presence in the room. I tried to throw off the covers and get up, but I was pinned to the bed. There was a weight on my chest. The more I struggled, the more I was unable to move. My heart was pounding. I strained to breathe.

The presence got closer, and I caught a whiff of a dusty odor. The smell seemed old, like something that had been kept in an attic too long. The air itself was dry and cool, reminding me of the inside of a cave.

Suddenly a shadow fell on the clock. *Omigod! This is no joke!* Something touched my neck and arm. A voice whispered in my ear. Each word was expelled from a mouth foul with tobacco. The language sounded strange, almost like English spoken backward. It didn't make any sense. Somehow the words gave rise to images in my mind: I saw rotting swamps full of toadstools, hideous reptiles, and other mephitic horrors. In my bedroom I could only see a shadow looming over my bed. I was terrified.

But I'm a scientist. I must see what it is. I suspected that it was a hallucination; either the type that occurs in the twilight just before falling asleep (hypnagogic hallucination) or the type that occurs just before awakening (hypnopompic hallucination). All I would have to do is either look at the image or touch it and it should vanish.

I signaled my muscles to move, but the presence immediately exerted all its weight on my chest. The weight spread through my body, gluing me to the bed. I was paralyzed. Still on my side, I was unable to turn my neck to see what was sitting on me. I looked at the clock on the night table. It was still ticking audibly. Next to the clock was the book I had been reading. A library card—my card, complete with coffee stains—marked my place. My eyes scanned the wall. I saw a spot that I had been meaning to fix because the paint had peeled. In the corner was a cactus plant I had been nurturing for years. This was definitely my bedroom and it looked normal. I was aware of my surroundings, oriented, and awake. *This is no dream! This is really happening!*

A hand grasped my arm and held it tightly. The intruder was doing the reality testing on me! The hand felt cold and dead. Now I understood how Ishmael, the narrator of Melville's *Moby Dick*, felt when, upon awakening and feeling a supernatural hand in his, he said: "I lay there, frozen with the most awful fears, not daring to drag away my hand; yet ever thinking that I could but stir it one single inch, the horrid spell would be broken." Neither Ishmael nor I could move.

Then part of the mattress next to me caved in. Someone climbed onto the bed! The presence shifted its weight and straddled my body, folding itself along the curve of my back. I heard the bed start to creak. There was a texture of sexual intoxication and terror in the room.

Throughout it all, I was forced to listen to the intruder's interminable whispering. The voice sounded female. I *knew* it was evil. It said something that sounded like "Deelanor . . . Deelanor." Later, I realized this was "Ronald" pronounced backward. At the time, all I could think about was trying to get out of bed.

It was then that I tried to summon my most powerful *kiai*,

a yell I had developed through years of martial arts training. But I couldn't fill my lungs. The intruder's heavy gelatinous body was crushing the life out of me. It was like breathing through a thin straw.

Fear released a memory buried since I was ten years old. My buddy and I had just seen a movie in which the hero eluded the villains by staying underwater in a swamp and breathing through a reed. We decided to try the trick and went to a nearby lake armed with a bunch of soda straws. I remember sitting underwater, sucking on a straw, and looking up through the surface. As I watched the sunbeams dance on the rippling surface, I marveled at how easy this was. All of a sudden I couldn't get enough air. Something was holding my shoulders down. Someone was yelling but the sounds were garbled. I lost consciousness. The next thing I knew I was lying on the bank, coughing up water. My buddy was laughing, the pinched straw still in his hand.

Now the intruder was squeezing me like a soda straw. My childhood fear of suffocation was returning. I started to lose consciousness. Suddenly the voice stopped. I sensed the intruder moving slowly out of the room. Gradually, the pressure on my chest eased. It was 4:30 A.M.

I sprang out of bed, grabbed a flashlight, and turned toward the bedroom door. There was nothing there. *Maybe it went into the next room.*

"Who's there?" I shouted. My lips were quivering.

There was no reply. I went to the bedroom door and stopped. Just around the corner there could be some hideous thing, waiting to pounce. "Hello?" I tried to sound as friendly as possible. "Anybody there?" The words came out with a slight tremble. There was no reply.

After several moments, I rushed through the door in police style, hugging the walls and holding my flashlight out with both hands. The flashlight sprayed the hall with a narrow beam of light. I had never seen my apartment in this particular way, illuminated in splotches, and it looked strange . . . almost alien. The flashlight created shadows everywhere. The shadows moved with the beam, and, in the corner of my eye, I caught the rocking chair rocking, the curtains shimmering, and the carpets creeping. When the shaft of light caught the bathroom mirror, the reflection startled me. I moved through the apartment, exposing every room and closet. There was no sign of an intruder.

Once the panic wore off, I became aware of my exhaustion. I needed sleep, but I was afraid I might miss a return visit by the intruder. I went to the kitchen, made a pot of coffee, and took it back to the bedroom. I remained at full attention, my eyes fixed on the bedroom door. But nothing happened. When the sun rose, I got dressed and went to the office.

I spent the day going through the motions of work. After a quick dinner in the hospital cafeteria, I hurried to my weekly graduate student seminar, which was meeting that evening at my apartment.

The students carried the discussion by themselves. I was unusually quiet, preoccupied with thoughts of my strange experience. But when someone started talking about the perceived reality of dreams, and how they are clearly different from waking perceptions, I had to disagree. I argued that when people are just falling asleep or in the process of waking up, it might be difficult to decide if an event was real or a dream. Then I blurted out my experience with the intruder. Since I had been awakened prior to the experience, perhaps it was a hypnopompic hallucination. Although I edited the story and omitted details about my panic reaction, I admitted that I was dumbfounded. Since my perceptions of the clock and the other items in the bedroom were of real objects, maybe there was *something real* about the presence that I perceived attacking me. The class stared at me in disbelief. I sensed I had lost their respect.

After the seminar ended, I struggled to understand what had happened to me. Did I just have a bad dream? I knew that intense nightmares, which occur during rapid eye movement (REM) sleep when the eyeballs flutter, can lead to spontaneous awakenings. Such nightmares are known as anxiety dreams and they endure for as long as twenty minutes *before* awakening occurs. When a person finally awakens from a nightmare, they may lie in bed, seemingly immobilized, as they replay the recent horror. But this could not explain my actual paralysis or the fact that my experience began *after* awakening.

If I hadn't had a nightmare, perhaps I had had a night terror. Night terrors are spontaneous awakenings from sleep followed by physiological signs of extreme fear: fast heart rate, rapid breathing, and heavy perspiration. But there the similarity to my experience ends. Whereas the sleeper awakening from a night terror screams in panic and makes desperate attempts to flee by walking or running out of the bedroom, I was unable to move. Furthermore, people rarely remember their night terrors and, even when they do, they cannot describe a specific image that frightened them. This is understandable because night terrors, which occur in non-REM sleep when the brain is not dreaming, are not dreams in the ordinary sense. Rather, they appear to be a result of a failure to control anxiety after being suddenly awakened from deep sleep. I decided I did not have a night terror. Besides, night terrors are almost the exclusive domain of children; I was an adult, a psychologist, and a university professor. I denied how childish I had been the night before.

Days later, after researching the phenomenon in the medical literature, I learned that I was not the first to be terrorized by such an experience. Throughout history many people have reported attacks by the *same* intruder. I was right when I said she smelled old. The Babylonians called her Lilitu, demoness of the wind, who seduced men by night. The Jews called her Lilith, the hairy night creature. She was the succubus of ancient Rome who leaped upon the sleeper and rode him to love or death. Then, in the Middle Ages, she became the witch Lamia. Finally, in Old Germany, she was known as the *mare*, the old, ugly woman who sat on the chest of the sleeper and produced the evil dreams we now call night*mares*. This nightrider also took on a male form, known in many cultures by the Latin name *incubus*. Psalm 91 called it what it really was: "the terror by night."

While feelings of seduction were a recurrent theme in the reported assaults, actual sexual intercourse was as fictitious as the wizard Merlin, who was said to have been born from the union of an incubus and a nun. During the Middle Ages, the Church taught that incubi were fiends of hell whose function was to tempt the frail. Inside cloisters of true believers, god-fearing virgins and nuns suffered epidemics of such attacks. But not all the attacks were strictly imaginary. The clergy often assumed the disguise of incubi. When a young lady of the fifteenth century cried out for help against an incubus, her rescuers found a local bishop under her bed. The bishop convinced everyone, including the victim, that an incubus had assumed his shape!

Clerical chicanery aside, some physical aspects of the experience are apparently genuine. My speculation that there was something real about the presence was correct in the sense that real physical changes occur in the body. Open eyes, muscle paralysis, and respiratory difficulty are reported by independent observers of the attacks. Afterward, the victims frequently appear pale and trembling. They show anxiety and fear despite the accompanying erotic sensations. These features have much in common with a state known as sleep paralysis, which can occur when falling asleep or when awakening. Sleep paralysis is characterized by inability to perform voluntary movements despite intense efforts to do so. But one remains conscious, and it is this awareness that gives rise to the feelings of horror. Afterward, there is complete recall of the experience.

Sleep paralysis provides a fertile setting for hypnopompic hallucinations. In the hypnopompic state, the brain cannot instantaneously switch from dreaming to a waking state, and the dream extends into the waking period. The brain circuits activated during dreams then send signals—such as an image of the succubus—to the cerebral cortex, where they are processed as if they came from the outside world. Thus, dream images extend into waking and the sleeper sees visual images (or has sensations in other modalities) within the context of the real bedroom.

Our brain knows what state it is in only from the surrounding context. In dreams, the context is of disorganized images, and this tells the brain it is sleeping. In the sleep paralysis/hypnopompic state, the context is of organized perceptions and the brain assumes that it is awake despite the very different nature of the experience. This, then, is how the brain is fooled by such dream hallucinations.

The best explanation for my succubus experience was that I was in a state of sleep paralysis *and* having a hypnopompic hallucination. The fact that I saw images of rotting swamps concomitant with awakening was a strong indication that some REM activity was continuing during the hypnopompic period. But why the specific succubus or incubus image? Jung believed it was a racial memory implanted in our genes eons ago when our ancestors awoke in a dark cave and panicked at the presence of a predator. Some contemporary psychiatrists believe it is a return to the frightening, looming shapes of the infant's perceptual world. While such explanations may account for the ubiquitous nature of the experience, it is likely that the general features of the succubus are suggested to the sleeper by specific physiological sensations. The brain tries to synthesize a meaningful explanation from this material.

What are these raw sensations, and how are they produced? Awakening in a state of sleep paralysis can cause the person to hyperventilate and experience feelings of tightness or heaviness in the chest. Hyperventilation, even in the form of sighing respirations, also diminishes the supply of oxygen to the brain. This can produce hyperacusis, whereby sounds seem especially loud. Simple background noises, ticking clocks, even one's own labored breathing can provide the seeds from which grow more complex auditory hallucinations such as opening doors, footsteps, and garbled voices. If the oxygen supply is sufficiently reduced, sexual pleasure centers in the brain may be affected for both men and women. This effect is utilized in autoerotic asphyxia, a bizarre practice of tying ropes or scarves around one's neck during masturbation in order to intensify the orgasm. Some sexual arousal may also be a carryover from REM sleep, which, for males, is accompaned by penile erections.

Intense efforts to move against the paralysis increase awareness of the rigid muscles, the body lying in bed under the covers, and the perspiring skin. In the hypnopompic brain, the restraint can turn into pressure from a grasping hand, the covers become another body folding itself over the sleeper, and the sweat nurtures gelatinous sensations complete with odors. Even the movement of the mattress and creaking of the bed were probably the result of my own struggles, not the intruder's. Autonomic nervous system changes in cardiac activity, skin temperature, and skin resistance can make additional contributions to the tingling, sensations of cold, and strong emotional responses.

Lying in my bedroom inside this paralytic terror, my brain was alert to the most subtle stimuli. I couldn't move, but my brain was using all its sensory modalities to probe the environment with intense scrutiny. Minor stimuli, usually unnoticed, were perceived so acutely that the brain attached major significance to them. For example, barely detectable shadows are normal in my bedroom, where a streetlight can be seen from the window. Looking through fear-dilated pupils, it would be easy to see these amorphous shadows, like inkblots, evolve into looming shapes from the id. And the smell of cigarette smoke, which periodically invaded my bedroom from the apartment below, undoubtedly accounted for the perception of tobacco breath. The smoke usually entered via my bedroom window, which was always open a crack, just enough to let in the cool air I thought arrived with the looming shape.

You don't have to have a medieval mind to see a succubus emerge from all these data points. One of the best cognitive "fits" the brain can make of these sensations is that someone or something is sitting or lying on top of the body. Yet knowing all this will not necessarily dispel the perceived reality of the succubus or the accompanying paroxysm of terror. Few persons, alone with such shadowy and paralyzing images, will be perfectly free from the idea that there is an underworld, a dark side of the soul, where Hypnos, Greek god of sleep, and his brother Thanatos, god of death, rule. It is no wonder that during the Middle Ages some dreamers, under the influence of the succubus, were literally scared to death!

As children we are told that the Sandman will sprinkle magic sand in our eyes and put us to sleep with pleasant dreams. Knowing that the dreaming brain can produce creatures like the succubus can change all that. We do not necessarily go gentle into that good night.

6

UFO

1

I sat in my den with Sherlock Holmes. Since I had several hours to while away before the seminar students would be arriving that evening, I decided to reread the stories of this famous detective who so entertained and influenced me throughout my schooling. Holmes was a creation of Sir Arthur Conan Doyle, who based the character on a real Edinburgh surgeon known for his diagnostic genius. The fictional detective was a master of deduction who possessed an extraordinary talent for observing minutiae. He was forever sleuthing his way through crimes by synthesizing the facts and reasoning backward from effect to cause. He once remarked to his good friend and assistant, Dr. Watson, that: "From a drop of water . . . a logician could infer the possibility of an Atlantic or a Niagara without having seen or heard of one or the other." As a behavioral scientist I had always felt that behavior was a mystery story in which I was the detective looking for a Niagara of causes. It was easy to admire the great Sherlock Holmes.

He was a brave and fearless man who would have ridiculed

me for my behavior when I encountered the succubus. When confronted by his own demon, the evil Professor Moriarty, Holmes was unflappable. I could almost see him puffing on his pipe and quietly laughing at me. He smoked incredible amounts of tobacco, using it as food for thought about a new case. Perhaps it was a pity I didn't smoke because the dilemma facing me now was what Holmes would have called "a three-pipe problem."

My students had failed to understand how real the succubus experience was for me. How could I explain that they, too, could be easily fooled by their senses? This was the defining essence of a true hallucination, and it was the most important lesson I could teach them. They had to understand that, in the right set (expectations and attitudes) and setting (physical and psychological environment), a false perception could have the full force and impact of the corresponding real perception. Holmes would have offered some convincing, well-reasoned proof. I decided to conduct a demonstration that I had used with spectacular results in other classes. It should be good enough to convince even the dear, skeptical Dr. Watson.

I made a list of items I would need:

> 2 large, clear plastic bags
> 1 roll of tape
> 1 box soda straws
> 26 birthday candles

Then I made two telephone calls and settled back to await the arrival of the students.

The class, all except Carol, arrived on time. We began. Thirty minutes later Carol came bursting into the room. "You're late," I said with uncharacteristic anger. She reddened, apologized, then explained that she was delayed by a mob of people who were watching a helicopter floundering over my apartment building. Since I didn't hear anything, I impolitely told her to stop making excuses and take her seat. "Look for yourself if you don't believe me," she said in a very loud, antagonistic voice.

I half-heartedly walked over to the window and peeked through the curtains. I saw a crowd of people in the courtyard pointing and staring at the sky.

"She's right," I said to the class. "I'm going to see just what's going on. Come if you want." I walked down the two flights of stairs to the outside courtyard. The entire class followed.

We looked up and saw Carol's so-called helicopter approximately three hundred feet above us.

"See? I was right, I was right," squealed Carol triumphantly.

Now, seeing anything in the smog-shrouded skies over Los Angeles is an event, but people rarely stand around and gawk. Even on the clearest night you will find only a faint star or two and the occasional lights from airplanes as they fly in ruler-straight paths miles above the city. Police helicopters sometimes crisscross the sky or hover over emergencies on the ground. This helicopter was different. It behaved like no helicopter made on Earth.

"What is it?" I asked the crowd.

"Dunno," someone answered. "It's moving at right angles. Just hovers along for a while, then zips to another altitude. Been doing that for the past ten minutes or so."

We watched the object dart about the sky, executing ninety-degree turns on a dime. Silently, we all knew that man-made helicopters can't maneuver that way at a constant high speed.

"Planes don't do that," added one of the students. "And look how it's glowing. There aren't any running lights."

"And no noise," someone noted.

"What is it?" I asked again.

"Looks like a large egg," came the first of many answers from the students.

"A giant lozenge."

"The Goodyear blimp."

"It's Superman!" someone joked. I heard nervous laughter all around. Then someone said the secret word.

"It's a *UFO*!"

Almost immediately, from out of the haze, a second UFO materialized. It seemed much higher than the first one.

"Look!" someone yelled. "They're chasing each other!" He was right. The lower UFO was following the higher one, executing the same quick turns and directional changes as they spiraled upward together, like giant fireflies caught in a secret courtship ritual.

The appearance of the second UFO triggered a new round of speculation. Weather balloons and commercial aircraft were quickly ruled out. Since the parallel maneuvering of the two crafts seemed so calculated and deliberate, the students started using words such as "flying saucers" and "intelligent ships." I could tell they were letting their imaginations run wild. The word "occupant" was mentioned more than once. Then, something really wild happened. Someone claimed to see shadows moving inside one of the glowing eggs!

Everyone was mesmerized. We watched the aerial acrobatics for several more minutes until, quick as a wink, the UFO lights went out. The UFOs vanished into thin air! I asked the students to return to the den and invited a man and woman from the crowd to join us.

When I got back to the den, a student was already on the telephone reporting the UFOs to the police and checking for any unusual radar sightings with the airport. Everyone was excited. Most were convinced that they had seen unidentified flying objects. A few students believed the crafts were guided by intelligence. One person said the shadows could have been life forms, perhaps extraterrestrial midgets. It was time to introduce our two guests from the courtyard.

Ray and Erin were laboratory technicians from the hospital. They were also my confederates. I had telephoned them earlier with instructions to come to the courtyard after the class started. The other call was to Carol. Ray's task was to put together the bits of straw and candles, then launch our homemade UFOs. The design was simple. The straws were stuck together in the form of a cross which formed the bottom of the UFO. Next, the birthday candles were placed in holes punched into the straws, so that the candles, three in each arm of the cross and one in the center, stood upright. Then the open end of a plastic bag (the type used by dry cleaners to cover hangers) was taped to the ends of the straws. After the candles were lit, the bag filled with hot air and rose slowly into the sky.

Once the two UFOs were launched, and gained a little altitude, the flickering candles produced an eerie, pulsating glow. They looked more like a pair of large glowing eggs than anything else. The UFOs appeared to "chase" each other because the currents of air and wind moved them along in the same way, just like any two ordinary balloons. Carol deliberately arrived late with her well-rehearsed remarks. Once the class ran down to the courtyard, Ray, who was already surrounded by a crowd of curious neighbors, pointed to the objects and made sure their peculiar behavior did not go unnoticed. Erin, acting out the role of someone in the crowd who believed in UFOs, made sure her opinions were heard by everyone. When the candles finally burned out, the UFOs were at a sufficient altitude to disappear from sight.

While everyone saw the same stimuli, no one saw them for what they actually were—hot air balloons. At least half of the class believed that they had seen real flying saucers. They were fooled by the demonstration just as I had been fooled by the experience of the succubus. I still smile when I think about that one frantic student calling the police and trying to describe what he had just seen. He was more than a little frustrated when the police did not take him seriously. It was a scene right out of a 1950s science fiction movie. Now the students knew what it felt like to be carried away by a false perception.

The balloons provided each person with the same sensory impressions. Yet the interpretation of these sensations was colored by the set and setting that I had engineered to insure a mistaken perception. While the demonstration was a good example of how a stimulus can be perceived as something it is not, this was a more elaborate illusion than a hallucination, which generally occurs in the absence of any real external stimulus.

What happened tonight, I told the class, can be compared to the wandering light illusion created by staring at an isolated star or other stationary spot of light in the night sky. This illusion can also be demonstrated indoors by placing a glowing cigarette in an ashtray at the far end of a completely dark room. If you fixate on the light, after several seconds you will see it moving. It will appear to wander around in an erratic manner, swooping in different directions, or oscillating back and forth. The patterns of movement may be further modified by suggestions from other people. With proper suggestions, the light can appear to move several feet. Despite such movements, the light always comes back to the original position. This illusion is caused by fatigue in the muscles of the eye as it fixates the object, resulting in slight fluctuations.

Our eyes can play other tricks on us, even in daylight. A particularly startling effect is the visual phantom. When real objects move around an empty region of visual space, vivid phantoms of these objects appear to move through the empty region. These phantoms originate in the brain and are due to the brain's normal tendency to fill in spatial gaps. Like the wandering lights, the phantoms are part of the visual system's normal operation. The perception of a visual phantom is an appropriate response to the moving contours around it. While the perception is erroneous, it is only an illusion because a real external stimulus (something moving around the empty region) is present. In the case of the UFO, the perception is also an illusion because a real external stimulus (the balloon) is present. To see a visual phantom or a UFO under these conditions is to err in the identification of the actual stimuli. Similar illusions can occur in any sensory modality.

Illusions can also be induced by real *internal* stimuli. Although such perceptions are sometimes considered hallucinations (because there are no external stimuli), they are as normal as wandering lights. Consider the visual phenomena created by floaters and phosphenes. Floaters are small particles floating in the aqueous humor in the front chamber of the eye. The floaters may drift about and be seen as objects flying across the field of vision. Phosphenes, those spots of light you see when you close your eyes or peer into a completely dark sky, are another source of internal stimuli. Blinking the eyes will not erase these spots but only flick them into rapid, right-angle turns. If you perceive these floaters or "flick phosphenes" as UFOs, the perception is still an illusion because there are real stimuli present.

While hallucinations may be influenced by such internal or external stimuli, they do not require any sensory information, illusory or otherwise. True hallucinations are strictly mental creations. The mental elements—the images, thoughts, fantasies, memories, and dreams—are the only building blocks necessary for construction of the final perception. These mental events are the reason why some people might see little green men inside a floating balloon, something the students speculated about but did not see. Of course, not all mental experiences, however vivid, fool us. It is easy to imagine a UFO that is much more detailed and realistic than any I could make from straw and wax. Picture such a flying saucer in your mind's eye. See it fly about, land in your backyard, and open its doors. Perhaps you can even picture occupants stepping out from the saucer. Why doesn't this mental image fool you?

Carol answered: "That's easy. The image is not real." Everybody laughed at the simplicity of the answer, but Carol was right.

"The hard question is what would make it real?" I said, then went on to answer the question. Current philosophical and psychological wisdom holds that there are certain properties or qualities that separate real perceptions from mental images, thoughts, fantasies, memories, and dreams. Real perceptions are more vivid, concrete, coherent, and vivacious than the rest. They have a quality of sensation whereby they produce the immediate feeling that something is seen, heard, touched, smelled, or tasted, as opposed to something imagined. Real perceptions convey the impression that the stimulus is external, that it exists, even if no one else perceives it. Furthermore, real perceptions are impossible or extremely difficult to alter or dismiss simply by wishing. When a mental event acquires these qualities, it becomes indistinguishable from a real perception.

Henry Maudsley, a famous psychiatrist in London during the time when Conan Doyle was writing the Sherlock Holmes stories, had an apt phrase that captured the impact of these qualities. A hallucination, Maudsley wrote, is "mental representation so intense as to become mental presentation." He noted that there were fine lines between mental experiences such as thoughts, fantasies, dreams, and hallucinations. These experiences can evolve into one another. For example, a dream, on awakening, may evolve into a hallucination; a thought, on falling asleep, may evolve into a dream. One can move along this continuum because the internal mechanisms of the experiences are similar.

We have already seen how visionary drugs, dreams, sleep paralysis, and hypnopompic states can endow mental events with qualities of reality, thereby generating movement along this continuum. Before I dismissed the class, I asked them to read several papers about hallucinations in clear states of consciousness. I repeated Maudsley's warning that when a person is sober, healthy, and awake, discovering whether a perception is real or not could challenge the best psychiatric detective.

2

I stood at my den window and watched the white-haired man walk haltingly across the courtyard below. He wore a red-checked lumber jacket, khaki pants, and a baseball cap. He kept glancing at a piece of paper he held inches from his eyes. When he disappeared into the entranceway below, I moved to the door. Seconds later, he knocked.

"Doctor Siegel?" he said as I opened the door.

"Yes, Mr. Wilson. Please come in." He appeared to be in his late sixties but with the rugged good looks of a Marlboro man. I offered him my favorite rocking chair, and I sat opposite him on the couch. A table with a cup of my favorite Jamaican Blue Mountain coffee separated us by a few feet.

"I take it you camped out last night in the desert," I said. Wilson stiffened and twisted his face into a question mark. "I can tell by the smell of a wood campfire on your clothes," I continued. "I always come back from camping trips smelling like that." He started to relax.

"But where are you staying now?" I asked. Despite his smelly clothes and unshaved face, Wilson's wet hair made him look like he had just stepped out of a shower. I assumed he had rented a room.

"At the St. Regis," he said. I knew the place. It was an inexpensive motel, not far from UCLA. The accommodations left much to be desired, but the management left you alone, never asking questions. I had heard that even the maids left the rooms alone. It was the perfect place to stay if you had just stepped off a flying saucer and wanted to travel incognito.

Mr. Jack Wilson—he insisted on the "Mr."—had called my office earlier in the day because he once heard me discuss UFOs on a radio program and *knew* that I would want to talk to him. I asked him why. "Day before yesterday I was on a UFO for seven hours," he said. I gulped, then insisted that he come to my apartment that night for a debriefing while events were still fresh.

He sounded calm on the phone, but I knew he was anxious to see me. There are sixteen steps (eight on each flight) leading to my apartment. I heard Wilson hit only four of them on his way up the stairs. He was in a hurry, all right. Before I could offer him a cup of coffee, he moved to the edge of the rocker, fixed me with the clearest blue eyes I've ever seen, and started describing his strange adventure.

Wilson was returning from Florida, where he had been visiting relatives. He had been driving all night when he hit the Arizona border. After stopping just long enough to fill up with gas and some extra bottles of water for the trip across the state, he resumed driving along a relatively isolated stretch of highway surrounded by high desert chaparral and distant mountains. He heard a strange "mechanical" noise coming from the rear, stopped the car, and got out to inspect the sound. As he stepped onto the shoulder of the road, he felt dizzy and faint. There was a blinding light somewhere overhead.

"That's when I saw it," said Wilson, leaning the chair so far forward it was on the tips of the rockers.

"The source of the light?" I asked. I found myself leaning forward on the couch.

"No. That's when I saw the little man," he said. Wilson said the man was humanoid but only three or four feet high. He was wearing a gray, seamless suit. He was inside some force field that made him appear blurry. A halo of glowing lights surrounded his head.

Wilson explained how he started to back away into the car, but the little gray man followed him. Suddenly, he felt paralyzed. His body became extraordinarily light, and he found himself floating, floating right up to the bright light. As he got closer, he realized it was a ship. "A god-damn gen-u-wine UFO," he said with emphasis. He assumed there was an opening because the next thing he knew he was inside, floating down a long corridor. The corridor was honeycombed with gleaming metal panels on the walls. There were intricate geometric designs carved on the panels.

"That must have been the cargo bay of their ship," Wilson said as he moved closer to the edge of the rocking chair.

He ended up inside a room at the end of the corridor. Something about the room reminded him of a hospital operating room. Several gray-suited figures crowded around him. They must have touched his head with something, he said, because he saw little stars, just like the ones he once saw when someone knocked him out in a fight.

"That's when . . . they drained me," he whispered. Mr. Wilson's voice was starting to break. This was the first sign of any emotion I had seen in the man. The rocking chair was teetering.

"How?" I asked.

"They took . . . my memories," he said. "They took my *fuckin' memories*!" I thought he might cry at any moment.

He explained that there was a large "TV" screen inside the operating room. As the aliens drained his brain, he saw images from his past flash across the screen. The images seemed disconnected, but he recalled a boyhood scene of fishing with his father, a picture of a ship he served on in the navy, then scenes from the recent Florida trip. The last picture showed him sitting in his parked car along the side of the highway. Then he discovered he was sitting in his car, the UFO was gone, and it was some seven hours later.

When Wilson finished telling his story, he picked up *my* cup of coffee and swallowed what was left. It must have been ice cold. I offered to get him a fresh cup and went into the kitchen to gather my thoughts while I brewed another pot.

My initial reaction was that Mr. Wilson's experience was a dream. The similarity of his account to dreams was obvious. Many so-called UFO abductees have first learned about their alleged abductions via such dreams. This fact always struck me as suspicious. Perhaps UFOs were nothing more than creations of the dreaming brain, literally flights of fantasy. Or, as Jung believed, they could be manifestations of a common unconscious process. This might account for the almost mythological appearance of UFO abduction reports throughout history. From the prophet Ezekiel, who floated into a "UFO" in the Old Testament, to the abductees of today, who emerge to tell their stories on the front pages of supermarket tabloids, the experiences are uncannily similar.

Some UFO abductions are discovered when people who have had unexplained blackouts are hypnotized and regressed, or taken back by the hypnotist to the time of the blackout. During these hypnotic sessions, the subjects report classic abduction scenarios complete with bright lights, paralysis, floating, tunnels or long corridors, geometric patterns, examinations, and a review of past memories on a TV screen. But when ordinary subjects who have no such blackouts or reported encounters with UFOs are hypnotized and asked to *imagine* a UFO abduction, they report identical scenarios! There are many individual variations to these reports, but the basic structure is common to both imagined and so-called authentic abductions. The true believer, of course, might argue that all such people were at one time captured and examined by aliens, whether they know it or not.

I preferred, however, to look for more parsimonious explanations. The notion of alien abductions required too many unproven assumptions. Extraordinary claims required extraordinary proof. Despite the claims of hundreds of abduction victims scattered around the world, there was still no concrete evidence that the experiences were anything other than mental. Indeed, most alleged abductees were dazed, in a trance, or asleep. This supported the notion that UFO abductions are generated somewhere along the continuum of internal mental events. I had a hunch that they happened during the dream state.

I tried to be candid with Mr. Wilson. "Sounds a little like a bad dream," I said as I returned with fresh cups of Jamaican Blue.

Wilson looked straight at me. The lines in his face seemed to deepen with conviction. His voice was firm and authoritative. "Friend, it was no dream," he began. "My son, Peter, was with me. They drained him, too."

This caught me off guard. Apparently there was an independent witness and co-abductee. The dream interpretation was no longer such an obvious explanation. I recalled Sherlock Holmes's famous line about nothing more deceptive than an obvious fact. I decided to approach this case from the point of view that what this man was saying was true.

"Well, when I said *like* a dream, I didn't necessarily mean it was a dream," I said, sheepishly retreating a bit from my earlier position. I told Wilson that it was not too late to try to gather some traces of physical evidence. Perhaps we could be the first to gather concrete evidence of a UFO abduction. I wanted to check out the car, talk to his son, and look for any lingering effects in both of them. After agreeing to meet them the next day at my office, I arose with a smile and outstretched hand.

He clasped my hand firmly. "Well, you're welcome to look at my Chevy, but you won't find any gray man in there. He's gone. But he was real, Doctor Siegel, *he wasn't a dream*." There was something about the way he said this that made me believe him. This could have been the Marlboro man saying cigarettes were good for you and I would have believed him.

"I believe you, Mr. Wilson," I said as I opened the door for him. I counted fifteen footsteps as he walked down the stairs. I knew that when I left for the office tomorrow I would do them in two giant leaps.

After he left, I drank the two cups of coffee that were still on the table while I paced in front of my bookcases. I kept about four thousand reference volumes in floor-to-ceiling shelves made from bricks and boards. I paused in front of the section on meteorology, selected a volume on atmospheric physics, and took it to bed with me.

The following morning I found Wilson waiting outside my office door as I arrived. True to my image of him, he was puffing away on Marlboros. The campfire smell was gone, as were the whiskers, replaced by a curious blend of tobacco and Old Spice aftershave lotion. I was glad to see him but disappointed to learn that his son had returned to his job in San Diego. Mr. Wilson wasn't sure how much longer he would be able to stay in L.A., so I decided to drop everything and work exclusively on this case for the next few days.

I started by taking a detailed personal and medical history. Wilson was fifty-two, retired from the navy, divorced, and lived in San Diego near his son, Peter, who was twenty-four. Their medical and psychiatric histories were unremarkable.

Next, I arranged for Mr. Wilson to have a complete physical examination including an ophthalmologic work-up. Although I told him that I wanted to know if the "blinding" light had done any ocular damage, I was more concerned about his need for glasses. He didn't wear corrective lenses, but I remembered that he had held the piece of paper with my address on it very close to his eyes. If he had poor vision, then his visual perception could have been distorted.

While Wilson was being examined, I went to the parking lot and checked out his car with the set of keys he had given me. In other alleged UFO-car encounters, there have been reports of physical "scars" such as dents on hoods, bumpers stripped of chrome, and scorch marks on the roofs. Wilson's car looked as dirty as his clothes, but neither the body nor the finish was damaged. I drove the car to a Westwood Village gas station, where a mechanic found that the electrical system and gauges (favorite targets for UFOs to tinker with) were operating normally. I filled the gas tank and drove the car back to the hospital parking lot. Before locking the car, I decided to rummage through the clothes and other articles strewn about the interior. Inside the glove compartment, I saw an item I wanted and slipped it into my pocket.

I walked over to the Jules Stein Eye Institute, part of the massive health sciences complex at UCLA, where I met Mr. Wilson after his examination. We went to lunch at Mario's, the only nearby restaurant with relatively private booths. While I picked at my food, Wilson ran down his story for me again. This time I asked detailed questions, such as precise locations and times, and studied his eyes as he answered.

In more than one case, Sherlock Holmes amazed Dr. Watson by deducing what he was thinking about from his facial features and the movement of his eyes. While Holmes's talents far exceeded any known facts about visual perception, sometimes it is possible to tell if a person is engaged in a fantasy or an actual reminiscence by the shifting of their eyes. Shifts to the left usually indicate that the person is imaginative and prone to vivid fantasies, while shifts to the right indicate that person has the information readily available from a minimal search of memory. When Mr. Wilson was not looking directly at me, he shifted his eyes to the right as he gave terse answers that I deduced were not fanciful elaborations.

Wilson could not add anything more to the abduction experience than he had already told me. However, he was able to describe the route he drove and where he stopped. I made a list of everything he had eaten and drunk for the past week. In addition to the cigarettes, the only other drug he used was caffeine in coffee and colas. His favorite snack food on the trip was Frosted Flakes, which explained the two empty cereal boxes I found in his car. I hadn't seen any tapes for the cassette player, and Wilson explained that he didn't care for music. But he liked to listen to sports on the car radio. When he mentioned that his favorite team was the UCLA Bruins, I picked up the check.

After lunch, I escorted Mr. Wilson back to the hospital, where I gave him a series of psychological tests. They confirmed my feelings that he was not particularly imaginative or creative. He was the type of person who had very few daydreams and almost no nightmares. Furthermore, he did not believe in paranormal phenomena, had never read a book about UFOs, and had not seen any of the popular movies, such as *Close Encounters of the Third Kind*, which have been credited with inspiring many UFO reports.

If UFO books and movies did not contribute to Wilson's abduction experience, I had much more work to do in finding other explanations. Besides, I still had to wait for the results from all the exams. I told Wilson to take the rest of the day off. Come back here first thing tomorrow morning, I said. As soon as he left, I put the item I had taken from his glove compartment on the table and started examining it. I knew it would be another long night.

"You're fit for duty, Mr. Wilson," I told him the next day. The physicians had given him a clean bill of health. All the blood and urine tests were within normal limits. I had ordered blood gases to be done because it has been alleged that anesthestic gases are used to paralyze UFO abductees. But these tests were normal, too. Wilson's skin, nails, and hair were as unmarked as his Chevy. He even passed the ophthalmologic examination with flying colors. The report noted that he was slightly photophobic and had some difficulty in a glare recovery task, but his eyesight was excellent. He did not need glasses. So I asked him why he had held the paper so close to his eyes when he was walking across the courtyard to my apartment. Wilson explained that he had been sensitive to bright lights all his life, and the glare from the sun setting over the courtyard wall was in his eyes. He used the paper as a sun shield because he had left his sunglasses in the car.

Mr. Wilson was smiling as I handed him report after report showing nothing wrong with him. To Wilson, this meant he was telling the truth and the abduction experience really happened. I was unwilling to go that far. Yet it was time to look just as systematically at the experience itself. I took him into an empty conference room and asked him to draw pictures of everything he could remember, including the gray man, the UFO, the inside corridor, and the examination room. He said he didn't have any artistic ability but agreed to try when I told him this would finally give us something concrete and *real* to work with.

I returned to the office. The written reports on my desk told only part of the story; they did not contain all observations made of Wilson's behavior. I was particularly interested in any anxiety or fear he displayed during the examinations. After all, he was very frightened when the aliens started to examine him. Could this have been his normal reaction to examinations? Was this any way for a navy man to behave, even one who liked Frosted Flakes? I telephoned the doctors and nurses who had examined Wilson. They described the patient as calm and easygoing. He even watched the needles going into his arm and the vacuum tubes filling with blood. I got the chills just listening to this.

By the time Wilson returned to my office with his drawings, I had planned a new course for the investigation. But I needed to buy more time. Would he be willing to stick around and take a few more tests? Wilson didn't want any more tests. He was ready to go back to San Diego.

"Just one more day, Mr. Wilson," I pleaded, "and we're all done."

"Then what, Doctor Siegel? You gonna tell me I'm crazy or what?"

It was a fair question. I had not thought this far ahead and didn't want to anticipate the outcome of my investigation. But Wilson had been extremely cooperative over the past days, sacrificing both time and vital fluids. Why? I suspected that, like many other alleged abductees, he wanted to feel important through the attention directed to him. Well, he still deserved an honest answer. I gave him one designed to fuel his motivation with the possibility of being not just important, but *famous*.

"If I cannot find a reasonable scientific or medical explanation by tomorrow," I said as I prepared to go out on a professional limb, "I will report this to the appropriate authorities, both the UFO groups and the FBI, as one *god-damn gen-u-wine UFO abduction*." I smiled as I mimicked his own description of the event.

Wilson smiled back. The bet was on. He promised to stay one more night, and I promised to pick up the entire tab at the St. Regis. I directed him to a staff psychometrician for a battery of assorted personality and intelligence tests that would occupy him for the rest of the day. Although I knew the tests not only were unnecessary but could not be scored for several days, such Sherlockian deception is sometimes justified. I threw his drawings into my briefcase, along with the item I had taken from the glove compartment, and raced to the airport.

The following morning I picked up Mr. Wilson at the St. Regis and we walked over to Uncle John's, a family restaurant located a half mile from the motel. On the way, we talked about the Bruin basketball team and shared a few jokes. By the time we reached the restaurant, Mr. Wilson did not object when I called him Jack.

We entered through a waiting room filled with fake Victorian furniture and antique style gas lamps fitted with electric bulbs. The waitress gave us a private booth along the back wall. Victorian-style curtains were draped around the entrance to the booth, but they were only decorations and could not be closed. Wilson and I sat opposite each other on comfortable imitation leather seats. One of those electrified gas lamps hung over the table. It was a perfect setting for a pretend Sherlock Holmes.

Despite the fakery, I liked Uncle John's because it was open twenty-four hours and served great breakfasts with all the coffee you could drink for the price of a cup. It was also very much a public place, which is where I wanted to be when I confronted Wilson with the results of my investigation. I was uncertain how he would react to what I had to say.

As we sipped our coffee and waited for our food, I turned on my tape recorder and started telling Wilson about my succubus experience. Such an act of self-disclosure can sometimes make a patient feel closer to a doctor, but there was a more important reason for my story. Once Wilson understood my explanation of the succubus, I told him that the succubus experience has been interpreted in many ways throughout history. During the Middle Ages, paralyzed sleepers thought they were being drained of blood by vampires. He smiled. The Eskimos believed the attacks were proof of the spirit world, which was out to get them. He chuckled. Some ufologists believe that these "bedroom invaders" are actually lustful aliens. Wilson's laughter finally told me that he not only understood but accepted the scientific explanation.

I pressed the pause button on the tape recorder as the waitress brought the food, then continued. Dreams can have many different interpretations, I explained, and they can be real enough to forge entire cultural beliefs. But, in the final analysis, succubi, like vampires and spirits, are only invading the mind, not the bedroom.

"Jack, I think some of the things you experienced really happened, but some of it you dreamed," I said, nonchalantly stuffing my mouth with French toast.

He was incredulous. "You think I was dreaming?" he said. "I was standing outside the fuckin' car, for Christsakes!"

"Only for a few minutes, Jack. I saw Peter yesterday in San Diego and he verified that." *Did I just destroy our relationship by going behind his back?*

"Didn't he tell you about the gray man?"

"Yes, he saw it too. That was the real part. Most of the rest was a dream, Jack."

"Stop calling me Jack!" he said. *There goes our relationship*, I thought. I knew he was irritated so I tried not to take his remark personally. I asked him to listen to my explanation. Then I promised I would listen to whatever he had to say. He mumbled agreement and started working on his cereal.

I pulled out the road map I had taken from the glove compartment. The Wilsons had used a felt tip pen to trace their entire route including the precise location of the UFO sighting. They had been taking turns driving for over thirty straight hours, but neither one had been able to sleep very well. Jack Wilson had been sitting behind the wheel for eleven hours before he stopped along the road to inspect the mechanical noise. According to the weather bureau, sunrise at that spot occurred two hours earlier. There was a light mist on the ground.

Mr. Wilson stepped out of the car and quickly stood up. He experienced an immediate dizziness. I reminded him that he had a past history of becoming faint and dizzy whenever he assumed an upright posture after sitting down for long periods of time. The condition, known as orthostatic hypotension, is actually very common. Many people experience it when they stand up after soaking in a hot bath.

The car was parked along the shoulder of the road, facing west. Once Wilson was outside the driver's door, he looked toward the noise at the rear of the car. He was now facing east, looking directly into the blinding light of the rising sun. His almost instinctive reaction was to turn around. Now he was facing west. His vision was centered on the antisolar point, a point in space that is directly opposite the sun from an observer.

"The antisolar point is where the little gray man materialized," I said excitedly. Wilson's eyes were glued to the sketch I was making, and I knew he was waiting for me to explain further. The explanation was first given by the philosopher Rene Descartes in the early seventeenth century, although I had only discovered it a few nights before when I was reading the book on atmospheric physics.

I drew a diagram showing Wilson, the car, and the sun. Since the sun was above the horizon and behind Wilson, the antisolar point was in front of him, on the ground. Actually, the point was marked by the head of his shadow on the ground. When there is mist or dew on the ground, light is focused in such a way as to create a special optical effect called a glory. A glory is a round halo of glowing light that is seen surrounding the antisolar point. When the angles of sunlight and reflected light from the droplets of dew are just right, the glory can sometimes appear as a circular rainbow. Atmospheric physicists call it *Heilgenschein*, a German word meaning "holy light." Glories can be easily mistaken for angels or aliens.

"The little gray man was simply your own shadow with a glory around the head. The mist in the early morning air caused the glory to spread out a bit, creating a secondary ring around the shadow. Combined with the indistinct and blurred boundaries of the shadow, this produced the force field you saw. The gray man followed you back to the car as any proper shadow would."

"Peter saw it?" said Mr. Wilson.

"Of course he did. He came out of the car when you appeared faint, stood behind you, and saw the glory around your shadow," I replied. "It was really there!"

Peter had told me how startled they were by the appearance of this phenomenon. Their sleepy eyes and tired brains either did not or could not recognize what they had witnessed. They returned to the car to discuss it. Peter wondered if it was some kind of radioactive creature prowling around. Maybe it was a ghost, perhaps—yes, he said it—a thing from outer space. They talked until they drifted to sleep.

Behind the closed eyes of the super-tired, there comes a series of hypnagogic images that precede sleep. Hypnagogic images are the germinal stuff of dreams, and they usually begin with flashes of light. Often, an illuminated circle, lozenge, or other generally round form appears to come nearer and nearer, swelling to a gigantic size. This particular image is known as the Isakower phenomenon, named after an Austrian psychoanalyst who first identified it. Isakower claimed the image was rooted in the memory of the mother's breast as it approached the infant's mouth.

"Doctor Siegel! Are you telling me I was attacked by a giant killer tit?" Wilson said, cracking up with laughter.

I laughed with him. Then I explained that, like illuminated inkblots, hypnagogic images can be interpreted in many different ways. Literally and figuratively, it's all in the eye of the beholder. The drowsy person in the hypnagogic state is just as open to suggestions as subjects in the hypnotized state. As Mr. Wilson and his son continued their drowsy conversation, floating off into sleep, the looming hypnagogic light was subconsciously transformed into the UFO.

When people start floating in the hypnagogic state, the amplitude and frequency of brain waves decrease. The alpha rhythms of wakefulness are progressively replaced by slower theta activity. This translates to a loss of volitional control, a sense of paralysis. As the person descends further into sleep itself, the outside physical world retreats to the fringe of consciousness and the new reality becomes the internal dream world.

For the next seven hours they remained asleep in the car. When they awoke, Mr. Wilson had strange dreams to tell his son. At first he described dreaming about gray figures like the one they saw the night before. Peter said that he also had a dream about the figure! Then Mr. Wilson described a series of disconnected images: geometric patterns, a tunnel, and scenes from the Florida trip. Peter remembered floating inside a long hallway, and seeing flashbacks from their trip, like pictures on a TV. Excitedly, they continued talking about their dreams, filling in the spaces between the disconnected images with a storyline that fit their bedtime discussion about the gray figure. By the time they arrived in L.A., the fleeting images of the dream had coalesced into a solid abduction story.

I finished my explanation by taking a stack of drawings from my briefcase. I put Mr. Wilson's drawings on the table next to a series I had asked Peter to prepare. The two sets were clearly very similar. For my finale, I showed Mr. Wilson dozens of drawings done by hypnotized subjects who had no significant knowledge of UFOs but were instructed to simply imagine an abduction. These "invented" drawings showed little gray men, long corridors, geometric patterns, examinations, and TV screens with memory scenes. They matched the Wilson drawings perfectly.

While Mr. Wilson was examining the drawings, I returned to my last, cold piece of French toast. Wilson now had all the data I had collected—well, almost all. I decided to withhold Peter's opinion that his father was swept away by the idea that *he*, of all people, would be selected for an alien abduction. He wanted to believe! Peter wasn't so certain it really happened, but he didn't want to argue with his father. Besides, there was the unexplained little gray man they saw outside the car. Although Peter admitted that they returned to the car and fell asleep, he speculated that it was possible that their physical bodies remained in the car while their *astral* bodies were taken aboard the UFO. Silently I wondered what self-respecting visitor to another planet would be satisfied with examining the astral body of an inhabitant when they could have the real thing instead.

The waitress returned with fresh coffee and the check. Wilson collected the drawings and handed them to me. He was forcing himself to smile but his lips remained pursed.

"Hell, I don't know what it was," he said. He sounded disappointed. "That glory thing is probably true. And if Peter says we talked about it and fell asleep, that's what we did. The boy doesn't lie. But, a dream? Dunno, maybe . . . maybe." Wilson forced another smile.

We walked back to the St. Regis and got there just in the nick of check-out time. After Wilson packed, we got into our respective cars, which were parked next to each other, and rolled down the windows.

"What caused the mechanical noise?" he shouted as he revved his engine.

"How should I know?" I shouted back. I didn't know.

"Hell, you're the detective," he hollered as he drove off.

7

DAYMARE

He felt his brain fill with a boiling mercury. . . . It no longer belonged to him. It was enemy territory.

—RAY BRADBURY,
"Fever Dream"

Alice woke up early Friday morning. She would have preferred to stay in bed, but the vacuum cleaner in the hallway outside her hotel room made getting back to sleep impossible. *They shouldn't be allowed to do that so early*, she thought, longing for the silence of the African plains she had left only two days earlier.

Now that she was up, the first thing she had to do was blow her nose. Grabbing the last Kleenex from the pack on her night table, she blew hard. Alice stared at the discharge in the open tissue. Even without her contact lenses, she could see the infected mass clearly. It was dotted with tiny black specks. The black specks were Alice's worry beads, signifying all those man-made pollutants that were slowly poisoning the planet.

Alice crumpled the tissue and tossed it at the wastebasket,

missing. That was the last of her Kleenex. She made a mental note to buy some more when she went out for breakfast. There were fifteen tissues in the pocket pack she purchased at Kennedy Airport when she arrived yesterday—fifteen reasons not to come to New York. Every six months when she visited the city, she blew her nose more and more. Every six months the air pollution seemed worse, the traffic thicker, the noise louder, and the price of Kleenex higher. Yet every six months she had to return in order to renew her visas and check in with the professors supervising her work.

Alice had been shuttling between continents for three years. She noticed that on each trip to New York her stay was always shorter than the one before. They were quick, but never painless. No matter how many times she did it, she always felt culture shock. There was never enough time to adjust to the change in environment, and she had long ago stopped trying. Alice remembered the subway signs when she was going to classes at Barnard in the sixties, NEW YORK: LOVE IT OR LEAVE IT. She had left, right after graduation, and entered the Peace Corps. They sent her to Africa, and she fell in love with the land and the people.

After the Peace Corps, Alice stayed in Africa, where she worked on several research projects for various professors. They encouraged her to enter graduate school. She returned to the States, completed the required classes, then selected a dissertation topic that took her back to Africa. Alice thought she could live there forever.

Somewhere in the middle of the street below a garbage truck started compressing its load. Traffic stopped and cars honked. The noise carried up to Alice's room on the tenth floor. She got out of bed, went to the window, and squinted at the scene below. Riverside Drive was a gray blur. But she could see clearly the black dust on the outside of the hotel window, which gave the city its bleak tones. *Another beautiful day in the jungle*, she thought.

She went to the bathroom, looked in the mirror, and decided to add some Visine to her shopping list. The red eye, of course, had to be from the city, not the long flight from Nairobi. She showered and shampooed her short, boyish hair, then stood under a cold spray until her skin prickled. For a moment, she was standing under a waterfall in Africa, bathed in thoughts of a less complicated world. When she could no longer stand the cold, she got out of the shower and dried herself with towels that were not much larger than washcloths and smelled of bleach. "At least they're clean," she said out loud.

Alice had a good, strong body, and she took a moment to admire it in the mirror. Her breasts were firm and she rarely wore a bra, except in the city. She thought five-five was too short for her broad shoulders, but all those years of playing field hockey in prep school and college were to blame for that. The weight training added bulk to her legs, but they were shapely enough to turn heads when she wore her short skirts. Miniskirts were not in style this year, but Alice was so accustomed to wearing shorts in the bush that she never could get used to anything clinging around her legs. Her great tan even eliminated the need for stockings.

She finished drying herself, then dabbed a little vitamin E lotion on the scar across her collarbone. There was no heroic story behind the scar, no fight to the death with a hungry lion, no Dian Fossey-style confrontation with poachers. It was just dumb luck. Alice had been surveying a section of forest that had been recently burned and cleared for new development. She was preparing to take a census of the dead animals when she tripped and fell against a tree stump. The charred remains of a huge branch speared Alice just below the collarbone. The branch angled up to her neck, threatening to rip her head clean off her shoulders. She remained frozen against the branch, afraid to move for fear the jagged edges might penetrate further. *Impaled by a tree*, thought Alice, *what a dumb way to die*. Then, a lucky reflex: Alice coughed and the branch popped out. It was only a minor wound, barely penetrating more than an inch, but enough to scare the devil out of her.

Despite the cold shower, Alice still didn't feel awake. She was bone-tired and decided to lie down before getting dressed. There was still time before her meeting at the consulate office. She would simply skip breakfast. It didn't matter because somehow she had lost her appetite.

The vacuum cleaner in the hall woke her up again. Reflexively, Alice looked to the door. It opened and someone came in, walked to the foot of her bed, looked at her, and walked out. *Someone from housekeeping checking on the room*, she thought, then realized she was naked and pulled a sheet over herself. She must remember to hang one of those DO NOT DISTURB signs on the doorknob.

It was time to get up, anyway. Alice went to her duffel and pulled out some underwear, a skirt and blouse. The clothes were wrinkled, and she chided herself for not unpacking when she first arrived. But she had been *so tired*. The jet lag had been particularly bad this time and she still felt it. After she returned from her errands, she would unpack and try to get the hotel to press a few items.

As she dressed, Alice went over the things to be done: see consulate; call professor; make dental appointment; stop at the drugstore. She also simply *had* to stop at the New York Public Library. It was her favorite retreat in the city. The giant stone lions on the steps outside the library always made her feel welcome. Inside, Alice could lose herself in books and forget she was in New York. She was hoping to finish her errands quickly in order to have as much time as possible for her library research. It was going to be a hectic day. Alice selected her most comfortable walking shoes, then sat on the edge of the bed as she laced them up.

The vacuum cleaner woke her up again. Alice rubbed the sleep from her eyes but didn't want to open them just yet. She groped for the Kleenex, couldn't find it, then blew her nose into the corner of the bed sheet. There was considerable discharge and she decided it was best not to look. But her eyes sprang open as soon as the door opened. At first she thought it was the house-keeper again, then saw it was a man! *Was this the person who had seen her lying naked on the bed before?* He looked old and frail. His skin reminded Alice of beef jerky. His clothes were tattered, literally falling apart. His face was black—not Negro, she noted—but covered with dirt and soot. He walked to the foot of her bed and looked directly at her. Alice froze. She might just as well have been pinned to the bed by the branch of a dead tree. The man stood there for several interminably long seconds, turned, and left the room.

The hotel management will certainly hear about this, thought Alice. She had purposely picked a room on the tenth floor to be as far away from the street as possible. Okay, there was nothing the hotel could do about noise. But homeless bums wandering into

the rooms was another matter. She blamed it on that pimply teenager who brought her room service last night. He had probably
forgotten to lock the door. She got up and checked the door and
found it was locked! Alice decided that the room service waiter
had failed to shut the door properly, leaving it slightly ajar.

She picked up the morning paper in front of the door and
took it back to bed with her. Today was Saturday and a good
day to see a movie. Alice didn't get a chance to see many movies
in Africa, and never any of the artsy ones she enjoyed. Usually,
her only choice was between a *Rambo*-style action film or some
gruesome Charles Bronson film. She looked through the listings
and picked Shakespeare's *Henry V* starring Kenneth Branagh.
Alice loved Shakespeare and kept a copy of his complete works
with her in Africa. The book, which had belonged to her father,
was beautifully bound in soft leather. He gave it to her just
before the cancer took him. It was her most treasured possession.
On the flyleaf he had scribbled:

To Alice, the Sonnet of my life.
"Thou art thy mother's glass, and she in thee
Calls back the lovely April of her prime."

> Love,
> Daddy.

Alice remembered how much her father wanted her to get married. "Perpetuate the gene pool," he used to say with deserved
pride. He was worried that she wouldn't meet anyone in the
African bush. The best she could do, he once quipped, was to
have some oversexed lion wander into her tent. But thus far,
the only man to walk into her life in New York was a homeless
bum. Alice decided to do something about that. She would call
an old boyfriend, the subject of one of her frequent masturbatory fantasies, and ask him to the movies. New York might be
dirty, but who said it couldn't be fun?

It was late Sunday morning when Alice woke up with a smile
and an appetite. She ordered breakfast from room service, then
got up to get the paper. The sun was shining through the window shade, promising a beautiful day. But Alice wasn't ready to
face it yet and pulled the curtains over the shade. Breakfast

arrived. She grabbed the glass of juice and downed it even before the waiter could set up the bed tray. Alice tipped the waiter with a five—or maybe she gave him a twenty by mistake—and reminded him to close the door on his way out.

Halfway through breakfast, the vacuum cleaner started again. "On *Sunday*?" Alice asked herself out loud. She decided never to stay at this hotel again. Something caused her to look up from the breakfast tray. The raggedy homeless man was standing at the foot of the bed. She could see him more clearly this time. His hair had been singed off, leaving scorch marks all over his scalp and forehead. The rest of his skin was parched and blistered. His clothes were little more than ashes. She looked at the man's eyes. The pupils were large and fixed, as they are in death. Alice had the horrifying thought that the man had walked out of a crematorium prematurely.

He must have left the door to her room open because the noise from the vacuum cleaner seemed much louder. Then she saw that the vacuum cleaner was in the man's hand. *No! That's not a vacuum cleaner!* thought Alice. *That's a chainsaw!* Alice certainly knew what a chainsaw looked like. She had seen enough of them in Africa, where ruthless developers and crazy lumber men used them to clear the forests.

A sardonic grin formed on the man's mouth. He raised an accusatory finger at Alice. The finger was long and crooked, like the twisted limb of a tree. He made a gesture by bringing his finger slowly across his neck, just above the collarbone. Alice screamed. Once. Twice. The man vanished.

On Monday the fever broke and Alice left the hotel room for the first time.

> *Is this a dagger which I see before me,*
> *The handle toward my hand? Come, let me clutch thee:*
> *I have thee not, and yet I see thee still.*
> *Art thou not, fatal vision, sensible*
> *To feeling as to sight? or art thou but*
> *A dagger of the mind, a false creation,*
> *Proceeding from the heat-oppressed brain?*
>   —WILLIAM SHAKESPEARE,
>   *Macbeth*

8

SHEILA AND THE SWASTIKAS

Inside the darkened lecture hall, a small object was barely visible in the right corner of the screen. The object resembled Venus as it appears in the eastern sky just before sunrise. "This is a typical hypnagogic image of a starlike dot as drawn by a subject who saw it just before falling asleep," I told the audience. I focused the red beam from my laser pointer on the dot to make sure that everybody saw it. Hypnagogic images are sometimes so faint that people miss them unless they are consciously watching for their appearance. I pushed a button on the podium to advance the projector to the next slide.

"And here we see two stars in the same position, the result of diplopia, or simple duplication of imagery." I pushed the advance button again.

A thousand points of light lit up the right side of the screen, creating a Milky Way that curved from the bottom to the top of the screen. The audience gasped. "This is the final stage, polyopia, the multiplication of the image, usually seen in one eye," I said.

These specks of light, I explained, are produced by electrical activity in the visual system and brain. One can almost imagine the specks representing electric sparks flying along the neural pathways of the brain. Here they look like stars, but they can also take the form of spots, circles, swirls, grids, checkerboards, or other figures composed of curves or lines. They are easy to see in the dark, but, in the light, they are on the borderline of perception. I turned on the house lights and the Milky Way faded away.

Even when the hypnagogic forms are not consciously noticed, they can still register as subliminal stimuli and influence subsequent image formation and fantasy. For example, a person may not notice some wavy lines moving about in the corner of the visual field. However, depending upon the subject's particular thoughts at the moment, the wavy lines could turn into blades of grass blowing in the wind, flames from a fire, or even snakes. Similarly, two lines forming the letter V, when duplicated, can become a row of menacing teeth. If presented upside-down, they can turn into a range of mountain peaks.

"So, the Milky Way could easily become . . ." I advanced the slide projector and dimmed the lights again. A brilliant shower of fireworks covered the screen. There were giant rocket bursts, pinwheels, and cascades of falling sparks, all frozen in mid-air. This slide had been prepared with special double refracting material, the same type used by commercial light show companies for creating moving displays. When I activated a switch that turned a polarized wheel in front of the projector lens, the whole fireworks display came alive. The rockets were shooting upward, the pinwheels were rotating, and the sparks were falling down.

The audience (the staff of a metropolitan Los Angeles hospital) clapped their approval. One hour and eighty slides later, the lecture ended and I was surrounded by several people asking questions. My eyes kept drifting to a nurse who seemed to be trying to catch my attention. After the others had left, and I was packing my equipment, she came up to the podium and handed me a folded piece of notebook paper.

"Has anyone ever seen one of these?" she asked.

I opened the paper and stared at a swastika drawn in black ink.

"No," I answered, riveted by the design. Until now, I

thought I had seen them all. "But there are many variations on the basic curves and lines," I explained. "The twisted cross could be a simple variation of a line or grid pattern." *If it was so simple, why hadn't anyone reported it before?*

"Did you see this?" I asked.

"*Oui*," she answered. "Many times."

"When you go to sleep?"

"*Non, jamais!*" I wondered why she was speaking French. Her words were pronounced poorly and sounded a bit affected.

I continued to stare at the bold lines of her drawing. The swastika gripped me with the same mixture of surprise and fascination that Hitler allegedly experienced when he first saw the Nazi flag unfurled.

"When do you see this? Where?" I asked.

"At work here at the hospital," she said without emotion.

I finally turned away from the piece of paper and took a long, hard look at this completely composed woman. Everything about her seemed to be arranged with careful attention to detail. Her thick, black hair fell to her shoulders with not a single hair out of place. The bangs were ruler straight. The makeup appeared to be expertly applied, and her blue eyes sparkled behind long, fake lashes. Her starched white uniform could pass any inspection, as could the shapely figure it outlined. Yet there was something wrong with this picture-perfect woman. There was no animation. Sure, she was pretty, but pretty like a Barbie doll outfitted in a nurse's uniform, complete with a tape recording of random French expressions. When she walked and talked, everything seemed mechanical.

"Are you seeing them now?" I asked. If she was hallucinating, that could explain the blank stare of her doll's eyes.

"No. *Non,*" she said with a smile. Her teeth were as white and perfect as her uniform.

"Do you use . . ." I started to ask.

"Drugs?" she said, finishing the question for me. "*Non.*"

Since she had some time before starting her night shift, I asked her to walk outside with me to my car so we could talk. We sat inside the car with two cups of coffee we got from a vending machine.

"Can a person pick up these images from other people who may be seeing them?" she asked.

This was a typical question from someone who did not suspect that they might be hallucinating. I told her that, while some parapsychologists believed it was possible, I had not seen any convincing scientific proof. But I encouraged her to tell me more about the swastika so I could decide how similar it was to a hallucination. *It already sounds different*, I thought.

Her name was Sheila and she had been a nurse at the hospital for several years. She prided herself on her attention to the details of good patient care, calling herself a model nurse. It was a judgment I could almost believe because she was dressed with such stiff meticulousness. She first noticed the swastikas about a year ago; they appeared as tiny, barely visible marks in the rooms of certain patients. The swastikas were either on the hospital gowns or on the bedsheets of the patients. She suspected that these patients were Nazis whose radiating thoughts produced the swastiskas. The swastikas would appear for only a second or two, but they always came back.

Sheila didn't discuss her findings or suspicions with anyone because she knew that other people, who might not be as sensitive as she was to the vibrations coming from patients, would not believe her. Besides, the hospital would never do anything about it for fear of losing business. Perhaps the hospital was part of a conspiracy to admit and care for these people. That's why she was thinking about finding another job. Did UCLA need any nurses?

Sheila's paranoid thinking was getting the better of her medical training. I wanted to tell her that, but I was afraid of losing a chance to study her. For all I knew, Sheila might interpret my disbelief as part of the conspiracy. I gently suggested that we should hold off on any drastic action until we understood exactly what we were up against. I purposely used "we" to indicate that I wanted to be on her side. Could she come to UCLA on her next day off? We could talk some more and she could check out the openings in the nursing office. She agreed. Before we said good night, Sheila asked if I was Jewish. Yes, I told her.

"*Dieu merci!*" she said with glee. Thank God, indeed. It was the first sign of emotion she displayed.

A few days later Sheila showed up at my lab after her interview at the nursing office. She wore a knit suit, matching high heel shoes, and a gold charm bracelet. It seemed a bit dressy for a nursing interview. I took a close look at her bracelet and asked about the Eiffel Tower charm. It was identical to the one my girlfriend had bought when she was studying at the Sorbonne. But Sheila had never been to Paris, although she had always wanted to go. She had taken French in high school, where she developed a romantic infatuation with the language and a burning desire to visit the country and mingle with the people. Her limited vocabulary, however, would restrict her travels to train stations and public toilets. When she asked in French for me to water down her coffee instead of add artificial sweetener (as she really meant to say), I knew her ability to order a decent meal would also be compromised.

None of this bothered Sheila. Her universe centered around her hospital job and extended only so far as her apartment and a nearby shopping mall. She had been happy until the swastikas appeared.

There was nothing about this woman to suggest that she harbored an abnormal interest in Nazis. Yet she shared the same fascination and repulsion that most people experience when they are exposed to images of Nazi horrors. Sheila recalled an especially disturbing movie about the Holocaust. After the movie, she was absorbed in replaying the images in her mind. Later that night, when Sheila went on duty at the hospital, she continued to think about scenes from the movie.

It was while she was adjusting the sheets on a bed that she saw a quick movement in the corner of her eye. She froze, her eyes staring straight ahead. Sheila had been noticing these movements ever since she started working the 11:00 P.M. to 7:00 A.M. shift. When the movement reappeared, she locked onto the object and tracked it as it passed through the top of her visual field. It seemed to slow to a stop for a moment, and that's when she saw for the first time that the object was actually a small swastika. Then it disappeared. Sheila insisted that the swastika was not some amorphous dot that only *looked like* a twisted cross. Rather, it *was* a perfectly formed swastika with thick black hooks. Once she identified the pattern, she started noticing it more. Most of the time it passed through the top of her visual field in less than a second. At other times Sheila saw the swastika going to and fro near the corners of the sheets, or darting in a set course across a patient's gown.

Her description of the swastika's movements resembled the movement patterns attributed to intraocular floaters, retinal phosphenes, and hypnagogic forms. While all of these phenomena appear as simple geometric figures, sometimes patients elaborate or interpret them as recognizable images. I recalled the story of one patient who saw phosphenes as white skunks with erect tails moving across the visual field. As Sheila described a few instances when swastikas duplicated and marched across the bedsheets, I smelled a skunk. Sheila smelled a conspiracy.

The most intriguing aspect of her report was the appearance of the swastikas as isolated phenomena. She denied any perceptual distortions, dizziness, or physical sensations. The swastikas varied somewhat—there were big ones and little ones—but they never developed into more complex hallucinatory patterns or scenes. I was puzzled by their apparent fixed nature. Some neurological disorders, such as migraines or seizures, might start off with simple fixed visual sensations but rapidly progress to auras, headaches, delirium, or hallucinations. Sheila's experiences occurred in states of clear consciousness and never developed into anything more serious. Her swastikas seemed like little more than pesky mosquitos that didn't even bite.

Since Sheila had attended my lecture, she must have considered the possibility that the swastikas were hypnagogic images. After all, most sightings were in the wee hours of the morning when she was probably sleepy.

"*C'est* impossible," said Sheila.

"*Pourquoi?*" I asked.

She explained that she was always wide awake, and, although she worked a night shift, it was the middle of the day for her. I got her to admit that working nights had been difficult and took considerable adjustment. But Sheila insisted that she didn't need a lot of sleep and, *merci* very much, managed just fine. However, I knew that any sleep loss can lower the threshold for detection of entoptic phenomena such as floaters and phosphenes. Even if one does not go to sleep, the fatigued brain can embroider these ambiguous forms with specific features. This could have happened to Sheila on the night when she was recalling scenes from the Holocaust movie. In the semi-darkened rooms of her sleeping patients, nighttime specks could have metamorphosed into Nazi swastikas.

Sheila had a different theory. If the swastikas were hypnagogic images, then they must be generated by her sleeping patients. Why shouldn't Nazis dream of swastikas? While Sheila agreed that "seeing" someone else's dreams was a bit farfetched, she felt that any admission of hallucinations was tantamount to insanity. She refused to believe that she was crazy or that something as evil as swastikas could be coming from deep inside herself. Her doll's eyes started to tear. *"Au secours, s'il vous plaît,"* she tried to whisper. She was asking for my help. It was the worst pronunciation I had ever heard. I felt like crying, too.

My first impulse was to give Sheila a full physical and psychological work-up. In my mind I ran through all the ophthalmological, neurological, and toxicological studies I wanted to run. My instincts told me to hold off and trust her statements as a nurse that she was healthy. Instead, I surrendered to my second impulse. I would try to capture a swastika with Sheila's help. I figured I couldn't lose. If I didn't catch one, as I suspected would be the case, and could convince Sheila that it was because they didn't exist, I might be able to save her from a runaway paranoid psychosis. And what if I was wrong and managed to catch one? The answer that came to my mind was as silly as the question. I recalled a lecture I once heard on the biology of the common blowfly. The speaker began by opening a mason jar filled with flies, allowing them to escape into the room. It got everyone's attention. Now I thought of an exciting addition to my slide show. I would open a jar filled with swastikas that would dart about the room for everyone to marvel at. My imagination never considered the possibility that the swastikas might capture me.

"C'est magnifique!" shouted Sheila when I presented my plan. I would initiate a psychological study of night-duty nurses. Sheila would be the pilot subject, and I would try to enlist the cooperation of her supervisor, explaining that it was important for me to conduct observations of Sheila while she worked. Of course, I would promise to be as unobtrusive as possible, but I also promised Sheila that I would be with her throughout the shift. She would tell me whenever the swastikas appeared, and I would record the precise time and location of their appearance. I told Sheila that this preliminary investigation should enable us to map the appearances of the swastikas as well as identify the

patients who she suspected were the sources. We had to know the enemy's habits, I told her, before we attempted the capture.

In a few weeks I had secured all the necessary permissions. I met with Sheila for a final briefing. Since this was going to be a real research project, I told her, we should obey standard medical protocol and start with a routine examination. She consented and I finally got the physical tests I wanted. Sheila was correct: her body was healthy. I didn't administer any psychological tests because I knew her experiences with the swastikas would tip the scales in favor of a paranoid disorder. Besides, I felt that a swastika, real or imaginary, was something to be justifiably afraid of. We would begin in three days.

I was already in the nurse's station, guzzling coffee, when Sheila arrived for duty. She complimented me on my uniform. I was wearing a starched white lab coat and regimental tie. My pockets were jammed with Nazi-busting gear: notebook, flashlight pen for writing in the dark, voice-activated microcassette tape recorder, and my trusty Minox spy camera. If only Sheila had not been in such a fragile state, I would have chanced a few laughs and worn my *yarmulke* and *tallis*.

Five hours later I was still guzzling coffee and getting bored watching Sheila watching patients. Night-duty nurses have an easy workload compared to nurses on day shifts, yet they make more money. Sheila spent most of her time monitoring the vital signs of her patients, distributing medication, and waiting for the rare occasions when a patient woke up and needed something. When she went to answer a patient's call at the end of the hall, I almost didn't follow, then ran after her. Inside the room I found Sheila helping an elderly woman get back into bed. After tucking the patient in, Sheila leaned across the center of the bed to straighten the covers. Suddenly she pointed her finger at a spot near the pillow at the end of the bed, jabbing her finger in the air again and again as if to say "There, There!"

I ran to Sheila's side and looked at where she was pointing. The old woman looked up at me, her toothless mouth forming a faint smile. Sheila was pointing to an area of the pillow next to the woman's face, but there was nothing there. Next, I looked at Sheila. She was staring at the middle of the bed, yet obviously watching something out of the corner of her eye. Her body was bent at the waist, with her feet on the floor and the rest sprawled across the bed, arms outstretched. Frozen in this position, Sheila looked more like a doll than ever before.

In a few moments she got up, straightened her skirt, patted her hair into place, and faced me. We had already arranged to speak in French in case the patients overheard. "*Partons* (Let's go)," she said. I followed her into the hall. Sheila had seen a swastika, one of the big ones, right there on the pillow. I dutifully recorded Sheila's description, the time, and the patient's name. *If that old woman is a Nazi, I'll eat my yarmulke.*

I asked Sheila if she noticed any other unusual activity in her visual field. None, she said. I ran through a quick symptom checklist and found that all her sensory systems seemed to be operating normally. She was certainly more awake than I was. It didn't take a sensitive nurse to notice that I was almost falling asleep on my feet. Sheila kindly suggested that I go home and get some rest. We would try again tomorrow. As I turned to leave, she cautioned me about running down the hall again because it had just been waxed and might be slippery. "*Merci*, nurse Sheila," I said as I walked away.

After sleeping most of the following day, I felt like I could tackle the full shift with Sheila that night, and I did. There were three more swastika sightings, all in the last half of the shift. Sheila saw one of the swastikas on the old woman's gown, and the other two appeared on the wall of another patient's bathroom. Apparently, even Nazis can't restrain themselves from putting graffiti on toilets. I saw nothing but unmarked tiles. Sheila didn't ask about my perceptions and, as during the previous night, I was careful not to reveal them.

I didn't sleep well that day, only about three hours. I met Sheila for dinner before the start of our next night shift. She was as perky as ever. But I hadn't felt this fatigued and befuddled since my organic chemistry finals in college. I drank enough coffee with dinner to stay with our conversation. Caffeine addiction was the only thing Sheila and I had in common. Sheila liked coffee but confessed that it stained her teeth. Then she reached into a pocket of her uniform, removed a blue-and-white box of NoDoz caffeine tablets, and swallowed two of them.

So this is why the doll never closes her eyes, I thought. The toxicology tests had screened for all the illegal stimulants but not caffeine. Amphetamines and related stimulants are highly abused by the medical profession, but high doses of caffeine can be almost as problematic. I learned that Sheila consumed as much as twelve hundred milligrams a day, the equivalent of twelve strong cups of coffee. When Sheila said she didn't have a problem getting to sleep after a shift but didn't dream much, I knew why. Tolerance to the caffeine would permit her to sleep, all right, but the quality of sleep is adversely affected. Caffeine, in doses as low as three hundred milligrams, produces a lighter than normal sleep with far fewer REM periods. Consequently, there are fewer dreams. While the chronic doses of caffeine might improve her alertness and work performance, they would continually deprive her of deep sleep. Caffeine does not cause hallucinations, but sleep deprivation does. This could keep her in a constant hypnagogiclike state where the swastikas could thrive.

Later that evening I found one of the signposts to that state. I literally tripped over it. I was running down the hall again when I stumbled. Luckily, I managed to catch myself before I fell. Sheila warned me about the wet floor. It didn't look wet at all. Actually, it looked dry and dusty. I checked with the janitor and found that the floors had not been washed that night. Yet they appeared wet to Sheila. *Voilà!* One of the early signs of sleep deprivation is a visual distortion whereby objects appear to shimmer as if covered by a thin film of water. These distortions or illusions are caused by blurred vision coupled with an increased sensitivity to light. I remembered that Sheila had warned me about the freshly waxed floors two nights before. A shining surface is another example of a distortion due to sleep deprivation. When the janitor said that the floors had not been waxed or buffed for more than a week, I knew that Sheila's eyes were not seeing the world correctly.

I started to watch Sheila from a new perspective. Not surprisingly, she saw several more swastikas that night. There was a big one on the old woman's pillow again and assorted smaller ones hovering around another patient's bed. All the sightings took place during periods when I observed Sheila to be somewhat dazed. Her behavior reminded me of my students, who often seemed a little "spacey" whenever they stayed up all night studying. The dazed appearance is due to brief lapses of awareness known as microsleeps. Microsleeps last only two or three seconds and are easily overlooked. There is a tendency for these lapses to become longer and more frequent as sleep deprivation continues. While there is no observable REM activity during microsleeps, the EEG shows the same activity as that found in the state between wakefulness and sleep, a state rich in hypnagogic imagery. Swastikas could erupt in such episodes.

Sleep deprivation also causes the fine movements of the eye to decrease, creating the tendency to stare. Lacking fine movements, the eye begins to move in a jerkier fashion, resulting in illusions of movement in the periphery of vision. Studies of sleep-deprived British soldiers found that they hallucinated armored columns moving across the horizon. While Sheila didn't see columns of Nazi panzer tanks, once the swastikas appeared, they did start blitzing the periphery of her visual field.

One sign of these episodes is the sudden loss of tone in the muscles maintaining body posture and the tendency to fall. I remembered that Sheila was leaning across the old woman's bed when she saw a swastika. At other sightings, she seemed to be a little unsteady, sometimes holding on to a bed or wall. Sheila said that the swastikas always upset her and made her uneasy. She imagined that it was all the doings of the Nazis. I suspected that Sheila was fighting off a different creature of the imagination: the Sandman.

In order to confirm that sleep deprivation was the culprit, I had to monitor Sheila's sleep habits. While I was willing to believe that she slept, I was equally willing to bet that it was probably very little. But how much? Did she have fits of microsleeps during the day? Did the swastikas attack her during the day? Somehow I had to clock her sleep time and observe her daily behavior.

At the end of the shift, I told Sheila that the preliminary investigation was nearing completion. The comings and goings of the swastikas had been charted for several nights. I had taken the names of the suspected patients. Before we started to kick them in the swastikas, I said in jest, it was necessary to rule out any daytime sources. I wanted to know everything about what she did during her time off. She agreed to let me stay at her place and monitor her daytime activities.

After breakfast I stopped to get some clothes and toilet items from my place, then drove to Sheila's apartment. She took the bedroom and I took the couch after reminding her to wake me as soon as she got up.

Sheila yelled my name. I sprang off the couch and grabbed my Rolex from the coffee table. It was only eleven-thirty in the morning! After two and one-half hours of sleep, Sheila was in the kitchen making a pot of coffee. I sat down at the table and watched her. My semi-slumbering mind was already telling me this was a bad idea. Her bitter-tasting coffee seemed to be saying the same thing. After a large mug of the stuff, I started to feel better.

We read the morning paper in silence. I studied Sheila's eye movements and decided she wasn't really reading. She glanced at the headlines and the comics, then flipped through the sections looking at the ads. Since sleep deprivation impairs fine eye movements and blurs type, her choice in reading material may have been forced upon her. She probably had a hard time even looking at the TV listings to find her favorite daytime programs. Then I picked up the business section and turned to the stock market report. It was all a blur!

As Sheila was getting dressed, I poked around the apartment, secretly hoping to find a book on Nazis. Her library consisted of about two dozen nursing books, a few oversized art books, and a French dictionary. A book on Leonardo da Vinci sat on the coffee table. The kitchen cupboards were well-stocked and orderly. Even the spices were arranged in alphabetical order.

Sheila emerged in a sweater, jeans, and spiked, high heel shoes. She grabbed another mug of coffee and turned on the television. I washed and dressed hurriedly, then returned to the living room. After sitting through several boring soaps, Sheila announced that she had to run some errands and I could come along. When we left her apartment, I couldn't help but notice the way she walked. She appeared to wobble on the high heels.

Her uncertain balance was reminiscent of a gruesome experiment carried out in 1927 on a dozen puppies. The puppies, from six weeks to three months old, were kept awake by experimenters who walked them frequently. After three or four days of sleep deprivation, the puppies lost all interest in their surroundings. Some developed a fear of light and attempted to get into dark corners when walked. It was while being forced to walk that the animals exhibited poor balance due to muscular weakness, a sure sign of severe sleep loss. The puppies flexed their front paws in such a manner as to give the appearance of being flatfooted. At this point the animals were allowed to sleep, but it was too late for some. Two died without awakening!

While I didn't think that Sheila would die in her sleep, I was concerned because her muscular weakness now completed the diagnosis of a prodrome leading to psychosis. The prodrome, or group of premonitory symptoms, includes microsleeps, staring, visual distortions, movements in the periphery of vision, and muscular weakness. There are also a variety of aches, pains, and tingling sensations that grow as the prodrome develops. A common sensation is a feeling of tightness around the head, the so-called "pressure band" effect. Although Sheila didn't complain about her body, I suspected that she was experiencing more than the usual number of discomforts. My evidence: I saw a half-empty bottle of five hundred aspirin tablets in her medicine cabinet.

The prodrome allows the mind to wander, creating difficulty in concentration and attention. This is particularly evident when a person is not working. At night, Sheila's duties kept her sufficiently occupied and these effects were suppressed. By day, however, when she relaxed, I fully expected to see some problems. Yet Sheila manifested no signs of cognitive dysfunction. When I followed her on the errands, I discovered the reason: she didn't relax. Sheila kept herself constantly on the go, shifting from one errand to another with the same semiautomatic performance she displayed when flipping through the morning paper. She was keeping herself from drifting asleep—and from falling into the prodrome's full grasp—in the same way the experimenters had kept the puppies awake by walking them whenever necessary. As I watched Sheila teetering on her high heels, I realized she was balancing on a fine line between sleep and wakefulness. Despite her list of daily errands, Sheila really didn't know where she was headed. My heart went out to this lost puppy.

Inside the apartment, Sheila kicked off her heels and announced she was taking a nap before dinner. I greeted the news with a silent prayer of thanksgiving. One hour later, her alarm woke us up. We had a light meal, then watched TV until it was time to go to the hospital. Before we left, she downed her usual pair of NoDoz tablets. I also took two. I had decided that as long as I was operating on Sheila's schedule, I might as well use the same fuel. From now on, I told her, I wanted to take a pill whenever she did. *Besides, I need them*, I thought.

It was a particularly quiet night at the hospital. Sheila's flat oxfords erased all signs of the uncertain footing I had seen during the day. She reported only one swastika: a small one zipping over the old woman's head like a shooting star. The other patients slept soundly, and Sheila spent most of her time inside the nurse's station, where she worked on reports. I spent the time chatting with Fred, the night janitor. His wife had just had a baby boy, he explained as he stuck a cigar in the breast pocket of my lab coat. I offered my congratulations.

On Sheila's next break, we both swallowed two more NoDoz tablets. Everything about the night, from the sight and taste of the NoDoz, and the distant memories it kindled, to my glassy-eyed view of a progressively blurring world, made me feel like I was back in college studying for an organic chemistry test. Somehow I made it through the shift and collapsed on the couch as soon as we returned to the apartment.

Sheila woke me a little after eleven. I had slept for three hours, or three and one half hours if I counted the time Sheila was putting on her makeup and I drifted back to sleep. We went to a nearby restaurant for lunch. The NoDoz was ruining my appetite, but I forced myself to eat the same tuna sandwich and fruit salad that Sheila ordered. We washed it down with iced tea, then went on another round of errands. Back in the apartment, Sheila surprised me by turning on the radio instead of the television.

The sparkling melody of a familiar piece filled the air. I couldn't quite put my finger on what it was. But then I was much too tired to even raise a finger, mental or otherwise. I closed my eyes and allowed the music to sweep me away. Perhaps it was the way the melody was carried by the violins, then answered by the horns, ebbing and flowing, rising and falling in great waves. Perhaps it was the rotating fan in the living room that blew a refreshing wind with regular intervals. It didn't matter. I would not risk losing this image by dissecting it. I was soaring in a hang glider. Below were the green hills of Earth, serene and beautiful. Above, cottony clouds covered the sky. Then a pair of trumpets blasted a hole in the clouds and a crescendo of strings lifted me through. Here, I flew round and

round in melodic circles, absorbing energy from a golden sun.
Then an announcer was saying something about a traffic jam on
the Santa Monica Freeway.

I came back to Earth. Sheila was talking to me. She told me
that I had a blank stare on my face and wouldn't answer her so
she changed the station to get my attention. I knew that I was
not dreaming because my eyes were open. The vivid fantasy
must have been a hypnagogic reverie. Even in the privacy of my
own thoughts I hesitated to admit that I was hallucinating. Sheila
was still the subject and I, dammit, was the experimenter.

We had a late dinner at the hospital cafeteria and went
directly to work. While I was aware that Sheila and I were beginning our fourth tour of night duty together, and the progressive
symptoms of my sleep loss were undeniable, I was determined
to avoid becoming a victim of her swastikas.

The old woman was up late that night watching TV. As
Sheila entered her room, a swastika appeared on the old woman's lips. It was a rare stationary one. I wasn't paying attention,
and Sheila had to pull me by the arm to look. By the time I
leaned over the bed to look, the swastika was gone but the old
woman was licking her lips as if she had just finished a satisfying
meal. Sheila and I laughed out loud together for the first time.
Only I couldn't stop laughing. Ever since I was a little kid, whenever I get overtired I succumb to giddiness. Sheila snickered and
brought me a cup of coffee. Strange as it may seem, it actually
quieted me down.

Sometime during the shift I visited with Fred. All he wanted
to talk about was his new baby. I offered him my congratulations.
Fred offered me a cigar, which I stuck in my breast pocket as I
walked away. When I saw that I had another cigar in my pocket,
I suddenly realized that we had had this conversation before!
Fred had been kind enough to ignore my lapse, but I still cringe
with embarrassment whenever I recall the incident.

During our next NoDoz and coffee break, I slipped on a
wet napkin and took a quick double step, spilling coffee on my
lab coat. Not only had I put myself in Sheila's chemical shoes, I
felt like I was walking in her high heels as well. I went to the
restroom to throw some water on the stains and on my face. As
I dried my face, I was alarmed by my zombie-eyed appearance

in the mirror. *They don't call this the graveyard shift for nothing*, I thought.

The rest of the shift was uneventful until 6:00 A.M. I was sitting next to Sheila in the nurse's station. In my left eye I saw a distinctive black form drift slowly into view. I took off my wire-rims. The form remained, telling me it was not a speck on my glasses. I studied it for several moments until it disappeared. I was afraid to move for fear of changing the optical conditions that allowed this to happen. In a few seconds, the form reappeared, drifting slowly over the same arc in my visual field. For the next several minutes, I sat in that exact position, turning this way and that, hoping to resurrect the vision, but the form was gone.

I had recognized the form at once. There were six black lines joined together in a ring. This had to be the structural formula for benzene, a form from organic chemistry that had been embedded in my brain during many all-night study sessions fueled by NoDoz. But it was actually nothing more than dots connected with black lines, the basic elements of a hypnagogic form. It would have been a simple matter to rearrange those six lines into the six lines of a twisted cross. This might have violated rules of organic chemistry, but the rules governing cognitive syntheses are much more flexible. When the form appeared, my sleep-deprived mind was reminiscing about my most nightmarish course in college. When Sheila saw her form, she was preoccupied by images of a different nightmare. Once she labeled the design a swastika, the symptom turned into a malady.

Although I said nothing to Sheila about my experience, I had enough information and decided to terminate the experiment in two days. Those next two days were her days off, and I still wanted to determine her sleep habits when she wasn't working. I found that Sheila had a respectable seven hours of sleep each day, which she said was typical for her days off. This amount of rest allowed her to recover much of the lost sleep. She never saw a swastika during these two days or nights, even in her dreams. This was good news because if hallucinations invaded her dreams, it was a sure sign of serious psychopathology.

Sheila's suspicious thoughts were still in the superficial prodrome stage and had not yet grown into a true sleep-deprivation psychosis. In the psychotic stage, hallucinations would become prolonged experiences instead of fleeting glimpses. All the prodromal symptoms would become more pronounced. Confusion and delirium would be more frequent as lucid intervals grew fewer and shorter. The final picture would be one of paranoid schizophrenia with wild mood swings and delusions of self-reference, grandeur, and persecution. Sheila was not there, yet. In fact, she appeared relatively free of symptoms when she started her new work week.

I stayed in touch with her by telephone. She reported that her first night back to work was swastika-free. *"C'est très intéressant,"* said Sheila, "it's always that way." Yes, it was interesting but understandable in light of her two days of rest. By the second night, as her sleep loss started to accumulate, the swastikas returned. They continued to reappear for the remainder of the week. I spent my time planning ways to stop the swastikas and the prodrome they triggered. Sheila could accomplish this herself by either sleeping more or going back to a normal day shift. Since I didn't think that I could convince her to give up her daytime activities or her night-duty bonus pay, I prepared a direct assault on the swastikas. I found everything I needed in the archeology section of the UCLA library.

Sheila came to my office on her next day off. She wore a white linen pantsuit, white silk blouse, and white high heels. It was the first time I saw her wearing the gold charm bracelet since our initial meeting. She looked well and rested. Even her French seemed more carefully pronounced.

I began by listing the effects of the experiment on *my* body: fatigue, lapses in attention, blurred vision, memory problems, and the movements of light in the visual periphery. Then I confessed to seeing a swastika! Sheila clapped her hands together and smiled in delight. I explained that my swastika had thick, black lines just like hers, but mine appeared more like a benzene ring than a twisted cross. Nonetheless, I insisted that both figures arose from the same elements and actions of the brain and visual system. When our sleep-deprived eyes started to see dots and specks in the visual field, our brains connected the dots, thus creating recognizable forms. In a sense, we made constellations out of the stars in our eyes. We saw the characters we were consciously or subconsciously looking for. After all, once we see the big dipper, it is hard to look at those points of light in the sky and *not* see the dipper every time.

Sheila was willing to accept my explanation that sleep loss probably caused the swastikas, but they still disturbed her. While I found the benzene ring amusing, Sheila viewed the swastika with alarm. Her reaction was based on the swastika's association with the barbarism of Nazism. It was time to rewrite history.

I dimmed the office lights and turned on the slide projector. The first slide showed a small pottery bowl with a swastika painted on the bottom. This bowl, I explained, was excavated from a site in western Iran. It has been dated to 4000 B.C., nineteen centuries before the Third Reich! The swastika is humanity's oldest symbol, and the word itself is from Sanskrit and means "object of well-being." The symbol spread from the Middle East to Greece, Rome, Europe, and Asia.

I advanced the projector. The next slide showed a clay female figure from ancient Greece. Swastikas covered her arms and shoulders like so many tattoos. In many cultures the swastika was a symbol of fertility, a charm for success in producing many offspring.

The next slide showed a swastika seal used as a symbol of good luck in ancient India. The symbol is still found in contemporary Hindu and Buddhist cultures. I advanced through a series of slides depicting good luck swastikas on public buildings in India, Tibet, China, and Japan. Lucky swastikas were also used by North American Indians. "Whoever heard of Navajo Nazis?" I asked sarcastically as I flashed slides of their pottery and weaving with the twisted cross motif.

Some cultures used the swastika as an astronomical or religious symbol representing planets or deities. To the Germanic peoples, the swastika was a symbol for the sun, a symbol of life. In parts of Austria, the swastika became a symbol of magical power. It was out of these mystical origins that Hitler and the Nazis adopted the swastika. However, the association of the swastika with Nazism accounts for less than 1 percent of its history. I showed the last slide of a Nazi flag for less than a second, then turned off the projector.

I had hoped that this little lecture would desensitize Sheila to the swastika. The rest was up to her. I appealed to her diligence as a nurse to consider all that I said. At the very least, I suggested she might consider Leonardo da Vinci's sleep diet. According to legend, Leonardo napped for fifteen minutes every four hours, limiting his total sleep to only ninety minutes a day without ill effect. A catnap or two might work far better than her coffee and NoDoz breaks at work. And recent studies have shown you can keep going this way without impairment for at least a week.

Before Sheila left I gave her copies of these studies as well as history papers about swastikas so she could study them at her leisure. She said goodbye. I found myself saying good night.

POSTSCRIPT

Sheila continued seeing swastikas, but, thanks to my history lesson, she came to recognize that she needn't fear them anymore. She never got a chance to try the catnap idea. Soon after our little experiment ended, she married a night-duty physician from the hospital. They honeymooned in France, and she is now raising twin daughters. Every year she sends me a Hanukkah card signed with a swastika drawn in red lipstick.

The melodic piece I heard on the radio was the ballet suite from Tchaikovsky's *The Sleeping Beauty*.

PART THREE

IMAGINARY COMPANIONS

9

THE GIRL
WITH
DRAGON EYES

When children are playing alone on the green
In comes the playmate that never was seen.
—ROBERT LOUIS STEVENSON,
"The Unseen Playmate"

"Don't you dare call it imaginary," yelled Mrs. R, "or she'll walk out!" Mrs. R was trying to coach me for my upcoming meeting with her daughter, Nancy, who had an invisible playmate.

Some children have imaginary playmates or companions that are as vivid and real to them as living ones. These playmates appear as actual visual and auditory projections that can be seen and heard. In this sense, the children are hallucinating. While many children come to recognize that their companions are not real, they may continue to engage in make-believe play with them. However, most imaginary playmates disappear when the child is about ten years old. The majority of parents view the phenomena as a normal event in a child's development. But Mrs.

R was concerned. Nancy had just turned fourteen and still played with her invisible friend.

Mrs. R had received one of the questionnaires I distributed to parents in an effort to locate and study children with imaginary companions. The questionnaire gave me much-needed background information before I met with the children. I was hoping that the children would introduce me to their imaginary friends and permit me to observe them in the act of hallucinating.

Most of the children I studied were between the ages of three and eight. The majority were either only children or first-borns, and they had no siblings at the time the imaginary companion first appeared. Although many of the children had access to toys, pets, and real playmates, they seemed to live lonely lives, spending much of their play time in self-initiated activities. I tended to agree with the parents that these children made highly creative uses of their time alone.

The children had invented a fantastic assortment of imaginary companions. In most cases, the companion was a person, usually of the same sex as the child. But there were animals, storybook characters, and even inanimate objects and toys brought to life by the child. One young girl's invisible friend was a little cloud called Puffy, which always made her laugh. During some play sessions, the girl would open the door so that Puffy could go outside and play with the other clouds, always reminding him to be back by bedtime. An eight-year-old boy played with an invisible train that followed him from his house to school every day. The boy would even hold the door to his house open for several seconds to allow all eight cars to pass (one car was added at each birthday). Other imaginary playmates included a talking doorknob, an elf, a pink giraffe, several miniature hens, and a baby Jesus Christ! After a few sessions, the children usually shared their companions with me. Then all three of us would engage in conversation and play. Almost all were friendly, and I never met an invisible playmate I didn't like, although the hens were more fun than Baby Jesus.

"Watch out for Chopsticks!" warned Mrs. R. "He'll rip your head off!" Chopsticks was the name Nancy had given her imaginary playmate, an eight-foot-tall dragon. Mrs. R assumed that any dragon that big had to be unfriendly. I asked her why she had left most of the questions about the imaginary companion blank.

"That's because Nancy rarely talks about him and I'm always afraid to ask," said Mrs. R.

I had a different reason for fearing imaginary dragons: the only other child I knew who had a dragon for a playmate eventually developed severe psychiatric problems. That dragon belonged to Belinda, a bright, artistic thirty-two-year-old patient at UCLA's Neuropsychiatric Institute. When Belinda was growing up, her parents were constantly moving around the country. The imaginary dragon became Belinda's only reliable friend and companion. He had wings for flying and humanlike hands for holding things. Belinda talked and played with the dragon in his imaginary castle for periods of fifteen minutes to three hours. These visits were the height of her pleasure. As Belinda grew older, the castle grew larger and was occupied by a variety of other imaginary creatures. Belinda spent more and more time exploring the dragon's world, sometimes dissociating from the real world for periods of three weeks. Although some imaginary companions function as "superegos," speaking to the child as a parent would, Belinda's dragon became powerful enough to rule most aspects of her behavior in the real world. Belinda consulted her dragon about every decision, from where she should go during the day to what she should say. She was caught in a tug-of-war between the dragon, who wanted her to spend the rest of her life painting murals on the castle walls, and her therapists, who were trying to keep her grounded in reality. The stress caused Belinda to become suicidal, and hospitalization was necessary. Belinda was kept from killing herself but stayed trapped inside the dragon's world. I still had the painting she gave me. It showed a world of gray shadows and ominous tones. A dragon flew overhead. In its claws it carried a cocoon with Belinda's naked body inside.

Since the behavioral problems surrounding Belinda's case were apparent at a very early age, I asked Mrs. R about any problems with Nancy. She said there were none. Nancy's health was excellent, and she was always well-behaved. When she played with Chopsticks, she seemed happy and in high spirits. The play was always quiet and reserved; Mrs. R was unaware of any arguments or disagreements between the two. At times, Nancy acted like a mime, as if she actually saw and heard the dragon. In preschool, there had been instances when the teacher saw Nancy playing with the invisible dragon, sometimes rubbing the dragon's imaginary tummy while laughing and giggling. But there had been no similar reports from grade-school teachers.

As a young child Nancy played with Chopsticks frequently but not every day. Almost all the play involved lengthy, whispered conversations. Sometimes Nancy talked with Chopsticks in the car when Mrs. R drove her to school. I asked Mrs. R if Chopsticks needed room in the car, his own chair at the table, or space in the child's bed. No, she told me, the dragon was apparently able to adapt to any physical situation.

Nancy never played with Chopsticks in public after her tenth birthday. She also stopped talking about him at home. As far as her mother knew, Nancy's play with Chopsticks was restricted to secret conversations held in the privacy of her bedroom. Mrs. R overheard some of these conversations, which she described as "eerie." Typically, Nancy would ask Chopsticks a question in her own voice, then answer in a high-pitched nasal whisper. Many of the children I studied carried on imaginary conversations with their companions, taking the part of both speakers. But I rarely learned much from these conversations because the children were usually only two or three years old. Nancy's continuing conversations with Chopsticks at the level of a fourteen-year-old promised to reveal much data about the nature of the imaginary beast. If I could get Nancy to talk with Chopsticks in my presence, it should be much more exciting than listening to a three-year-old talk to her brood of miniature hens.

After agreeing that Mrs. R could monitor the sessions via closed-circuit television, I arranged for her to bring Nancy to my lab. As a final word of advice, Mrs. R suggested that I have plenty of beer nuts available.

"Nancy likes beer nuts?" I asked. It seemed like an unusual snack.

"It's the only thing Chopsticks will eat," answered the mother.

I wasn't sure how to handle a teenager who still held on to an invisible playmate. My approach was geared to much younger children. I usually began by having them play several games in order to help me determine how firmly they believed in the reality of their imaginary companions. Until they are four or five, children do not understand the distinction between appearance and reality. The games I used were designed to function as "reality tests." In one test, I presented the children with several objects and asked them to inspect each one and tell me what it was. The objects were either real objects, such as a milk bottle or telephone, or rubber models of the same objects, which I purchased in novelty stores. One of the fake objects was a sponge rock that looked like a solid piece of granite, but felt soft and squeezable like the sponge that it really was. The very young children I tested could not always tell that the sponge rock was fake, even when they squeezed it. I found that the children who believed most in the separate reality of their imaginary playmates had the most difficulty in making such discriminations.

The children's favorite test was one I dubbed the M&M Game. A child would sit in a chair at a special desk. On the desk would be two M&M chocolate candies. At least that's what they looked like from the child's perspective. Actually, only one M&M was real; the other was a three-dimensional projection arranged by parabolic mirrors hidden inside the desk. The illusion was remarkably convincing. The two candies looked much the same in terms of color, size, and shape. When the desk was pushed up to the chair, the children could easily reach out and grab the real M&M; if they reached for the illusory M&M, their hands would only go through the projection!

In order to grasp the real candy correctly before the desk was pushed back out of reach, the children had to discriminate between the real and the illusory M&M. The real and illusory objects differed from each other along very subtle dimensions. Real M&Ms were more vivid, brighter, coherent, and concrete than their unreal counterparts. It is precisely these dimensions that distinguish real perceptions from fantasies, dreams, and hallucinations. Real perceptions, like real M&Ms, are more solid and veridical than make-believe dragons or mirages of chocolate candy.

When I tested very young children, from three to six, who had imaginary playmates, they all had difficulty in discriminating between the real and illusory candies. This difficulty paralleled their strong belief in the reality of their imaginary companions. When I tested young children of the same age who did not have imaginary playmates, they grabbed the real M&Ms almost every time. Older children, from eight to ten, who understood that their imaginary playmates were make-believe, also had no difficulty in selecting the real M&Ms. However, since most children older than ten, with or without imaginary playmates, performed extremely well on this test, it seemed like a waste of time to try it with Nancy, even if I substituted beer nuts for the M&Ms.

Since Nancy had an extremely high IQ and was an outstanding student at a demanding school, I knew that I could not use the usual tests with sponge rocks and M&Ms. Imaginary dragon aside, Nancy was not likely to appreciate such childish tricks. But one thing that should work, even with big kids, was the approach pioneered by Mr. Wizard on his weekly television show. The show usually opened with Mr. Wizard, played by Don Herbert, absorbed in an intriguing experiment. A young boy or girl would arrive on the scene and immediately start asking questions. Mr. Wizard would engage the youngster in a half hour of fascinating experiments that demonstrated some scientific principle. As a child, I found myself mesmerized by the program. Now, as a scientist, I decided to act the role of Mr. Wizard and relive those magic years with Nancy.

Nancy knocked on the door to my lab.

"It's open. Come on in!" I yelled. If my voice sounded muffled, it was because my head was literally stuck in a hole in the wall. I was sitting in a chair with my head inside a plastic hood. The hood was the shape of an ice cream cone and my head was in the large end, facing the small end of the cone, which was attached to the wall.

I purposely ignored Nancy and concentrated on the milky plastic screen at the far end of the cone. "Jesus, this is great!" I said in a stage whisper. "Really great!" After a long period of silence, during which I heard Nancy sit down on the chair next to mine, I pushed myself away from the hood and swiveled around in my chair to face Nancy.

The first thing I noticed was her long red hair. There were small waves on top, but the sides were so straight I thought they had been ironed. Tiny diamond studs in her ears kept flashing through the fine red strands. It was an effect that highlighted her green eyes. She wore a matching green skirt and a baggy sweatshirt that failed to hide her chubby frame. Nancy seemed totally at ease, sitting with her feet propped up on her school knapsack, audibly chewing a piece of gum.

After saying hello, I immediately started telling Nancy about the piece of equipment I was testing. Some of the things I told her were true, but I had to mislead her in order for the device to help me find out about Chopsticks. I called it a Perky Hood in honor of the turn-of-the-century psychologist who invented an earlier model (true). Perky was interested in studying imagination (true) and built a device that helped people visualize things that they were thinking about (only partially true). I invited Nancy to take my seat and look into the hood. After she was properly positioned, I instructed her to look at the far end and try to imagine a common object. "Try to imagine a banana," I said.

The far end of the plastic hood contained a screen that was flat against the wall. Unknown to Nancy, my lab assistant was on the other side of the wall, inside an acoustically isolated room. The assistant operated a special slide projector that enabled images to be rear-projected on the screen. The brightness, duration, and focus of the projected image could be varied by special electronics attached to the projector. Although the room shielded the sound of the projection equipment, my assistant could hear everything going on in the lab via an intercom. At my signal, the assistant silently projected the first slide for a couple of seconds at an illumination that was initially subliminal but gradually brightened to a level that was barely visible. The slide showed a yellow banana designed to mimic the properties of a vague mental image of a banana: it had fuzzy edges and oscillated slightly. Perky had found that when subjects expected only mental imagery, they did not recognize that an external stimulus was present. The subjects were often surprised by the perceived intensity of their images. One subject reported that "If I hadn't known I was imagining, [I] should have thought it was real." Subsequent researchers have found that the decision to call an image real or imaginary is a function of expectancy as well as intensity of the stimulus.

When I asked Nancy to describe her image, she was astonished at how vivid it appeared inside the Perky Hood. "I was thinking about this yellow banana in my mind, and it just came right out of me!" she exclaimed.

I asked her to imagine several other items including a tomato, orange, green leaf, lemon, pencil, even a cigarette. Each time a slide was projected, and each time Nancy reported extremely vivid, almost concrete visual images. She never suspected that there was a real external stimulus on the screen. Once in a while I asked her to imagine an object without projecting a slide. I did this in order to determine the vividness of her normal mental imagery. Nancy could visualize distinct images when the screen was blank, but she described them as being less vivid and solid than when I used the slides. On one of these "blank" trials, I asked Nancy to imagine Chopsticks.

"Tell me what you see," I said after a few seconds.

"Chopsticks."

"Can you describe the image?" I asked softly.

"I can picture him but it's kinda faint," she answered. "Normally he's a bright royal blue. This is washed out . . . very pale. . . . There's the pointed ears. . . . I can't see the white spot on his belly."

Nancy pushed her seat away and said she didn't want to do this anymore. She said she was tired.

Despite the weak imagery, Nancy was giving me exactly what I hoped she would: a detailed description of the imaginary dragon. I pressed her for more data by asking how the image in the Perky Hood differed from the real Chopsticks. She explained that she had never tried to visualize him before; he always just appeared or said something. When she did see him, he was huge, eight feet tall. But he could squeeze his body like an accordion and shrink down to Nancy's size or smaller. Did he have pointed ears like her image of him?

"Yeah. But I couldn't make out his eyes," she said.

"What color are his eyes?" I asked.

"Green. Just like mine," said Nancy as she batted her eyes with mock flirtation.

"Can you call the real Chopsticks here now?" I asked.

"No," she screamed. The scream almost took my head off.

Just when I thought that we were getting along so well, Nancy stated that she didn't want to talk anymore about Chopsticks. "It's private," she said. I hesitated to risk losing ground by asking more questions. Instead, I took Nancy on a tour of the lab, explaining various experiments that were in progress.

She had a good time and seemed genuinely excited when I invited her to come back in two days.

At the door, Nancy remarked, "That Perky, he must have been a genius."

"She," I corrected. "Perky was a woman."

Nancy smiled. "Next time," she said.

After she left, I noticed that the bowl of raisins and beer nuts on my desk had been disturbed.

I was intrigued by Nancy's difficulty in visualizing Chopsticks on demand. The majority of children I studied were able to form elaborate visual images of their companions. Sometimes the images became animated, immediately engaging the child in play. That didn't happen to Nancy. She said that the "real" Chopsticks was much more vivid than her imagined visual image of him. Imaginary playmates are more real than characters in typical daydreams or fantasies, but children vary in the degree to which they regard the playmates as actual solid substances. Older children don't see them as solid. Nancy believed that Chopsticks was not only solid, but would appear suddenly on his own, further proof to her of his independent existence. However, the only truly spontaneous and sudden manifestations of imaginary companions are the occasions of their first and last appearances to the child. During the intervening years when these invisible playmates are around, almost all children can summon their companion at will. I knew that Nancy's refusal to call Chopsticks for me was an act of her will, not his. I needed to structure a situation wherein Nancy would allow him to appear.

The primary reason imaginary playmates appear to children is to provide friendship and companionship. Even when other living playmates are available to the child, the imaginary companion is usually more agreeable and easier to manipulate than an actual playmate. Another reason the imaginary playmate appears is to give approval to the child for both real and imagined acts. The companion may also appear when a young child is rehearsing skills such as verbal behavior, functioning as a partner with whom to practice and test oneself. Some children may even use their playmates to act out forbidden impulses such as fighting.

Everything that Mrs. R told me suggested that Nancy was using Chopsticks as her best friend, literally someone to talk to.

The snippets of conversation overheard by Mrs. R concerned the same topics a child might discuss with a close friend or sibling, although Nancy had neither. School gossip, boys, and parental rules were frequent subjects for discussion. If Nancy was listening to music or doing homework, the conversations might turn to those ongoing activities. Since almost all the conversations with the dragon took place when Nancy was alone in her room, I knew there was no practical way to observe this. In order to persuade Nancy to bring Chopsticks out of the bedroom and into the lab for me to study, I needed to make her feel that she would be making an important contribution to science. I decided on Mr. Wizard's direct approach: I would enlist Nancy as a co-investigator in my research.

Nancy arrived early for our next session. "What's up, Doc?" she said in a Bugs Bunny nasal voice.

I was still arranging some apparatus on a lab bench and asked her to help. All the equipment was designed to demonstrate afterimages, those visual images that persist long after the original image disappears. I asked Nancy if she had ever had her picture taken with a flashbulb and then continued to see a bright light after the picture had been taken. Many times, she said. That was an afterimage, I explained, caused when the photopigments in the retina are bleached by bright light. It takes time for the photochemicals to return to normal, and during this time there is continuing firing of the retina and optic nerve. So after the flash, you continue to see a bright white afterimage.

"But when I tried it just before you arrived," I said, "the afterimage was dark. You try it." Nancy positioned herself directly in front of the camera flashbulb I had set up. "Smile," I said as I triggered the flash. Immediately, I asked her to look at the wall and describe the afterimage.

"It's dark, a black blob," Nancy said with surprise.

I turned off the overhead lights and triggered another flash. This time Nancy reported a white afterimage. I explained that the white afterimage is only seen in the dark. But in the light, the afterimage is dark because the bleached area of the retina is less sensitive to light. When looking at a lighted surface, such as the lab wall, it can't see very well so a dark patch appears for a few moments.

Then I set up several different color filters in front of the flashbulb and, following each flash, asked Nancy to describe her afterimages when looking at a neutral gray screen. After a red flash, she reported a green afterimage. A blue flash caused her to see a yellow afterimage. Another flash with a different blue filter produced a pink afterimage tinged with orange.

The fun part about afterimages, I told Nancy, is that everybody has them but you can only see your own. While I could know the color of the flash, I could not know the precise afterimage she would see. In order for me to know what color she was seeing, she had to tell me. Although these afterimages were private events, they were just as "real" and genuine as the flashbulbs which produced them. I emphasized this point several times. While I couldn't see her afterimages any more than I could see her friend Chopsticks, Nancy could let me see them through her descriptions.

I explained that I was interested in finding out about the friends that visit people when they are alone. Lots of famous people have had invisible friends like Chopsticks. Christiane Ritter, an early explorer of Antarctica, had a male friend, "Karl," who visited her during the long polar night. Admiral Richard Byrd, another famous explorer, played cards with his invisible friend. And there were others who had invisible playmates as children. The author Stephen King called his invisible childhood friend "Jerry." Some people kept their special friends with them throughout adulthood. Robert Louis Stevenson, who wrote *The Strange Case of Dr. Jekyll and Mr. Hyde*, talked with little invisible people he called "brownies." The brownies dreamed up stories for Stevenson, who wrote them down. Machiavelli, the notorious politician and writer, even held long dinner conversations with his invisible guests. I told Nancy that almost every one of the adults and children who had these experiences were *very* intelligent and talented people. They were also brave enough to share their private experiences with others so we could all learn from them.

In many ways, they were as courageous as my team of psychonauts, whom I described to Nancy as explorers who volunteered to describe things that they saw when alone. I showed her the isolation room used by the psychonauts. The room was now set up for children. There was a small desk, a bean bag chair, and comfortable oversized pillows on the floor. Colorful posters decorated the wall, and everything was bright and cheery. Most of the psychonauts had been students at UCLA, where Nancy wanted to go after high school. Would Nancy like to be a psychonaut? "You betcha," she said.

I invited her to make herself comfortable in the room. She could take her book bag in with her and do homework if she wished. "Stay as long as you like, do what you want, but try to get Chopsticks to visit with you." I told her I would be watching and listening via a closed-circuit TV so if she needed anything, just to let me know. Before she entered the room, I handed her the bowl of beer nuts and raisins from my desk.

Chopsticks didn't show up that first day, but Nancy was much more willing to talk about him when she was alone in the room and I was only a disembodied voice on an intercom. I learned that Chopsticks had little rooster feet and a face that looked more like a poodle than a reptile. His entire body was covered with blue skin except for "a little white beer belly." I assumed this was actually a beer nut belly, not unlike Nancy's. Chopsticks liked to do the same things Nancy did, and he never made her do anything she didn't want to. I took this as a healthy sign that Chopsticks was not threatening the child in the way that Belinda's dragon had when he tried to trap her inside the imaginary castle.

Nancy couldn't remember when Chopsticks had first appeared, but she remembered that he had been her friend for a long time. They grew up together. When Nancy acquired new skills, Chopsticks developed the same ones. As Nancy grew taller, Chopsticks sprouted to gigantic heights. He developed the ability to adjust his size, which was a good thing because the ceiling of the psychonaut room was only six feet. Despite his bulk, Chopsticks remained invisible to everyone but Nancy. She surprised me when she said that sometimes even she didn't see him when he was talking to her. When I asked Nancy what Chopsticks sounded like, she did her Bugs Bunny imitation for me again.

"Will I be able to hear him?" I asked.

"Kinda," said Nancy. "I sorta talk for him."

"Could you do that now?"

"Next time," said Nancy as she prepared to leave the room after staying for more than two hours. A respectable first try for a psychonaut, I told her as we said goodbye.

After she left I discovered that only raisins were left in the snack bowl. For the next session, which was scheduled on a Saturday, I eliminated the raisins and filled two bowls with beer nuts. Nancy was prepared to spend the entire day doing her homework inside the room. I gave her several cans of soft drinks just before I closed her door and settled down at my own desk to do some paperwork.

Nancy worked diligently for several hours. After a restroom and lunch break, she asked if she could take a nap. I dimmed the lights in the room as she curled up on the pillows. The low-light lens of my Sony videocamera continued to record her every movement. Forty minutes later she sat up and started humming to herself. The humming turned into a song. The song turned into a question.

"Like it? Like it?" asked Nancy. She was just sitting on the pillows looking around the room. Neither I nor anyone else answered. "There's more math to do ... English ... Spanish ... *cabré, cabrás, cabrá, cabremos, cabréis, cabrán*. Pretty good, eh Choppy?"

"Pretty good," said Nancy in Chopsticks' nasal voice. "Whatsya gonna do first?"

"Math," answered Nancy normally.

Then Nancy stood up, turned up the illumination in the room by herself, and settled back to work at the desk. She began working on an algebra problem, reading out loud each step as she wrote it down.

"Stupid Nancy," she said to herself as she started erasing.

"Stupid Nancy," echoed Chopsticks.

I had to disagree with both of them as Nancy breezed her way through the solution, all the while reciting various equations. I was reminded of what the famous child psychologist Nathan Harvey once wrote: "No stupid child ever had an imaginary companion."

A little later, Nancy blurted out, "I love you, Chopsticks. I love you very much." There was no answer. When several minutes went by with no further conversations, I interrupted Nancy on the intercom and asked if Chopsticks was still there. Nancy said he was.

"Can I talk to him?" I asked.

Nancy started giggling.

"No way!" said Chopsticks.

"Please?" I pleaded.

"No way!" yelled Nancy. The yell was amplified by the inter-com and nearly ripped my head off. I lowered the volume and left Nancy alone for the rest of the afternoon. She made a few more comments to Chopsticks about the silly doctor. When Chopsticks said that he liked me, I knew I had at least one friend in the room. He might be imaginary, but basic researchers, like lonely children, can't be too picky.

The third and fourth sessions were very similar. I was disap-pointed that the conversations with Chopsticks never reached the sophisticated level promised by Nancy's age and intelligence. Her remarks to him sometimes seemed to be generated by force of habit rather than any desire to engage in meaningful dia-logue. On many occasions, Chopsticks would simply echo Nan-cy's words or make nonsensical remarks. At other times he sounded like a parent, reminding her not to wiggle her foot while sitting or chew her food with her mouth open. I was thank-ful for this parental role when Chopsticks told Nancy not to stick her gum under the desk in the isolation room.

Nancy jealously guarded my access to Chopsticks. I learned from her mother that even as a small child, Nancy never shared her imaginary playmate with other real friends. While such pos-sessiveness was not unusual, I took it as a personal defeat that I wasn't able to gain Nancy's complete trust. Why was she keeping Chopsticks from me? Children might hide their imaginary com-panions from others when the companion is used to express hidden wishes and impulses, but that didn't seem to be the case here. Nancy's behavior with the dragon was as tame and inno-cent as any I had studied. I suspected that Nancy was at the age when Chopsticks was losing importance to her as a friend and companion. She probably had some awareness of his declining role in her life and was starting to view him as a vestige of younger days. Unwilling to let go of him, Nancy could have been embarrassed to let me see her interact with him.

Since imaginary companions often visit when children are alone in their beds at night, as Chopsticks frequently did with Nancy, I decided to reduce the illumination in the room for Nancy's fifth session. But how much illumination should remain? Dimming the lights for her nap had prompted a brief conversation with Chopsticks. Would even less light generate more talk? I knew that blind children have stronger imaginary companions than sighted children. I was also aware that boredom prompted imaginary play. Therefore, I decided to put Nancy in total darkness with nothing to do. An infrared lens and light source kept me in constant video contact. I encouraged her to let Chopsticks appear. There was nothing to do but watch and listen.

Nancy tossed and turned on the pillows, hummed a tune, chewed three successive sticks of sugar-free bubble gum, and twirled her hair around her fingers. She was a total fidget . . . until Chopsticks showed up. Nathan Harvey was right when he said that a large amount of nervous energy in a child initiates the production of the imaginary companion. The first sign was Nancy's laughter. Then a whispered "O Choppy" as she rolled over on her side and faced an empty area of the room. More giggling. More whispering into the pillows. Then silence.

For the next thirty minutes I watched Nancy making faces, moving her lips, and shaking her head in gestures of yes or no. I decided on a bold step. I grabbed the intercom microphone and said: "Psychonaut Nancy! Report!"

"I've been talking with Chopsticks," said Nancy with the cool aplomb of a more seasoned psychonaut.

"Tell me about it," I said.

Nancy described a lengthy imaginal dialogue with Chopsticks. They spoke about a new dress and a watch she wanted. Then they started to plan her "sweet sixteen" birthday party, discussing what she would wear and who she would invite. She told me that most of her conversations with him were not actually vocalized but took place inside her head like this one had. Sometimes she repeated things he said, but, if there was much to discuss, it was easier to do it without speaking out loud.

Throughout these dialogues Chopsticks never talked about himself. Although he had a distinct carefree personality, he was subordinate to Nancy. She dictated the terms of their play and the topics for discussion. In a very real sense, she was the dragon's creator and master. He was the puppet and she was the puppeteer. She never lost her autonomy, and Chopsticks, unlike Belinda's pathologically aggressive dragon, never took control. Nonetheless, Nancy kept him endowed with enough reality to justify her continuing imaginal dialogues.

Imaginal dialogues are common in both children and adults. Many people engage in private, unspoken thoughts with themselves and others. Some may even speak aloud to themselves in a mirror, to a photograph, or to a pet dog. When young children engage in such dialogues with their imaginary companions, however, they avert their eyes from other people present and orient toward an empty area now occupied by their invisible friend. Their nonverbal actions and gestures describe in clear terms the presence of the companion. If the child speaks, the loudness of speech is reduced to low voices or whispers. In Nancy's case, she rolled over on the pillows and faced the empty wall when she started whispering to Chopsticks. Then she nuzzled the pillows and hugged them as if she was playing with a big dog.

The voice of Chopsticks as heard by Nancy was probably very similar to the imaginal internal dialogues we all hear ourselves engage in from time to time. Such "voices" are experienced in internal psychological space. But when Nancy repeated out loud what Chopsticks said to her, the voice became part of the external objective world, and she could verify its existence with her own ears. The fact that Nancy's conversations with the dragon had become progressively more unspoken over the years suggested that Chopsticks was gradually moving from the externalized world of the hallucination to the internalized world of imagination where it was born and, eventually, would die.

Inside the isolation room, Chopsticks was, literally and figuratively, only a whisper in the dark. I wondered what remained of his blue dragon body.

"Well, Nancy, can you tell me what Chopsticks looks like now?" I said in my best Mr. Wizard voice.

She giggled.

Silence.

"Psychonaut Nancy! Report! What do you see?"

Loud, hysterical laughter.

"What's so funny?" I finally asked, holding back a few contagious giggles of my own.

"I can't . . . [laughter] . . . see. It's dark . . . [laughter]," said Nancy as she gasped for breath.

The brilliant Mr. Wizard had forgotten that the lights were out in her room. While darkness brought out the longest conversation with Chopsticks thus far, the auditory sensations were enhanced at the expense of the visual. Chopsticks was primarily a visual image during the day and an auditory image at night. Nancy was accustomed to seeing the visual image of the dragon in environments that were visually perceptible to her. She never endowed Chopsticks with magical visual properties such as the ability to glow in the dark. He was just as invisible to her in the dark as he was to me in the light.

While the slip with the lights was embarrassing, it caused me to stumble across a unique property of Nancy's imaginary companion. Unlike the visual images or hallucinations produced *in darkness*, the visual image of her dragon was forged *in light* and snuffed out by darkness. Apparently, imaginary companions need perceptible visual space in order to be seen, although they can still be heard. This is particularly true with very young children, who often use visual props to represent the imaginary companion. Such props may include a doll, a toy, or even a finger. In the dark, Nancy may have been using the pillows as tactile props when she nuzzled them and whispered to them.

After informing Nancy that I was entering the room in order to change the video camera and lights, I opened the door and gradually turned the room light on with the dimmer switch. Nancy was sitting in the corner on the bean bag chair. She was clutching one of the pillows in her arms. As I busied myself with the camera, I heard Nancy grab the bowl of nuts and start eating.

"Want some?" she asked.

I turned around, ready to grab a handful. Nancy did not look at me. She was staring at the floor.

"Thank you," said Chopsticks, his voice slightly altered by the beer nuts in Nancy's mouth.

I sat down in the opposite corner of the room and watched. Nancy continued to ignore me while she chewed. When children are engaged in dialogue or play with their imaginary companion, they usually do not consider other children or adults present as part of the audience. They maintain a distance and rarely respond to the others. This behavior was typical of three- and four-year-olds, but I did not expect it from a teenager. I decided to test it and waited patiently for the next remark.

"More?" asked Nancy, after finally swallowing the last pieces in her mouth.

"No thank you," I answered.

"More," said Chopsticks, ignoring me. Nancy popped several more nuts into her mouth.

"Thanks," said either Chopsticks or Nancy. It was hard to tell because of all the chewing.

"Nancy. Would you like something to drink?" I asked. There was no response. Nancy was still averting her eyes, looking about the floor of the room. I started to feel uncomfortable, like an intruder who was crashing someone's private party. As I tiptoed out of the room, I thought I heard Nancy whisper, "Good." It couldn't have been Chopsticks. After all, he said he liked me.

The session ended shortly after that brief interlude. But not before Nancy gave me a detailed description of the dragon, now collapsed like an accordion to a mere two feet. Other than his size, he never changed: blue body, green eyes, and pointed ears. When I asked Nancy how vivid and solid he was, her answer sounded more like a psychonaut than the child I had just seen sharing nuts with a make-believe dragon.

"He's not like the pillows or desk. Kinda like those afterimages from the flashbulb," she said.

Bingo! I said to myself. *You've just graduated, Nancy.* Inside the dark isolation room, Nancy's imagination had produced an image of Chopsticks so strong that she continued to hear, then see it in the light. It not only resembled an afterimage of a flashbulb in terms of vividness and concreteness, but it blocked out perception of other things as it continued to "flash" in her mind's eye.

We had a few more sessions in the weeks that followed. In a particularly relaxed session, conducted in dim light, I recorded an unexpected and revealing exchange.

"Am I pretty?" asked Nancy.

"Beau-tee-full," answered Chopsticks.

"Boys say I'm fat."

"Beau-tee-full," repeated Chopsticks. "Beautiful hair, beautiful eyes."

"I'm fat," protested Nancy.

"Beautiful, inside and out," said the dragon, repeating something I had heard Nancy's mother say.

"O Choppy. If you were a boy, I'd fuck you!"

"You're very fuckable," replied the dragon.

"Very fuckable," repeated Nancy wistfully.

One day I took Nancy to another lab for an EEG. It was normal. Then, while Nancy was engaged in one of her imaginal dialogues with Chopsticks, who she said was physically present at the time, we used a photic stimulator to keep flashing a bright light in front of her eyes. Flashing such lights produces a visual evoked response, a characteristic pattern of electrical waves from the part of the brain concerned with vision. Nancy's response as seen on the EEG tracings showed a slight reduction. I called it normal at the time.

Originally, I thought that these EEG studies had been a monumental waste. Many years later, a colleague told me about Ruth, a psychiatric patient who was tested in a similar way while she was hallucinating. When Ruth said she was seeing a hallucination of her daughter, her visual-evoked responses to a flashing light were reduced. In other words, her brain was reacting as if something (the hallucinatory image) was partially blocking her vision of the flashing light. I dug out Nancy's original records and compared them with Ruth's. The diminished evoked responses obtained when Nancy was seeing Chopsticks and when Ruth was hallucinating her daughter were similar, although Ruth showed the more dramatic effect. Both Nancy's and Ruth's brains were reacting to their hallucinatory images as if they were real perceptions.

Neurophysiological researchers have now confirmed that there is a similarity between processes underlying visual perception and those occurring while vivid visual imagery takes place. When a visual image arises in the brain, impulses activate retinal elements, excite muscles in the eye, and suppress some of the brain's own bioelectric activity, including evoked responses. Since perceptions of real objects involve the same mechanisms, the strength of these stimulations, coupled with feedback mechanisms between the eye and brain, can transform a visual image of the imagination into a visual image of perception. In other words, an imaginary dragon like Chopsticks can become vivid enough to fool the brain into thinking it has seen something real.

Why children are so much better at this process than adults has always been a mystery. The session in the EEG lab with Nancy did not answer the question. In a way, it didn't matter. I was not about to slay Nancy's dragon with neurophysiological explanations even if I could. Time would do that. And, at fourteen, Nancy was showing signs it was about to happen.

At the end of the EEG session, which was our last, Nancy left. She put her knapsack over one shoulder, turned, and cheerfully hummed her way down the corridor. I could almost imagine Chopsticks lumbering after her, humming along in his Bugs Bunny voice. Nancy waved from the end of the hall. I yelled thanks and waved back to Nancy and her companion, whom she finally let me see.

I heard that Nancy had a wonderful sweet sixteen birthday party. Chopsticks was not there. Like Peter Pan, who flew off to Never-Never Land when Wendy came of age, Chopsticks disappeared suddenly. He was never seen or heard from again.

10

CHANNELING

The path into the forest ended abruptly. I stood perfectly still and listened. Shafts of sunlight cut through the trees, dappling the ground with light and shadow. Every direction looked the same—scary and wrong. The woman back at the day care center had told me to listen for the sound of a flute and follow it. I could hear my own panting respiration from the long hike but nothing else. The ground sloped down to the left and I decided to follow it, downhill being the path of least effort.

It was slow going. Here, inside a forgotten corner of a California forest that few people saw, the roots of the trees grew unabashedly on top of the dirt, a network of booby traps for the unsuspecting. This was a good place to hide a secret. I was taking my time stepping over the roots when I heard the flute. The sound was from the northwest and I headed toward it. I found another path and followed it. The flute was getting louder.

The path turned uphill. I plodded on, wishing Steve had been at the center back in town where he told me I could find him on most days. Steve did volunteer work supervising the playground at a children's day care center. He was good with the children and seemed to enjoy the swings and seesaws almost as much as they did. Everyone liked Steve, and the director of the center would have gladly paid him a small salary if only they had the funds. Not that Steve ever asked for money. He had all he needed. Steve made a comfortable living growing marijuana. That was why I wanted to meet him. I was studying the various pests on marijuana plants and hoped that Steve would give me access to his secret garden.

I was also hoping that I wouldn't get shot before I could identify myself. The path disappeared in some rocks, and I began scrambling over them. As I stood on a large boulder I saw Steve's A-frame in a small clearing up ahead. He was still playing his flute, although I couldn't see him. I assumed the safest position I knew when approaching marijuana growers on their own turf: I stripped naked and stood in the open.

"Yo, Steve!" I yelled. "It's Ron Siegel."

The flute stopped and Steve peered through an open window. "Come on up," he said with a wave of the flute. I dressed and went to the door, where Steve greeted me. He wasn't wearing much himself: a pair of torn swimming trunks and light-weight Nike hiking shoes. His hair was long and stringy. When he smiled, I could see a row of crooked teeth in need of considerable attention. He was skinny and, despite the outdoor life, pale. The feature I liked best was that he was unarmed.

We talked over a cup of the worst coffee I ever saw. Steve poured coffee grinds into a stained cup that had flecks of dried soup on the rim, then added hot water from his propane stove. I let it sit untouched on the table. I had had cowboy coffee prepared from grinds before, but brewed in a kettle and served in clean cups. Steve's coffee looked as awful as everything else inside his house.

The place was a mess. Clothes, tools, and dirty dishes were strewn on the floor. Shelves were cluttered with food, books, and gardening equipment. The cabin, which Steve had built himself, had only one room, but this was no excuse for the chaotic condition. It was also filthy. A layer of dust covered everything. Cobwebs dangled between the wooden beams overhead. Stained Mexican blankets covered the redwood furniture. The kitchen alcove was coated with grease. The windows had pretty yellow gingham curtains with little embroidered flowers. But the glass was so dirty that the sun cast a gray haze throughout the cabin. Steve lit a cigarette. The smoke was barely visible.

Steve told me that his wife, Helen, had died suddenly a few years earlier. He pointed to the bed where she "passed over to the other side." She was pregnant at the time, far enough along that they knew it was going to be a girl. They had already picked a name—Star. Steve's eyes brightened and he smiled as he told me that Star had been conceived when the sun was in Aquarius, a good sign. I felt sorry for Steve and hoped that his neglect of the cabin did not extend to his marijuana garden.

"Where's the pot?" I asked, hoping to change the topic, which was depressing me more than it seemed to affect Steve.

He led me to a deck in the back of his house. The deck was built several feet off the ground. It provided a spectacular view of a large marijuana field, carefully camouflaged between rows of small trees. They were spread out over at least a quarter of a mile. The marijuana plants were carefully manicured and I could tell, even from this distance, that Steve was growing high quality sinsemilla, a variety that requires considerable attention and work. How much help did he have?

None, he told me. Didn't it get lonely up here? "She's still with me," he said with bright eyes and a broad smile. I assumed he was referring to his memories of Helen. The poor man was drowning in bereavement, I thought. But as Steve rushed into a long discourse on his communication with the spirit of his daughter, Star, I began to suspect that he might be smoking too much of his own weed. Then I realized he was describing a very unusual hallucination, even for a chronic marijuana smoker.

He explained that Star was now three years old. He didn't say she *would have been* three if she had lived; he said Star *was* three. She was born "on the other side," in a fourth dimension. Since she could travel at will through time and space, she visited him often. Steve not only heard Star, and spoke to her, he saw her just as clear as day. She had sandy brown hair just like her mother.

This sounded like a typical hallucination suffered by people who mourn a loved one. Many of these experiences occur in the elderly who suffer the loss of a longtime spouse. Bereavement hallucinations often take the form of imaginary companions.

One eighty-four-year-old widow said her dead husband had come back to live with her within a few days of his death. She didn't want to upset him with questions so the woman continued to carry on her usual life with him. Suddenly, he disappeared. The widow suspected that he might have found another woman. Similar hallucinations occur when a child mourns a parent or when parents mourn their children. I had read one case of a woman whose dead father sat on her shoulder and talked to her at great length. The woman recognized that he was dead, and, like many older adults who have imaginary companions, spoke to him internally rather than audibly.

Steve had both internal and audible dialogues with Star. Of course, Steve's explanation was that his daughter was not dead. She merely had passed on to another level of being, moving from the physical to the astral plane. Bereaved individuals, who are unaware of their susceptibility to hallucinations yet hold strong beliefs in the paranormal, might reach such a spiritual conclusion when visited by the imaginary companion. Some parapsychologists deny that these experiences are hallucinations, saying that imaginary companions are real spirits that transcend time and space. A quick glance at the books in the cabin told me that Steve was well-read in this area. I recognized several titles, including *The Secret Life of Plants*, Linda Goodman's *Sun Signs*, and *Phone Calls from the Dead*. Of course, that really didn't prove anything because I had the same books on my shelf.

Star's initial appearance was sudden and confusing to Steve. He realized that she came back not only to share the spiritual knowledge acquired in the fourth dimension, but to experience the childhood that she missed. Therefore he started working at the day care center so Star could have a place to play. Steve was honest and rational enough to admit that playing with her was something he needed as well. No wonder the preschool children on the playground adored Steve. He and his imaginary playmate were just like all the other kids. Steve was comfortable, too. No one would suspect he was playing with the ghost of his daughter any more than they would know he was growing dope.

It was apparent that Steve's imaginary daughter brought him much solace and comfort. I would no sooner try to rid him of his bereavement hallucinations than I would bust him for growing marijuana. In fact, my interest in his marijuana plants was now overshadowed by my desire to keep Steve's hallucinations alive for study.

The communication between Steve and Star took the form of classic channeling. Channeling refers to the alleged process of receiving information from some level of reality other than the ordinary physical one. Like mediums of a bygone age, New Age channelers claim to speak for spirits of the dead whom they call entities or channels. The channelers speak in a psychobabble laced with terms from quantum physics, neurophysiology, religion, and philosophy. Their messages are full of neologisms like "biocosmic resonators," "ascended masters," "parapsychiatry," and "radionics."

J. Z. Knight, a housewife in Yelm, Washington, claims to channel "Ramtha," a man who lived thirty-five thousand years ago. Rosemary Brown, a housewife in London, England, claims to channel Liszt, Beethoven, and Debussy. Others have opened channels with the spirits of the rich (William Randolph Hearst), the famous (John F. Kennedy), the brilliant (Albert Einstein), the artistic (Rembrandt), the holy (Jesus Christ), and the obscure (Tom MacPherson, a sixteenth-century pickpocket). Channelers have also communicated with an assortment of nonhuman entities including dolphins, angels, cherubs, elves, fairies, and daffodils.

Perhaps the best insight into what channeling is all about was provided by the ventriloquist Edgar Bergen, who worked with a wooden dummy named Charlie McCarthy. One day, a visitor came into Bergen's room and found him talking—not rehearsing—with Charlie. Bergen was asking Charlie a number of philosophical questions about the nature of life, virtue, and love. Charlie was responding with brilliant Socratic answers. When Bergen noticed that he had a visitor, he turned red and said that he was talking with Charlie, the wisest person he knew. The visitor pointed out that it was Bergen's own mind and voice coming through the wooden dummy. Bergen replied, "Well, I guess ultimately it is, but I ask Charlie these questions and he answers, and I haven't the faintest idea of what he's going to say and I'm astounded by his brilliance—so much more than I know." Bergen had simply opened a channel into an area of his own mind.

Steve prepared to demonstrate his channeling with Star. He

sat on his knees in the middle of the deck. Then he rolled a splinter-thin joint of marijuana and lit up. His upper chest swelled with the first inhalation, and I watched the skin tighten around his bony ribs. After several seconds he exhaled, put the joint down, and closed his eyes. I retrieved the tape recorder from my day pack and switched it on, despite Steve's warning that it would be a waste of tape. While he would speak to Star out loud for my benefit, she would only talk to him internally. And, although she had great knowledge that was light years ahead of our own, she still had a child's vocabulary and could only answer questions with a yes or no. I thought it was very strange that Steve had chosen to keep something as important as a channel to the fourth dimension locked inside the body of an imaginary three-year-old with a retarded vocabulary.

"Hi, baby," said Steve. His eyes remained closed.

"Star?" I asked.

Steve bowed. I had a feeling of déjà vu about this whole scene. Suddenly, I remembered! Popeye! As a child I had read all the Popeye comic books I could get my sticky little fingers on. One of the most lovable characters in the books was Eugene the Jeep, a magical animal supposedly from Africa. He looked like a small puppy with a big red nose. The Jeep was described as a fourth-dimensional animal with a fourth-dimensional brain, capable of appearing out of thin air whenever Popeye needed his special talents. Those talents included the ability to foretell future events. Eugene had a vocabulary limited to "jeep jeep" sounds, but he could answer questions with body language. If he didn't move, the answer to the question was no. If the answer was yes, the Jeep would bow down, like Steve just did.

"The universe," began Steve, "is full of holes. Tiny worm-holes from a higher dimension. That's how Star gets here. It's as easy as crawling through the tunnel at the playground." He reached for the joint and sucked on it again.

"Do you see her now?" I asked.

He had his eyes open but closed them when I asked the question. He nodded a yes, opened his eyes, and continued. "She is here as a sign of eternal life and love. So we should know there are higher levels that go on. Consciousness goes on, merges with everything and becomes part of everything, part of the universal vibration. I prepare myself by vibrating at the same frequency.

Smoke the righteous herb; eat organic fruits and vegetables. Her consciousness and mine become one."

Steve's discourse sounded a little like the comic-book Professor Brainstine, who tried to explain to Popeye what a Jeep was. The professor said that some Jeep cells slipped through the dimensional barrier into our world. Since the electrical vibrations of these cells were the same as the cells of the African "Hooey Hound," they fused and grew into the Jeep. Before Steve got too carried away with his own New Age hooey, I tried to bring the conversation back to Star.

"Can Star come out and play?" I asked. I really didn't mean to be cute, but I was totally unprepared for an encounter with a Star child and didn't know how else to ask Steve to show me his imaginary playmate.

Steve opened his eyes and started to bend over. At first I thought he was signaling yes. But he was only reaching for the joint on the deck. He sucked away until there was only a tiny roach left, then ate it.

I tried another tack. Since Steve considered Star a little girl, I decided to talk to "her" the same way. "Star, is your mother with you?" I asked.

Steve bowed slowly.

"Are you in Heaven?"

No response.

"She's part of the mind of God," said Steve. "God does not play dice with the universe." Steve was getting loaded.

"Star, do you like visiting with your daddy?" I asked.

Steve nodded and smiled. His eyes were still closed.

"Do you like to play with him?"

Another nod.

"What do you like to do the most?"

"She likes the seesaw," said Steve. *Now we're getting someplace*, I thought.

"Steve, do you think we could go back to the center and let Star play?" I asked.

"She's tired now," he said. I didn't know entities got physically tired in the fourth dimension. However, I knew that three-dimensional daddies stoned on marijuana aren't too motivated.

"Star, do you need to sleep?" I asked.

No response. A good ten minutes elapsed without a word

or movement from Steve. *Maybe she crawled back into a wormhole,* I thought.

"Are you hungry?" I asked. Even the Jeep had to eat, although he lived on a diet of orchids.

No response. I had a chocolate bar in my pack, and I thought about offering it to Steve. There's nothing better for the munchies. But I decided not to break his trance with Star.

"Star, will marijuana be legalized?" I asked. After all, she should be just as capable of foretelling the future as Eugene the Jeep.

Steve bowed all the way down so that his forehead touched the deck. The Jeep's tail stood straight in the air. When Steve returned to an upright position, I hit him again. "Star, will the plants be ready for harvesting soon?" Both Steve and I knew they were not ready, but did Star?

"She says no," replied Steve. "Not until November."

"Star, what is your favorite color?" I asked, forgetting for a moment that she could only answer yes or no.

Steve did not forget and gave no response. Was he too stoned or too absorbed with Star to hear me? I could imagine the Jeep answering by pointing to the marijuana field. Steve's breathing became slow and deep, a sign of the drug's progressing effect. If his intoxication was anything like what my psychonauts experienced, he should be prone to hilarity and laughter at anything that was the least bit funny.

"Star, do you ever have to go wee-wee or doo-doo on the other side?" It almost cracked me up as soon as I said it—and I wasn't the one smoking. But Steve remained ramrod straight. He opened his eyes, tilted his head in my direction, and stared. His eyes were totally white! He had rolled his eyes up into his lids so only the whites were showing. The effort caused the muscles around his eyes to flutter slightly. It was a cheap parlor trick my uncle used to do for me at holiday dinners when I was a little boy. It fascinated me but ruined the meal for everyone else. Now Steve was trying to intimidate me with the same crazy look.

Steve eventually closed his eyes again and continued his channeling: "Star says that the earth plane is connected to the astral plane. The body is the barrier. Death frees the soul to join the God energy flow. . . . God gave the herb to man to know these things . . . to know past lives . . . and future lives . . ." *All this he learns from yes and no questions?* I thought.

Then Steve announced it was time to eat. He went inside and came back with several tomatoes and a Buck knife. I didn't want any and Steve didn't offer any. As he ate, he gave me a vivid description of the inner workings of his digestive system. He had fasted recently and prided himself on how smoothly and cleanly everything now went through his body.

"I eat only once a day," he said as he put a tomato wedge in his mouth. "I can feel the food flowing through me." He used the knife blade to trace a path from his throat, down the middle of his chest. "It comes out as a single pebble, regular as the sun," he continued with a proud smile.

Speaking of the sun reminded me that it was getting dark and time to head back. I thanked him and said goodbye. I had already decided not to study a marijuana garden haunted by a child from the fourth dimension.

I lost the path again on my way back. Then I heard Steve's flute. I knew enough to walk away from it.

11

ALONE

Loneliness weighed on me no more than it does on a healthy child. Like a child, I peopled nature with my friends.

—HANNES LINDEMANN,
Alone at Sea

In a solo voyage across the Atlantic in 1955, Hannes Lindemann, a respected physician and mariner, found his boat caught in a constant and terrible roll. He misinterpreted the gurgling of the water as voices of men and women. "They shouted and whispered, laughed and giggled, tittered, coughed, and mumbled," he wrote. "Their voices became so clear that I finally joined in the discussions." When Steven Callahan was adrift in the Atlantic in an inflatable raft, and faced with an unappetizing meal of gelatinous nuggets and fluids from the inside of a fish, an invisible Jewish mother coaxed him to "Eat, eat. Go ahead, my sick darling, you must eat your chicken soup to get well."

Imaginal dialogues of these sorts can provide welcome entertainment, but the lonely eyes of sailors hunger for visual company as well. Lindemann strained so hard to see someone, anyone, that he finally could make out a blurred shape—a phantom—speaking to him from across the water. Walter Gibson, adrift for days in a lifeboat, wanted company so badly that when he saw a hallucinatory figure on an imaginary beach, he encouraged the figure to swim toward him. Gibson's figure vanished, but other imaginary companions have managed to make it aboard, especially when the boat is caught in difficult circumstances.

Captain Joshua Slocum, sailing alone in the south Atlantic at the turn of the century, was helped through a storm by an imaginary companion. When the companion first appeared on the deck, Slocum took him to be a pirate because of his strange dress. The man assured Slocum that he was not a pirate but the pilot of Columbus's *Pinta*. The companion chanted songs to Slocum and gave him advice on sailing through the heavy seas. When the storm ended, the companion told the captain that he would return whenever he was needed, then disappeared as mysteriously as he had come. Slocum assumed he returned to the phantom *Pinta*. The companion's actual quarters were more likely to be found in the pages of the Columbus biography that Slocum kept on board for pleasure reading.

The imaginary companion who visited Captain Jack Jones arose from the pages of Jack's own childhood memories. The companion took Jack back into a child's world of make-believe pirates and stolen treasure, then left him there.

Jack stopped to pick up a nickel half-buried on the beach. He brushed the sand off with his fingers and put it in his pocket. Jack had always had a remarkable eye for details, whether it meant scanning the ocean waters for telltale signs of fish below or combing his charter ocean yacht, *Promise*, for needed repairs. He was also a stickler for following instructions, especially from cash-paying clients. So when Manny gave him five crisp one-hundred-dollar bills as a deposit on a charter, Jack followed his orders, as crazy as they sounded.

Manny, a huge bear of a man who could whistle audibly through the hole in his nose, operated a Miami tobacco store where Jack bought his cigars—the superior Cuban ones that no one else could get for him. The store also sold paraphernalia for marijuana and cocaine users. While Jack did not approve of these items, he liked Manny for his sense of humor. In a glass frame in the shop was a hundred-dollar bill—Manny always joked that it was the first hundred through which he had snorted coke. One of the devices he sold was a no-spill cocaine spoon shaped like a shovel. Ask Manny how much it held and he'd answer "Never enough! Never enough!" punctuating each phrase with a pretend toot and whistle from the shovel. Although he never actually saw Manny use coke, Jack thought the moves were too well-practiced to be just pretend. He also didn't think Manny was fooling when he passed him the money and told him to go to the Fontainebleau and walk north along the beach. "Juan will meet you," Manny had said.

The deposit was nonrefundable, and all Jack had to do was meet with the prospective client, Juan, and listen to the deal. If he didn't like it, he could walk away five hundred bucks richer. So Jack was taking a well-paid stroll along Miami Beach. He would have preferred to be out on the water on such a beautiful, calm day. The salt water in the air pulled him closer to the ocean, and he took off his sandals to walk along the tide mark where the foaming surf disappeared into the wet sand. He played a little game, skipping away from the rushing waves and jumping over the dead jelly fish. He passed dozens of hotels this way until a tall, dark and emaciated man, wearing a khaki fishing vest, approached him. Juan told Jack to follow him into a nearby hotel.

Manny greeted him inside the room with a warm hug. He introduced George, a fat, balding man with frizzy hair on the sides that made him look like a clown. George was wearing a T-shirt emblazoned with an American flag, which hugged the rolls of his belly. Jack noticed a fine detail—the flag had tiny marijuana leaves instead of stars.

Juan disappeared into the bedroom and a shorter dark-haired man wearing an identical khaki vest came out and introduced himself as Juan. Jack looked puzzled but Manny laughed it off by saying "They all call themselves Juan. Ain't got no imagination."

The shorter Juan carried a pencil-type beeper in one of the outer pockets of his vest. Jack would later learn that the vests had been modified by Isabel, a plump, almost bearded Spanish woman who provided special tailoring services to drug couriers in Miami. The hidden pockets and Velcro seams allowed Juan to carry large amounts of drugs or cash without a bump or sag on the outside. For the moment, Jack took the fishing vest and beeper to mean that Juan was the businessman who wanted to charter the *Promise* for a private fishing party.

To Jack's surprise, Manny did all the talking. A coastal freighter was bringing in a load of marijuana from Colombia. It would stop offshore, just outside the government's jurisdiction, where smaller crafts would shuttle the cargo to the beach. Trucks would be waiting. Juan's people would take care of all the logistics. They never failed. Manny called them the Magic Juans.

"Jack, they need another boat to off-load," said Manny. "I'm doing you a big favor, kid. You always wanted to be a pirate."

Manny was right. Jack had often told Manny how he played pirate with his best friend, John, when they were growing up. They went out in their little rubber dinghy and pretended they were plundering other ships. They even buried a small treasure chest behind John's house. The chest was empty, but they planned to fill it up when they got older. John never got the chance; he was killed in an auto accident just after high school graduation. Jack went on to take over his father's charter boat business after the old man died from alcoholism. His father and Manny were friends, and Jack always looked upon Manny as an uncle. It wouldn't be the first time Jack had ventured into a shady deal with Uncle Manny. Sometimes Manny supplied female escorts to accompany Jack's clients on fishing or cruising trips.

"It'll be fun," said Manny when he saw Jack hesitating. "How fast is the *Promise*?"

"She'll do better than forty knots," said Jack.

"Whew!" said Manny, glancing at Juan. "That's over fifty miles per hour. Jack, you'll be in and out in no time."

Jack knew that Manny was exaggerating the conversion from nautical miles to statute miles in order to impress Juan. It was more like forty-six miles per hour and Manny knew it. Apparently he was going all out to help Jack make some money. Jack didn't want to embarrass his friend. "I don't know," said Jack, hesitating to say much more. He was eyeing fat George, who was eyeing him, hanging on every word. George looked like a narc.

"It'll take one night. Juan will pay your regular charter rate . . . for two weeks!" added Manny, sweetening the pot, so to speak.

"One week," said Juan with a thick accent.

Manny glared at Juan. "Two weeks!" he said loudly.

Juan smiled. "Two weeks," he said.

After Jack agreed, Juan pulled out a plastic bullet, a hand-held device for delivering pre-measured plugs of cocaine directly to the nostrils. Juan took two hits and passed it to Jack. Jack passed it to George without taking any. George took two for himself, then another two for Jack. "The wonderful thing about America," said George, "is she's got room for everyone's tastes."

Manny whistled twice when he took his hits; then everybody left the hotel room and went their separate ways. There was much to do. The freighter was arriving that night.

The transfer started just after dark. Jack had never seen so many guys all called Juan in one place. They each carried portable phones or two-way radios and spoke in whispers. When the whispers became so rushed that they sounded like steam hissing through every radio, Jack knew something had gone wrong. Everybody was upset that the other off-loader did not show. Just to be on the safe side, the Juans changed the rendezvous point and off-loading spot at the last moment. Jack was forced to make a number of roundtrips between the shore and the freighter with bales crammed into every square inch including the master stateroom and head, but the *Promise* came through. Jack estimated he off-loaded several million dollars worth of marijuana. The marijuana bales had a strong smell, and Jack knew he'd have to give the boat a thorough cleaning when it was all over. He made his last run just before daybreak, gliding in without running lights, right past a Coast Guard cutter. Jack felt a rush.

He got his payment the next day, along with a gold Rolex and a big vial of cocaine. The vial was the size of a large test tube. "The Juans were *mucho* happy," explained Manny. Jack slipped on the Rolex and wondered if the treasure chest in John's backyard was still there. *Wish you were here Johnny boy*, he thought.

Jack wanted to celebrate. He certainly didn't feel like cleaning the boat. Instead, he went on a busman's holiday and took the *Promise* out to sea early the next morning. It wasn't often that he got a chance to go out alone; it was too expensive to run the boat without a charter. Jack was always scrambling for money by taking people fishing, diving, cruising, or whatever. Now the whatever had paid for the next two weeks, and Jack was determined to enjoy it.

He put the *Promise* on a setting due east, into an area known as the Bermuda Triangle. The triangle is roughly bounded by a line from Miami to Bermuda to San Juan in Puerto Rico. According to legend, numerous ships and planes have disappeared mysteriously in this area. But according to Jack, the triangle was a place where "the cruisin' is easy and the fish is jumping." Never mind those tabloid articles about mysterious time warps, reverse gravity fields, death rays from Atlantis, and other nonsense. This was Jack's backyard.

Jack had everything he needed for the voyage. The full load of fuel was good for more than two thousand miles. There was plenty of food and drinks in the galley. The water tanks were low, but his electric watermaker could crank out gallons of fresh water every hour. The state-of-the-art electronics, ten-inch radar, autopilot, and other navigational aids were in perfect running order. He went below, shoved a Jimmy Buffett cassette into the tape player, popped open a beer, and toasted the receding skyline of Miami.

By nightfall the *Promise* was passing the Bahamas on the way into the Atlantic. Nassau was only a glow on the southwestern horizon. The sky was clear and full of stars. Jack took out the sextant his father had given him and tried to remember how to use it. In this modern day of plotting courses by navigational satellites, there was little need for such ancient devices. Jack remembered how his father used to read all those pirate stories to him at bedtime. His father was the one who had taught him how to sail and wanted Jack to be able to navigate "by the seat of your pants and a wet finger in the wind." Jack could do that, all right, but becoming a master of celestial navigation like his father was another matter. He put the instrument back in the hardwood case, then lit a cigar, something he did as well as his old man.

Jack remembered the vial of cocaine and found it in his

windbreaker. He started snorting. Tonight the stars seemed brighter than ever. Jack felt like he was right up there with them. Jimmy Buffett was singing for him:

> Life is just a tire swing. . . .
> Who'd figure twenty years later
> I'd be rubbing shoulders with the stars.

Jack stayed up on his swing all night.

He saw the sunrise's first light above a cloudbank. That usually indicated a wind was coming. The morning sun broke from behind the clouds and turned into a scorcher. That could mean thundershowers in the evening. *Maybe it'll get the damn pot smell off the decks*, thought Jack. Later he noticed a number of deep scratch marks in the teak floor of the salon, undoubtedly caused by the Juans. Jack set about repairing the damage. First he found a deep scratch and filled it with cocaine, which he snorted up through a straw. Then he rubbed the scratch with superfine steel wool, refinishing as needed. He moved methodically from scratch to scratch. The cocaine made it fun. It also allowed Jack's eye to zero in on the most microscopic imperfections, turning each scratch into a Grand Canyon of faults. A twenty-minute job took him half the day.

By then he remembered to eat. He fixed himself a cheese sandwich and washed it down with a couple of cans of Gatorade. In the afternoon he fussed with the engines, checking gauges and oil levels, then ran ten miles of open ocean at full throttle just for the hell of it. Toward evening, he noticed that he had been doing cocaine for a day but the vial still looked almost full. The stuff was pure and densely packed. The Juans really appreciated his talents.

There was a faint reddish hue to the sunset that night. When Jack checked the barometer, he knew that rain was coming. But there was still time to enjoy the sunset. Jack ate his dinner—a bagel and a bottle of wine—in the pilot seat rather than in the galley. He had a commanding view of the open sea. In the distance a thunderstorm cracked the black sky with veins of white lightning. Jack saluted the power of nature with a pile of cocaine snorted off the back of his hand.

He studied the bolts of lightning. Their forked paths resem-

bled a road map. Where did they go? Here and there where the
paths seemed to end in the sea, tiny balls of fire rose from the
ocean and climbed the bolts. Jack ran below and grabbed his
low-light Steiner binoculars. The bright optics enabled him to
see the fireballs in detail. He decided that they were UFOs of
some sort, maybe flying saucers. Using the Steiner's built-in
scales and illuminated compass, Jack determined that the UFOs
were eight miles to the northeast. He turned the *Promise* to the
new course and went below to get into his foul-weather gear.

The sea was rough as Jack approached the lightning. In
order to stay on course, he had to run into the breaking head
seas, causing the *Promise* to pitch. Slamming through the waves
in this way put strain on the hull. But Jack knew it would not
be dangerous if he reduced speed and took the heavier waves
slightly on the bow. Still, it was wet and sloppy going. Jack defi-
antly lit a cigar.

As he got closer Jack could see that the UFOs got their
energy from the electrical storm. They went right up inside the
clouds and drew it out. One of the UFOs came down near the
boat, hovered, then disappeared below the surface. Jack felt his
skin crawl with electricity.

I am really privileged to be here now, thought Jack. *I have been
singled out for a special purpose. God has chosen me to see this. He
wants me to know these things. There are powers and realities and all
kinds of weird shit happening out here.*

Jack chased the lightning all night long. There was a little
rain at first, but the wind was still growing. This was more than
a local thunderstorm, where most of the wind dies down before
the rain. Now the waves were building to tremendous dimensions. These were the giant trochoidal waves of deep water. The
Promise looked like a matchstick. The waves started to break at
the crest. Jack found that he was actually running before the
waves, the most dangerous of any position at sea. At any moment
the boat could be lifted by the stern, wind up broadside to the
seas, and be rolled over. Jack worked the steering and throttle
controls, carefully compensating for the yawing and broaching.
He knew that he had to keep the stern to the sea and abruptly
reduced his speed.

*Every decision I make is the right decision. I can't do anything
wrong. I am a god out here on the ocean.*

Now the lightning moved to another part of the sky. Jack turned the boat around. Although the *Promise* was holding steady, forward progress was almost impossible in this new direction. Jack was not about to let a little bad weather bring him down off the swing. He positioned the boat to keep the bow heading into the seas and went below to ride out the gale.

The first thing he did when he got below was to snort more cocaine and swallow a handful of vitamin pills. Then he secured the loose items in the galley and made sure everything was locked in place. Inside the master stateroom he saw a lamp that had tipped over and decided to leave it there because the boat was still rolling. But there were no leaks. *A great boat and a great captain*, thought Jack. The cocaine kicked in and made him feel even more euphoric. Somehow he was still tired. *Too much wine*, he thought. He stretched out on the queen-sized bed for a moment.

The *Promise* gave Jack a wonderfully secure feeling. It was just like when he was a little kid and his mom would tuck him into bed at night. Nothing could hurt him. Or when he and John set out on their rubber dinghy to conquer the seven seas. They were invincible.

"Jack! . . . Jack! . . . Jack!" The voice was coming from the deck. There are many sounds inside the hull of a small boat in a storm. The howling wind, the thumps of the waves, the creaks of the cabin, and the shifting contents of lockers all combine to create a cacophonous symphony that only a god of the sea could love. But Jack had never heard the sea talk before. He rushed to the deck.

As soon as he got on top, he realized he never should have left the helm. *God, these seas come up fast*, he thought. The wind was thirty knots now, up from twenty just a few minutes ago. Some of the gusts were at least thirty-five. Waves were breaking everywhere. Black water was pouring over the deck. Jack knew all the tricks for handling such head seas. He eased the throttles as the bow started to lift to a wave. This stopped the bow from flying off the top of the wave. Then he opened the throttles again to get the bow to lift to the next wave. He kept repeating the delicate maneuver, steering the *Promise* up and down the giant mountains. It was a great ride!

"Jack! . . . Jack! . . . Jack!" This time Jack located the sound.

It was coming from the side of the boat. Each time the waves slapped against the boat they cried out his name. *Are they praising me?* he asked himself. He looked out over the waves. The wind was carrying other voices, all chanting his name.

Jack strained to see who was yelling his name. The storm limited visibility, but he thought he saw a figure in the water. Reflexively, he grabbed the Zodiac liferaft and tossed it overboard. In four seconds the plastic suitcase popped open in the water. Eight seconds later the liferaft was almost fully inflated. In another eight seconds the self-erecting canopy had been deployed. Someone was moving into the raft.

"Hey!" called Jack. It looked like a man was standing in the raft, holding his finger in the wind. It couldn't be his father, could it? The raft was still next to the *Promise*. Jack grabbed the sextant and tossed it into the liferaft.

"Thanks, kid," came back his father's voice. The voice trailed into laughter as the Zodiac disappeared from sight. Jack had just thrown his liferaft and sextant to a hallucination.

While Jack suspected that the figure might have been a hallucination, he wasn't worried about it even if it was a real person. The Zodiac had a complete survival kit, insulating double floor, stabilizing water-ballast chambers, and everything else necessary to ride out this storm. Any occupant could survive. But Jack was becoming concerned about his own safety. A giant rogue wave picked up the *Promise* and slammed it down, hard. Numbing cold water found its way into Jack's Gore-Tex suit. A minute ago he was sweating; now he was freezing. The wind was blowing at fifty knots. He threw the storm drogue over the stern. This bucket-like device was designed to drag behind the boat and help dissipate the sea's energy, keeping the boat steady and steerable. Jack steered in and out of the waves, avoiding as much punishment as possible.

It's a good thing it was dark because Jack couldn't see how high the waves really were. At sunrise he saw that they were monsters. They were so steep, his speed down them was faster than he wanted. This caused the bow to bury in the base of the wave ahead, and the *Promise* started to take water over the bow right up to the pilot house. "Damn!" yelled Jack. His cigar had just gone out with spray from the last wave. He considered putting up the storm flaps on the open sides of the pilot house, but that would reduce visibility even more.

Jack had to fight to keep the *Promise* from getting a little sideways and rolling over as he raced down the waves. When it got lighter, he looked around and saw that the storm drogue had been tossed back on board. It was hung up on one of the aft cleats. *No wonder I'm going so fast*, thought Jack. He quickly freed the drogue and tossed it back in the water. Immediately, the boat started to brake and Jack was back in control.

The third day passed quickly. Jack made several trips below to check on the engines, grab some food, and visit the head. He noticed that the contents of the cocaine vial were finally starting to disappear. On his last trip below, Jack dropped a small amount of cocaine on the galley floor. As he was snorting it up off the floor, the boat rolled violently, sending him headfirst into the stove. A deep cut opened on his forehead and started to bleed. He put some styptic powder on it, then wrapped a bandana around his head like a sweatband. He was still squinting from the pain when he climbed back into the pilot house. It was getting dark again.

"Jack fell down and broke his crown," said the voice. It sounded like a child teasing him. Jack started to look around for the speaker, but a new set of monster waves was demanding his total concentration.

"Blackjack!" said the voice.

Only John called him that! But John was dead!

"John? Is that you?" Jack was yelling into the wind. He was still looking straight ahead as he tried to keep the bow out of the water. There was no answer. Several minutes later there was a lull in the weather, and Jack felt it was safe to look around. He climbed down to the deck. A light spray filled the night air. John stood in the middle of the spray. He was wearing his yellow slicker, black galoshes, and boyish smile.

"Johnny! You're dead! You're dead!" cried Jack.

"A pledge is a promise. Remember?" said John.

Jack remembered. They were maybe ten or eleven at the time. John had just swiped a pocketknife from the local five and dime while Jack stood guard. When they got back to the safety of John's backyard, they decided to become blood brothers. John made a cut in his thumb, then Jack did the same. They placed their thumbs together and, as the drops of blood mixed, pledged to be best friends forever. A pledge is a promise, they told each other.

"John!" exclaimed Jack. He didn't know what else to say.

"Cut the . . ." said John. The roar of the waves drowned out the rest of his words. But Jack *knew* that John was telling him to cut the drogue loose. Otherwise he'd never make any headway out of the storm. He pulled out his knife but, at the last moment, decided to haul in the drogue instead.

Jack returned to the pilot house and checked out his position on the electronic chart. He saw at a glance where he was. Almost in the middle of the Bermuda Triangle. He decided to go south and quickly plotted a new course for the *Promise*. He was now moving into some rough seas, but the radar helped him pick out patches of breaking waves ahead in time to avoid them. The coke helped him count them. In rough seas there should be about 6 waves every minute, 360 every hour. Jack counted two hours and came up with 418, only 209 every hour. This made him feel like things were getting better.

"Don't sleep, don't sleep," chanted John. The voice startled Jack out of a lapse in attention, just in time to avoid a forty-foot rogue wave. He went below, downed some vitamins, and took some hot coffee back to the pilot house. Jack usually didn't drink coffee but tonight he felt he needed it. Combined with the cocaine, it was putting his brain into overdrive.

But he still needed something else to keep his mind occupied in order to avoid another lapse. He had to maintain vigilance and sharp reflexes. "Let's sing," said Jack to John.

Jack started with "Row, Row, Row Your Boat." The waves joined in with John's refrain. Then Jack switched to a medley of advertising jingles, including "Ajax, the foaming cleanser," which made the boiling seas seem like a big joke. He and John started laughing.

Throughout the night John remained a loyal companion. He stood behind Jack, singing his silly songs and reminding him to check a gauge or ease back on the throttles. It was like having another crewman on board. Jack really didn't need any advice on handling the *Promise*, but he did need the company, even if it was only a ghost.

Jack passed the night by flipping through the pages of his

own childhood memories with John. When they played pirate, Jack was always in command while John was first mate. Sometimes they would invent a make-believe crew to help with some of the bigger battles. Jack ruled his rubber dinghy with an iron fist. If someone tried to mutiny, Blackjack would make them walk the plank. He remembered the time when John lost a paddle and he forced him to jump and swim back to shore. Jack felt so bad about doing this that he jumped in the water and, towing the dinghy with a rope, swam alongside John all the way back.

Now they were together in the proverbial soup again, only the *Promise* was no rubber dinghy. And Jack was no longer a little boy. The near hurricane conditions on the ocean, together with the cocaine storm in his brain, made Jack feel more like a man than ever before. Already the winds were down and there was less spray coming over the bow. The *Promise* was performing like a ship worthy of a god. He and John were going to make it again.

"We're gonna make it," said John.

"We're gonna make it," echoed Jack.

Jack started to think about how it was possible that he could communicate with John. He knew John was dead. But he believed John's spirit was with him. His thoughts turned to the earlier encounters with the freak lightning and the UFOs. God had singled him out to see all this. Now, alone in the ocean, where the waves and hum of the engines were in harmony, where the seas sang his praise, perhaps he had entered a mystical place. This mystical place was the reason why he could communicate with the dead! Jack suddenly realized this was the only possible explanation. He shivered in the grip of a peak experience. It felt wonderful. If he could only keep his cigar lit, it would be perfect.

Jack was still glowing when the sun came up on the fourth day. The morning gray sky told him there was going to be good weather ahead. It was calm enough for the *Promise* to handle herself on autopilot again.

"Better eat something," said John.

"Better eat," echoed Jack as he climbed below.

The first thing Jack did was to get out of his Gore-Tex suit and take a shower. He decided not to shave but slapped on some after-shave lotion anyway. Then he did something he had always wanted to try. He poured a huge line of cocaine on the edge of a table, put his nose on one end and moved along the line, snorting it up just the way Al Pacino did in *Scarface*. The vial was still half full. Jack started to feel sexually aroused as he got dressed. He rummaged through the stateroom and found a copy of *Penthouse*. After masturbating he put on a clean pair of shorts and T-shirt and went to the galley.

Jack drank half a carton of slightly bitter orange juice as he fixed an enormous meal of bacon, cheese, eggs, muffins, and a can of fruit cocktail. He ate the fruit right out of the can, but picked away at the rest of the food.

"Gotta keep strong," said John from somewhere on the deck.

"I'm full," said Jack.

"Should drink more," John coaxed.

"I'm full," snapped Jack. He was irritated with John, who was only trying to help like any decent imaginary companion would. But there was another invisible force overruling Jack's appetite—Mama Coca, the mythical goddess of cocaine who seduces all users and bestows upon them a hunger only for herself. Jack snorted another two lines and went topside.

The day was shaping up to be sunny and clear. A few feathery cirrus clouds were visible. Jack reduced his cruising speed in order to save fuel. Fighting the storm had used up more than he thought. In the afternoon he stopped the *Promise* to try his luck at fishing. Much to the chagrin of his clients, Jack never cared about catching anything. It was the meditation of fishing that turned him on. He used to tell his friends that it was the only time he really relaxed. But fishing with Mama Coca meant that, while your body was sitting still in a fighting chair, your brain was racing with thoughts and images.

Jack passed several hours in reviewing images from the past. He thought about his family and friends. Then he remembered he had never told his girlfriend that he was going away for a few days. Now he regretted not inviting her along. But maybe if he did, he might not have wandered into the lightning, seen the UFOs, and spoken to John. While Jack was certain that these were not hallucinations, and his girlfriend would have seen and heard the same things if she had been aboard, he *knew* that he had been singled out to see these visions for a special purpose. He was destined to become a very powerful person.

In the distance a boat crossed the ocean and smiled at Jack. The profile resembled a tugboat, but Jack could see it was no ordinary tug. This one was bright red and fully animated, like a cartoon. It even had little porthole eyes that turned and winked at the *Promise*. Then a giant hand grew out of the tug's side, reached up to the top of the boat, and pulled a rope activating the foghorn. Jack smiled back at the tug. It was all part of his new destiny.

Jack spent the night cleaning the *Promise*, writing in a diary, snorting coke, masturbating, and singing songs. By morning, the sleep deprivation was starting to show. Jack was making mistakes. He discovered he had left too much equipment on and was draining one of the batteries. It had discharged more than 50 percent, which meant that even when he recharged it, which he proceeded to do, it would shorten the battery's life. After tending to the battery, Jack cut his finger on a can opener, then accidentally dropped a wrench overboard.

On the fifth day, the tugboat came back, all by itself. It paralleled the *Promise* for a few moments, tooted its horn, smiled, then turned away.

That night Jack tore apart the *Promise* looking for John, whom he hadn't seen all day. Then he saw John in his yellow slicker run into the galley. Jack searched the entire galley, opening every cupboard and locker, even removing a panel from the wall, but he couldn't catch him. John was playing the haunting game, the ghostly version of tag. When John started whispering inside the second stateroom, Jack turned over all the furniture and searched every panel looking for his friend. John egged him on but refused to be caught.

On the sixth day Jack decided to head back to Miami. He would be there in less than twenty-four hours. One day more but only one stinking cigar left. He lit the cigar and set the course. At least there was still plenty of cocaine in the vial. And plenty of planning ahead. Jack was anxious to do more deals with the Magic Juans. He daydreamed of running commercial tankers, not small coastal freighters, and off-loading them with a fleet of fishing trawlers. A caravan of refrigerated eighteen-wheelers would complete the distribution network. Together with his newfound power, and John as his spiritual partner, Blackjack the Pirate was destined to once again conquer the seas.

When the stars came out that night, Jack had been up for six days and nights, the same amount of time that Robert Louis Stevenson took to write *The Strange Case of Dr. Jekyll and Mr. Hyde* under the influence of cocaine. Jack looked at the stars and regretted throwing the sextant away. He peered into the radar screen. A green glow bathed his hands and face. He studied his hands. They looked more like animal claws. The knuckles were big and gnarled. Green veins, a good half-inch in diameter, pulsated with green blood. The fingernails were pointed and hooked. Jack imagined what his face must look like—green and evil just like the Wicked Witch in *The Wizard of Oz*.

"You think you can get out of the Devil's Triangle, my pretty?" teased John's voice.

"Watch me," answered Jack. And with that he switched off the radar, the compass, all the running lights, everything but the engines. Like Captain Ahab, who threw away his sextant and compass in mad pursuit of the white whale Moby Dick, Jack was determined to captain his ship into port the way his father had taught him—by the seat of his pants. Never mind the crowded traffic near the coast, Blackjack was out to prove himself a seaworthy son and smuggler.

The water was as smooth as glass. Jack glided the *Promise* across the imaginary line marking the western border of the triangle and toward the lights of Miami. It was a religious experience for Jack: the still night, the distant twinkling stars, the glow of the city, and the cocaine. The soft sounds of a Jimmy Buffett ballad, "Trying to Reason with Hurricane Season," drifted over the water.

> Now I must confess
> I could use some rest,
> I can't run at this pace very long.
> Yes, it's quite insane.
> I think it hurts my brain.
> But it cleans me out
> And then I can go on.

POSTSCRIPT

Jack was indicted for conspiracy to import marijuana and is now serving time in a federal prison.

I worked on the case and interviewed John's parents. Jack had paid them a visit sometime after he returned from the Bermuda Triangle. He told them not to worry; John was alive and well on the other side, and he loved them. When I saw John's parents they were each wearing gold Rolex watches, identical to Jack's. I knew better than to think that they had dug up John's treasure chest.

12

TAKE
A
PICTURE

The canyons that slice through the Los Angeles basin are as pretty as a picture, but I don't trust them. In the rugged hills of Tujunga Canyon, north of the city, two women reported having been abducted by a UFO. In Decker Canyon, near Malibu, I spent several weekends visiting with John Lilly, who claimed he was splashing around in a sensory deprivation flotation tank with extraterrestrials. Later, Lilly was found floating face-down in his tank, half-dead. In Laurel Canyon, on a road called Wonderland Avenue, not far from the house where I was visiting with Timothy Leary, four people were bludgeoned to death with a steel pipe. One of the murder suspects was a drug user I had once interviewed. Then, in Tuna Canyon, police subdued a deranged man armed with a .357 magnum. The man was on a mission to kill the one person he believed responsible for all the strange happenings in the canyons. I was his target!

After that last incident, it was hard to trust the canyons. I promised myself I would go there only when it was absolutely necessary. This was one of those times. I had to save Roger's life. Roger had taken enough LSD one night to send the entire population of Topanga Canyon on a trip. It was all because he had lost his girlfriend. He said he was looking for insight and understanding. What he found was a bad trip during which he tried to kill himself. He was threatening to try again. That's why I decided to drive into Topanga Canyon looking for Marjorie. In order to help Roger, I needed to hear her side of the story.

I drove up to a secluded house surrounded by trees and dense brush. It was an ideal setting for Marjorie and her room-mates, all disfigured women recovering from reconstructive plastic surgery. Many of the women had endured scores of oper-ations in order to rebuild bodies literally ripped apart by acci-dents or diseases. Most were out-of-towners who came here to avoid family and friends while they healed. But they opened their house to the local hippies. The hippies in Topanga not only looked like their counterparts from the sixties, but espoused the same philosophy of acceptance and love for all people, no matter how different. They greeted Marjorie and the other patients with open hearts.

After parking the car, I walked to the backyard, where Mar-jorie said I could find her. A party was in progress. Tie-dyed clothing, flowered hats, and bright umbrellas were everywhere. Everyone was smiling and laughing. A little girl, looking very much like a cherub, was wearing a garland of fresh flowers in her blond hair, and nothing else. She was carrying a stuffed Mickey Mouse doll that was as big as she was. Someone was banging on a congo drum. A skinny, long-haired man in white pants was dancing by himself. He seemed to be in a trance. I saw a woman with white make-up talking to a man with a shaved head. Nearby, a biker wearing black leathers and a handle-bar mustache seemed mesmerized by a young man juggling colorful silk scarves. Two little boys were chasing a puppy around the yard. The blond-haired girl and Mickey Mouse joined them.

Now I know how Eddie Valiant felt when he drove into Toontown, I thought as I flashed on scenes from the cartoon movie *Who Framed Roger Rabbit?* I made my way to the food table. Raw vegetables, seeds, nuts, some crackers that looked like dog bis-cuits, and puddles of mysterious dips. *Toon food!* I tossed a few seeds to a peacock strutting nearby. Then I noticed a young woman wearing a long pink dress that came down to her bare feet. She had a large straw hat that shielded her face from the sun, but there was something very unusual about that face. The angles were . . . cubist. Some parts appeared normal while other parts seemed rigid, almost mannequinlike. I couldn't take my eyes off her. When she looked up and smiled at me, her facial movements were robotic. I smiled back at Marjorie.

She kissed me on the cheek. It felt funny, like someone kissing you with a pair of wax lips. I caught a hint of Opium perfume. "Welcome," she said. "I'm glad you found us." She seemed sincere but the staccato pronunciation gave it a slightly mechanical sound. "I've had my face rebuilt," she said up front. "New cheekbone . . . a plate here . . . this eye's not quite right yet. It's okay to stare if you want. They said we should get used to it."

I *was* staring, all right. But I couldn't tell there had been such massive reconstruction. "They did a wonderful job," I said and meant it.

"My doctor's a genius," she gushed. "I'm really lucky to have him. Why, he took some bone from over here and . . ."

Marjorie launched into a step-by-step description of her surgeries. She recited all the details including the brand name of the bone saw that her surgeon used, the types of skin flaps, even the number of sutures. Perhaps a medical student would appreciate her enthusiasm, but I was overcome with a strange mixture of pity and nausea. As Marjorie started to describe how her sinuses had to be cut away, I blocked out her words. I focused on her one good eye—the other looked like it had been poached—and tried to concentrate on the key ring I was squeezing in my pocket. By using my sense of touch, I tried to identify the door that matched each key. After getting halfway around the ring, I tuned in to Marjorie again.

". . . all new teeth and they're perfect. I'll never have a cavity again. Isn't that great? It's a small compensation, but they said we have to take what we can get," she said.

I tried to make some idle conversation, but Marjorie wouldn't let me. "Have you seen Roger? How is he? Does he ever ask about me? You know I still love him. He used to call me Bunny," she said in her rapid-fire way.

I said I was worried about Roger, who was having a difficult time recovering from a bad drug trip. He had told me about their relationship. It might help to hear her side.

"I will do anything I can. I'm still his Bunny, you know. Of course, Judy was his first Bunny. Even when he called me Judy, it didn't bother me. I mean, we all fantasize, you know. It's all part of love, you know."

"Hold on," I said. Marjorie was going too fast for me. I recognized what she was talking about from my conversations with Roger, but I wanted to hear the whole story chronologically. Couldn't we sit down and take some time to understand this step-by-step, I said, appealing to her obsession with detail. We found a shady spot on the lawn, where Marjorie spread a blanket. The hours went by as we sat and talked. Actually, Marjorie did most of the talking while I simply tried to keep her on track. As she spoke, I juxtaposed her version with Roger's, trying to decipher exactly what had happened. I ended up with an edited version that was as shockingly different from what Roger had told me as Marjorie's new face was from the original.

Roger had never had a girlfriend until his senior year at UCLA. None unless you count Brigitte Bardot and Natalie Wood, the two subjects of his frequent masturbatory fantasies. Roger didn't have any pictures to look at; he simply recalled their images from movies he had seen. He always had the ability to recall memory images with amazing clarity. As a child his remarkable memory prompted his parents to take him to a psychologist for testing. The psychologist found that Roger possessed eidetic imagery—the capacity to retain memory images of objects with photographic fidelity. It was an ability he never lost. Now his images of the movie stars were so vivid that they seemed almost real as he projected them against his pillows or onto the bedroom ceiling. The images were better than the girlie magazines that his roommate used because Roger could make his imaginary sexual partners do anything he wanted.

Then he met Judy, another senior. They were both virgins, but not for long. Roger thought Judy was the most beautiful girl in the world. She had Natalie Wood eyes and sexy, pouty lips like Bardot. Her hair was styled like Bardot's, only darker. Roger convinced her to bleach it. Now, in Roger's eyes, sex with Judy was picture-perfect. They went at it like the proverbial rabbits, and Roger started calling Judy by the pet name Bunny.

After graduation, Roger and Judy took an apartment together. Roger got a job in data processing while Judy took summer school classes in preparation for graduate school. According to Roger, they talked about getting married. He showed me a picture of Judy wearing a little silver rabbit pin with ruby eyes. Instead of a fraternity pin, Roger "pinned" Judy with the silver rabbit. "That meant that we were engaged to be engaged," he said. His emotional dependency on her grew deeper. He told Judy he wanted to have a family—he thought that two kids were ideal—and even talked about how they should raise the children. Judy's only response to questions of marriage or family was a guarded "maybe." She didn't bother to tell Roger that she had applied to graduate programs out-of-state. And she certainly didn't tell him she wanted to see other guys.

The summer was almost over when Judy was finally accepted to a graduate school in New York City. The letter came on a Wednesday. On Saturday she told Roger she was leaving. The movers were coming that day to take her things to her parents. She wanted to leave right away, but Roger cried and pleaded for her to stay one more night. They had sex and Roger held her tightly all night long. On Sunday Judy left. Sunday night Roger had sex again with Judy, only this time it was a masturbatory fantasy. Every night after that was the same.

Roger wrote a stream of letters to Judy. She never answered. When he called, she was always busy and couldn't talk. He asked if he could visit her for a long weekend. "Maybe," she said, "we'll see in a few weeks." The weeks stretched into months. Finally, Roger made a surprise visit to New York. He showed up at Judy's apartment with flowers, a giant bag of her favorite Famous Amos chocolate chip cookies, and a stuffed rabbit. She refused to let him in. They talked outside, in a light drizzle. Roger didn't hear the words. All he could think about was how beautiful, how sexy, how perfect Judy was. He didn't try to kiss her, but he did put an affectionate hand on her arm. Judy moved back and the hand slipped away. She was saying something about moving on with her career, a new life.

All Roger could do was hold out the flowers and other gifts. "I love you," he said.

Judy took the gifts inside and returned with the rabbit pin. She handed it to Roger.

"Can't we still be friends?" he asked as he tried to give the pin back.

"We knew each other, but we were never friends," she said, almost spitting out the words. Roger was devastated.

When Roger returned to Los Angeles, he couldn't bring himself to remove Judy's photograph from his night table. He thought it was such a great shot. Judy's face was turned slightly to the side so that her Bardot lips were almost in profile while her Natalie Wood eyes were looking coquettishly at the camera. Her silk blouse, open to the waist, hugged her breasts. The nipples were erect and clearly visible through the blouse. Roger liked the fact that Judy never wore a bra. He also liked where she chose to wear the rabbit pin for the photograph: directly above her left nipple. It gave the picture a three-dimensional effect.

Roger went to the closet and took out Judy's blue silk polka-dot dress. She had left some clothes that she didn't want anymore and had told Roger to throw them out. He kept them all. Now he spread her dress on the bed. He rubbed his hands up and down the dress, feeling the material, remembering how sensuous she looked in it. Roger took off his clothes and lay down next to the dress. He would have liked to put it on, only it was too small. Judy's size had always been an advantage. When they were having sex she would get on top of him. She was so light that he could literally lift her up and down in the air with his arms. Judy could have multiple orgasms in that position. Roger could almost hear her moaning as he began masturbating.

The masturbation took him into a trance. He forgot about the real world. Judy's physical presence in faraway New York became unimportant, forgotten. Roger's entire attention was concentrated on Judy's image on top of him. He saw her unbuttoning her blouse, smiling mischievously, then licking her lips with her tongue. She started riding him, telling him how much she liked the way he felt. Orgasm released Roger from his trance.

"It seemed like a half-dream," Roger explained to me in one of our many meetings. "Somewhere in the back of my mind I knew I was masturbating, but at the same time I was *really* with her. It was some of the sweetest sex I ever had with her, or anyone."

At first, these fantasies were confined to Roger's masturbatory sessions. They soon became a daily ritual. Roger would come home from work and eat dinner. After dinner he would open the closet and ask Judy what she would like to wear tonight. Then he would select an outfit and put it on the bed. Before masturbating, he would spend many minutes looking at the clothes, feeling them, and imagining Judy's face and body inside them.

Gradually, Judy's image became more solid, and Roger invented a solid relationship to go with it. He told both his friends and co-workers that he was still engaged to Judy. Any prospective dates soon learned that Roger was unavailable. He took all of his vacations in New York. While he never went to Judy's apartment, he always hoped that he would bump into her. He even rehearsed what he would say. Meanwhile, he spent his time in New York shopping, touring museums, and walking aimlessly around the city. Toward evening he usually cruised Times Square. The porno movies and sex parlors excited him. He ended each night back in his hotel room in a wild sex scene with his imaginary partner.

On one of these trips to New York, Roger thought he saw Judy window-shopping on Fifth Avenue. He studied her from across the street. It had been over a year since he last saw her but, yes, it was Judy. She was shopping with a taller woman. They went into a store. Roger used the time to cross the street. Judy emerged, walked right past him, and ducked into another store. Roger waited. After about thirty minutes, they came out and walked toward another store. Roger ran after them and grabbed Judy by the arm. "Judy, Judy," he said.

She turned to the taller woman and said, "Did you touch my arm? Someone touched my arm!"

"Judy, I did. It's me!" said Roger excitedly.

She turned toward Roger. "I don't know you," she said.

Roger couldn't believe what he was hearing. He was staring right into Judy's face. The Bardot lips and Natalie Wood eyes were twisted into a strange expression of anger and fear.

"Stop following me!" she shouted.

"I'm sorry," Roger heard himself saying with disbelief. "I thought you were someone I knew a long time ago."

As the two women hurried away, Roger heard Judy say to

her friend, "He grabbed my arm! I don't believe he grabbed my arm!" Roger couldn't understand why Judy was acting that way.

After that incident, he stopped going to New York. Back in Los Angeles, he thought he saw her several times, but it was always at such a distance he couldn't be sure. Then, one day while he was driving along the Ventura Freeway, Judy passed him in a car. She smiled. Roger smiled back. She waved at him as she zipped past him in the high-speed lane. He followed the car for many miles, way past his own exit, until he lost it in traffic. He would have liked to know what she was doing that day in Los Angeles. But her activities at night were never in doubt. In fact, that night his sex with Judy was the most realistic that he had ever imagined.

Five years went by this way. Roger eventually started dating a few women, but the relationships remained platonic and non-sexual. Some of his dates probably thought he was gay, but Roger didn't care. If only his little Bunny could talk, she would tell him how great he was in bed. Over the years Roger had perfected his act. The clothes and photograph were no longer necessary props. Gone were the nightly rituals after dinner. Roger could now have sex with Judy any place, any time.

In the mornings, when he awoke with an erection, he could actually *feel* her body next to his. She would nuzzle him, then wrap her legs around him as they lay side by side. He could feel her lips against his, her tongue pushing deep inside his mouth. Sometimes he could feel her licking him while he was in the shower. There, with the sound of the water drowning his voice, Roger cried out to Judy, telling her that he loved her and wanted to marry her and have a baby with her. At night, as his hands caressed his own groin, he could feel her pubic hairs brushing against his, hear the slapping sounds of her skin against his, and smell their sex mixed with the Opium perfume she always wore.

Sex had always been the primary aspect of Roger's relationship with Judy. Imaginary sex with her remained as satisfying as the real thing because it seemed so real. But when Roger started dating, he began wishing Judy was more than just a silent partner. The wishing caused him considerable loneliness, depression, and anxiety. Like a lonely child, Roger sought escape by creating a more complete and satisfying companion. His wishful imagination, which had already created Judy as an imaginary partner in bed, was now about to make her walk and talk.

Roger met Marjorie at a trendy café that catered to the business lunch trade. He had just gone through the food line and was looking for a table. The place was crowded, but he saw an empty chair next to a small woman with beautiful natural blond hair. Marjorie said that the seat was not taken and he was welcome to sit there. She thought he had an unusual pick-up line.

"You know, if you took off your glasses, your eyes are just like Natalie Wood's," Roger said.

Marjorie blushed. She was too embarrassed to take them off, but thanked him for the compliment. They started talking about their work. Marjorie had just graduated college and was working as an administrative assistant. It was a dead-end job, she said, nothing more than a fancy secretary. Roger told her that she should go on to graduate school, move on with her career. He said she was obviously too intelligent to spend her time locked into a glorified secretarial position. She liked the interest he was showing in her. By the time he asked her out, she had taken off her glasses and was waiting to say yes.

Their first date was a movie. Afterward, they bought ice cream cones and walked around the Santa Monica Pier. Roger liked the way Marjorie ate the ice cream cone. She didn't lick it, but puckered her lips and more or less sucked on it. It made her thin lips look pouty and sexy. He told her this and she blushed.

They started to date regularly and had sex for the first time a few weeks later. During their lovemaking, Roger called her "Bunny" several times. Aferward, as they were lying in bed, Marjorie asked him why he used that name. He explained that he thought she made love like a little rabbit and the name just popped out. Marjorie didn't think her lovemaking was so hot. She felt awkward as she always did the first time she slept with someone. But Roger seemed so comfortable, so at ease with her. It was almost as though he had known her all his life. She started to relax. Yes, it was almost as though they belonged together. She had finally met someone who, instinctively, felt right. And he was so gorgeous! Marjorie snuggled up to Roger just like her nickname. For the first time in her life, she was falling in love.

The next day Roger gave her a bottle of Opium perfume, and they made love all day long until Marjorie was too sore to continue. They saw each other almost every day thereafter. Roger always wanted to make love. He couldn't seem to get enough of her. Marjorie was swept away by the physical attention. Nobody had ever told her that she was attractive. Certainly, no one before Roger had ever compared her to Natalie Wood. Marjorie just couldn't understand what he saw in her. But she told herself that love was blind and it didn't matter.

They became inseparable. Marjorie was constantly snuggling and cuddling with Roger, whether they were in bed, standing on line at a movie or a bank, or even waiting in the dentist office. They were like Siamese twins, nuzzling face to face, oblivious to the rest of the world. Whenever people gawked, as happened often, Marjorie would smile at them and yell, "Take a picture!" In her eyes, the love affair was picture-perfect.

Several months into the relationship, Roger called her Judy. Marjorie ignored it since it was in the heat of passion. Then it happened again when they were sitting on the sofa watching television.

"Who's Judy?" asked Marjorie.

There was a long pause. "Oh, she was my fiancée, who was killed in a car accident," he lied. "It was a long time ago. I had a hard time getting over it. Guess I still do." He choked up and started crying. Marjorie's heart melted. She snuggled against Roger and cried with him. It was then that she decided to do anything necessary to ease Roger's pain. She was part of him now.

The next time Roger slipped was at a picnic on Santa Monica beach. He was chatting with a couple on a nearby blanket when Marjorie emerged from her swim. Roger introduced her as his girlfriend Judy. Marjorie didn't bother to correct him. A few nights later, at one of those L.A. restaurants where waiters insist you call them by their first name and they do the same with you, Roger introduced Marjorie as Judy. Marjorie thought it was cute. Then he began to call her Judy in bed. Marjorie couldn't begin to count the number of times. It was becoming as much a pet name for her as Bunny. She accepted it. After all, she was his "one and only honey Bunny," wasn't she?

One day Marjorie was browsing through the books on Roger's shelf when she came across his college yearbook. She looked up his picture. Handsome as ever, she thought. Then she came across Judy's senior year picture. It was signed "with love, Bunny." Marjorie started crying, partly because of the inscription, and partly because Judy was so pretty and now she was dead. Poor Roger, she thought. She could not bring herself to mention it and risk throwing him into another depression. Marjorie knew that her relationship with Roger had lasted longer than his engagement with Judy. The way she figured it, she was more his Bunny than Judy ever was.

Marjorie looked at Roger with lovesick eyes. She still couldn't believe someone so handsome would be going with her. It was enjoyable to simply admire his good looks. Sometimes when she was staring at him, she would hold her hands up so that they formed a box around her eyes. Then she would look through the box, smile, and say, "Click!"

"What was that all about?" asked Roger the first time she did it.

"Taking a picture," said Marjorie. He was so gorgeous. She was so happy. She wanted to take loads of pictures.

All of Marjorie's friends started to notice how happy she had become. There was a constant smile and glow on her face. Marjorie also started to feel sexy for the first time in her life. Roger bought her some daring lingerie, a see-through white silk blouse, and a blue silk dress. She didn't care for the blue dress with the gaudy polka dots, but when he pulled it up to her waist and made love to her right there on the living room floor, she decided to wear it for him whenever he wanted.

They celebrated their one-year anniverary with champagne and dinner at Fennel, a new gourmet restaurant in Santa Monica. Marjorie was wearing the white silk blouse, without a bra as Roger had requested, with a black blazer and matching slacks. She was shy about removing her blazer at the table but did it for Roger. He surprised her by reaching across the table and putting a pin above her left breast. It was a beautiful silver rabbit with ruby eyes. He said he loved her.

"Click!"

After dinner they walked across the street to the Santa Monica Pier, the scene of their first date. They rode the carousel, played a few arcade games, and walked hand-in-hand around the pier. Marjorie stopped in front of a little pink hut with a PSYCHIC ADVISOR sign in the window. Doreena, the resident palm reader, encouraged her to come inside. Roger gave Marjorie the three dollars but refused to go inside with her. It's nonsense, he said. Marjorie was giggling when she went inside. She returned in a few minutes wearing a somber expression. All she would say was that Roger was right, it was a bunch of nonsense. Roger took her hand and led her to the bumper car ride. Marjorie jerked her hand away and said no. Something Doreena said was obviously bothering her.

They decided to have their pictures taken together inside one of those coin-operated photo booths. Marjorie was delighted with the pictures; they looked just like her and Roger. Roger said it didn't look at all like her and complained about the cheap camera they probably used. She wanted him to have her picture as a souvenir of their anniversary. No, he said, it wasn't a good likeness. But he didn't have any pictures of her, she reminded him. He laughed it off saying he didn't need one; he had a photographic memory and could picture her all the time. He could see her beauty better than any cheap camera.

"Why, that five-and-dime piece of junk couldn't possibly capture your Natalie Wood eyes and Brigitte Bardot lips," he said.

Brigitte Bardot lips! Marjorie thought that Roger had had a bit too much champagne. She cuddled next to him and told him he was a terrible poet, but she loved him anyway. "Take Bunny home quickly," she whispered.

The following weekend Marjorie decided to visit her parents in San Diego. She had never been very close to them but felt that it was time to tell them about Roger. After all, there might be a wedding in the future. There was a terrible accident. Marjorie was driving alone when a drunk driver in a van crossed into her lane and hit her head-on. The front of her small car collapsed, and Marjorie was pushed through the windshield. Her right ear was severed and most of her face was ripped off by the jagged glass and metal. Luckily, she lost consciousness immediately.

Her next memory was of lying on a hospital gurney with all kinds of hurried activity around her. A friendly voice was telling her that they were taking her into surgery. Although her eyes were bandaged shut, Marjorie didn't think she was badly hurt. Inside the operating room, they started removing the bandages. Marjorie was feeling no pain because of the pre-operative medication. The surgeon entered the room, leaned over the table, and looked into what was once Marjorie's face. In the twilight of her consciousness, Marjorie heard him say, "Jesus! Take a picture of this before we start!"

Marjorie's parents arrived at the hospital just as she was moved from the recovery room to intensive care. Did she want them to call anyone? they asked. Just her boss, Marjorie mumbled. She wanted to tell Roger herself but would have to wait until she could speak more clearly. While nobody would say much to her about her injuries, something was telling her it was serious. And that something was also telling her that Roger would not react very well.

When Marjorie failed to return after the weekend, Roger called her office. They told him only what her parents had said: Marjorie had been in a car accident. She was in the hospital in San Diego.

Roger showed up the next day. He was carrying flowers and a bag of cookies. A nurse confiscated the cookies before Roger entered the room. He didn't understand why Marjorie would be unable to eat them.

"Hi, Bunny," Roger said in a loud voice as he bounced into her room. Marjorie's mother gave him a stern look and motioned for him to be quiet. Her daughter was sleeping. Roger didn't see Marjorie. He saw a body draped in I.V. lines and electronic monitors. The head was wrapped like a mummy. One eye was completely covered with bandages. The other eye was black and swollen shut. The mother took Roger outside. He asked a million questions. She tried to explain what little the doctors had already told her. Roger heard phrases like "extensive damage," "lost an ear," "more operations," and "several months." The word "disfigured" echoed again and again inside Roger's head until that was all he could hear. It pushed out all other thoughts, creating a feeling of emptiness and panic that seemed at once both familiar and frightening.

"You're friends with Marjorie?" asked her mother. She didn't know.

Roger reached deep down inside his panic and found an

ancient response. From a detached distance he heard himself say, "We knew each other but we were not close friends." He gave the flowers to Marjorie's mother, wished her well, and left.

Later, Marjorie showed no emotion when her mother told her about Roger and what he had said. The tear ducts in her one good eye were still messed up. And with wires holding her mouth closed, no one heard her screaming.

Now, in the fading light of Topanga Canyon, Marjorie appeared calm as she recounted her story. At first she had refused to accept losing Roger. They talked on the telephone, but he didn't want to see her. She thought that once she recovered he might take her back. The thought gave her the will to continue with the long process of reconstructive surgery. At one point she even wanted to modify her face to look more like Judy. She asked the surgeon to inject silicone into her lips. He refused. Instead, he convinced her to stay as close as possible to her natural face. He worked off the most recent photo of Marjorie taken at the Santa Monica Pier.

"Ironic, isn't it?" said Marjorie. "I only had that picture because Roger didn't want it. He said I looked like Judy. Did you ever see what she looked like?"

"Yes," I said. Roger had shown the Judy picture to me once.

"Crazy, isn't it?" she continued. "We look like day and night."

I agreed. Day and night. Reality and dream. Marjorie was the real woman in every sense of both words. Judy was some gauzy boudoir photograph that Roger was in love with. Somehow, Roger's imagery was so strong that he had been able to project Judy's features onto Marjorie's face. These projected features, combined with a few physical resemblances such as the blond hair and large eyes, created an imaginary-living face that took on the same emotional intensity and sensory vividness as Judy's face.

"Actually I knew I wasn't as beautiful as Judy," Marjorie was saying. "My mouth was always too big. The ideal mouth is fifty percent of the width of the face at mouth level, you know. Now, it's worse and my cheekbones are still too small. But they taught us tricks to compensate, like smiling a lot."

Someone came over to the blanket and gave us a couple of

those outdoor candles in jars. In the flickering light, Marjorie's new smile was genuinely beautiful. The rest of her face was in shadows. I tried to imagine Judy's features superimposed on the shadows, the way Roger always saw it. It didn't work for me, but I didn't have Roger's experience of living for five years with the imaginary Judy. Roger had finally realized that was exactly what he had been doing when he took the LSD. During the trip he became aware of the fact that he was still in love with Judy and, in a sense, was never really close to Marjorie. The trip ended in two guilty nonlethal slashes across his wrists with a razor blade.

My clinical instincts told me that Marjorie would heal much sooner than Roger. Maybe Roger would discover that he really did love Marjorie for qualities that remained intact, deep beneath her skin. Although it was trite, I told her that it takes time for some people to see the beauty in others. I didn't know what else to say so I stood up to leave.

Marjorie pressed the rabbit pin into my hand as she kissed me on the cheek. "For Roger," she whispered. I could feel her tear ducts working again.

"God bless you, Marjorie," I said as I took the pin. I only wished it was a simple matter of destroying this pin to free Roger from his imaginary partner, and, in the process, to save other Marjories.

On my way back to the car I threw the pin into the woods. Roger would never know. And I could trust the canyon to keep a secret.

POSTSCRIPT

Marjorie recovered from her surgeries and eventually returned to her old job in Los Angeles, not far from where Roger continued to work. She never married.

Therapy and medication finally eliminated Roger's anxiety and suicidal thoughts, but he never stopped fantasizing about Bunny. He never married.

13

SERGEANT
TOMMY

Imaginary companions sometimes go bad and lead their real playmates astray. In the 1914 book *Una Mary*, a remarkable work about the inner life of a child, author Una Hunt described how her own imaginary playmate turned into an outlaw. Hunt called her playmate Una Mary, acknowledging that the playmate embodied part of her own identity but with far more freedom to act out feelings and fantasies. "I only had to set Una Mary free, to let her come outside, and she could do anything," wrote Hunt. She described one incident in which she was being teased by Harry, a neighborhood bully. Hunt bore the teasing meekly until Harry bit a hole in Jemima, her favorite doll. Immediately, she released Una Mary, who flew at Harry like a wildcat, "ready to fight to the death." After a thorough beating, Harry never bothered her again.

Una Hunt's imaginary playmate stayed with her throughout adolescence. Such long-term relationships seem to be common with children who later show creative ability in writing, although no one knows why. Perhaps the imaginative processes that create invisible characters for lonely children or for adult writers are the same. Although most children learn to separate the real and fictional worlds, a rare few become victims of their own mental creations. The imaginary companion can start writing its own plot, a Frankenstein turned loose by a child's wishful thinking.

Chris Sizemore, whose true story was immortalized by the movie *The Three Faces of Eve*, was a classic case. Chris kept a little red-haired girl as her childhood imaginary playmate. It was the little red-haired girl who got into mischief doing things Chris knew were wrong. When Chris was six, her mother brought home twin baby girls from the hospital. The little red-haired girl flew into a jealous rage and attacked the babies, poking and biting them. Hearing their screams, the mother rushed into the room. Chris was delighted because now her mother would see the little red-haired girl doing the mischief and realize that Chris had been innocent all along. Although Chris was certain that her mother had seen the red-haired girl, she was still spanked. The shock of this injustice left her confused and powerless. The little red-haired girl took over, eventually giving way to the multiple personalities known as Eve Black, Eve White, and Jane. It took Chris a half-century to work her way back into control over her own body.

Perhaps the most infamous and twisted example was provided by Mark David Chapman. Chapman played with thousands of "little people" who lived in the walls of his living room. He created an entire imaginary world in which the little people worshipped him like a king. Chapman was a benign ruler who frequently staged imaginary Beatles concerts for his subjects. But if any of the little people dared to get out of line or anger him in any way, Chapman would kill them by pressing an imaginary destruct button on the arm of his family sofa. When John Lennon angered him, Chapman discussed plans to murder the ex-Beatle with the little people. "They were shocked . . . they didn't want any part of it," Chapman later told his psychiatrist. So Chapman went to another imaginary figure, Satan. He prayed to Satan to steady his hand as he pressed the trigger, emptying a snub-nosed .38 special into Lennon.

Now meet Henry Hammer, a quiet boy of fifteen who never got into trouble in his life. At least that's what he told me when

I first interviewed him in the Los Angeles County Juvenile Hall, where he was awaiting trial on charges of attempted murder.

"*Oy vey!*" his mother said upon hearing the news of his arrest. "Not my son! He's a *shainer yid* (good Jew). And a real scholar, not a second-rater like all the other children in his school."

In his blue crocheted skullcap and black horn-rims, Henry certainly appeared to be everything his mother said. He was the top student in his high school class and showed exceptional talents as a creative writer in English. His mother didn't care about writing skills; she wanted Henry to be a doctor. "You'll be a famous brain surgeon, God willing!" she always told him. That's why she wouldn't let him play any sports—he might hurt his hands. However, she didn't stop him from writing. Henry filled several notebooks with short stories and essays, several of which were read aloud in class and received extra credit. But Henry's best work, the project he had been working on for several years, was kept secret. It took the occasion of a substitute teacher to give Henry a chance to show off his masterpiece: Sergeant Tommy, decorated Vietnam sniper and all-around he-man, a real *mensch*.

Henry was an only child, the pride and joy of his parents, Abe and Yetta, who were observant Orthodox Jews. They were also overly protective of their son and never allowed him to have friends over or engage in extracurricular activities. Any free time had to be spent in Hebrew school or studying the Talmud. One of Henry's two main recreations was eating. Evidence of this was easy to see in his chipmunklike jowls, jelly roll belly that hung over black trousers that were always too tight, and wiggly behind. Mrs. Hammer was unable to keep Henry on a diet and was always confiscating pieces of strudel and other sweets hidden in his room.

"You eat like a horse," she would tell him.

Henry's other great pleasure was playing with an imaginary happy-go-lucky friend called Tom-Tom. Originally, Tom-Tom was invisible and stayed just behind Henry's right ear, where he whispered smart-alec remarks about Henry's mother. When Mrs. Hammer caught Henry with an unauthorized candy bar, she yelled: "You're going to swell up like a mountain and *plats!*" referring to his intestines bursting.

"It should happen to you," whispered Tom-Tom. The imaginary remark caused Henry to smirk, bite his lip, then laugh out loud hysterically. And that caused Mrs. Hammer to smack Henry with a very real hand across his face.

"God will punish you," she would say after delivering her own secular penalty.

"Kiss my *tokhes* (behind)," whispered Tom-Tom. He always got in the last word, which is why Henry liked him so much.

Henry knew he was not the only one who admired Tom-Tom. In his mind, all the little girls liked Tom-Tom. They all wanted to play with him and kiss him on the lips. Sometimes they fought among themselves as to whom Tom-Tom liked best. Henry loved these fantasies. But he began to envy Tom-Tom's ability to play all the time while he had to go to school. That's when he decided to start taking Tom-Tom to school with him. Tom-Tom became Tommy, best-looking and most athletic kid in the class. Henry was fat and slightly effeminate looking. Tommy was trim and virile. Henry had a small penis, a *petseleh* his mother once called it, using the term for an infant's penis. Tommy had a *shlanger* that would scare a snake. Henry played the tuba. Tommy could play all the hottest tunes on the piano and sing them as well! Henry couldn't do one single pull-up in gym class whereas Tommy held the school record. They became best friends.

The years in grade school went by. Henry got smarter and fatter. Tommy got stronger and more cunning. Henry wasn't allowed to join the Boy Scouts so he sent Tommy. Meanwhile, Henry spent time in the library reading adventure books. He was particularly fascinated by stories about secret agents and combat heroes. Sometimes Tommy would come into the library, silently creeping and crawling among the stacks. Tommy became so accomplished at doing this undetected that he could even crawl under the tables and look up the skirts of the girls. Henry could only imagine what Tommy saw. Whenever Sharon, the prettiest girl in the class, was in the library, Tommy would creep up behind her and feel her breasts. She never knew. But Henry knew, and he giggled to himself.

One day, the boys in Henry's class were passing around a small pornographic magazine with actual photographs of intercourse. Tommy managed to swipe it, hiding the magazine inside

Henry's Hebrew school bookbag where nobody would think of looking. That night Tommy and Henry stared at the pictures in open-eyed wonder. In the morning Mrs. Hammer found the magazine while cleaning Henry's room. She went into a rage of yiddish.

"Vos iz mit dir?" (What's wrong with you?) she asked over and over again as she waved the magazine around in the air. Every time it came near her face, she closed her eyes, then opened them again as her arm carried the magazine above her head. Henry thought he would be walloped any minute.

"Look! A flying fuck!" whispered Tommy.

Henry cracked up.

Mrs. Hammer began wailing. *"Oy! Vey iz mir! A klog iz mir! A brokh tsu mir!"* (Woe is me! A curse on me!)

"Mama, stop talking yourself into illness," said Henry with genuine concern. He always felt she would die with her mouth open, yelling at him.

"Your father will hear about this!" she said with finality.

"He doesn't frighten me," whispered Tommy.

Henry's father came into his room that evening. He told Henry to take off all his clothes and stand on a chair. Henry obeyed. Now he was looking directly into his father's piercing eyes. His father reminded Henry why observant Orthodox Jews wear a *yarmulke*, or skullcap. It's to indicate that someone is above them. That someone is God. The God of Abraham, Isaac, Jacob, and Henry. He watches you all the time, and sees everything, his father said. Henry looked above his father's head. There, for the first time, he saw Tommy sitting on top of his dresser!

"You can vomit from this," said Tommy.

Abe Hammer continued lecturing Henry. When he was finished, he told Henry he must stand on the chair all night reading the Talmud. In the morning, he would be asked questions about the readings. If he answered correctly, he could go back to school. The following day Henry shuffled back to school.

"Do your legs hurt?" asked Tommy.

"What, I'm as strong as a horse," answered Henry.

"They don't let you live," said Tommy. Henry agreed.

The boys at school were in a panic looking for the lost magazine. They confronted Henry in the hall. Someone accused him of stealing it. Henry told them a partial truth: he didn't know what had happened to the magazine. They started calling him names. "Liar!" "Fat ass!" "Jew boy!" Henry was sweating now. Everybody could see he was guilty. Someone threw a punch that connected with Henry's jaw and knocked him to the ground. The crowd scattered. Immediately Henry got up, brushed his black trousers as best he could, and went to his next class. He didn't say a word. Henry was no whiner.

After that incident, Henry was always being picked on by the same group of three boys. They taunted him about the magazine. He called them the "Three *Shlubs* (jerks)." He never told them that his parents had confiscated the magazine, but somehow they must have figured it out because they were always insinuating that his mother and father mimicked the poses in the photographs. Henry tried to ignore them.

One day, as Henry was sitting down at his desk in science class, he felt a sharp sensation in his behind. The pain grew more intense as he lowered himself to the chair. Henry knew that he was sitting on a tack of some sort. The "Three *Shlubs*" were staring at him. He knew they were responsible. Henry refused to wince or whine. The pain was not getting any better, but at least it wasn't getting any worse. He tried to avoid the hot flashes and concentrate on Tommy, who was outside the class window. Tommy had a Tommy gun. Henry indicated with his eyes to waste the jerks. Tommy saluted.

"*Shmuts* (slime)," yelled Tommy as he began spraying the classroom. The three jerks were torn to ribbons. Then Tommy slipped through the window and walked triumphantly down the aisle, kissing all the girls on the lips and squeezing their breasts. A just reward, thought Henry.

At the end of the class, Henry went to the restroom and removed a one-inch upholstery tack from his backside. When he pulled it out, there were a few drops of blood. Henry packed his underpants with toilet paper to make sure nothing would get stained. He didn't think his mother would notice the tiny hole in his black trousers. Then he walked out of the restroom and acted as if nothing was wrong.

Henry was bar mitzvahed the following year. His father gave him a black briefcase made of real leather. Take care of it and it will last through high school and college, his father said. And medical school, God willing, his mother added. Henry liked it because it looked like the type secret agents would use.

The briefcase was the only outward change in Henry's appearance in high school. He would have liked to wear stylish shirts and designer jeans like the other boys, but his parents made him wear the same black trousers, white shirt, and skull cap. Tommy also wore a uniform—a Boy Scout one! While some of the other boys were Eagle Scouts and proudly displayed their merit badges on gigantic sashes worn over their shoulders, Tommy was in a class by himself. His badges, which were sewn onto his shirt sleeves and not some sissy sash, told the story. On his right shoulder was the insignia of the Special Forces, a gold sword with lightning bolts. Below that was the blue-and-white patch marking him a Jungle Warfare Expert. On his left shoulder was the skull and crossbones insignia of an 18th Airborne Sniper from Vietnam. His breast pocket displayed a tiny Star of David, presented to him by the prime minister of Israel in recognition of his services in wiping out the "Three *Shlubs*." Henry started calling him Sergeant Tommy, a go-anywhere do-anything soldier who obeyed Henry's every command.

Henry ordered the sergeant to patrol his classes and act as a bodyguard. The classes themselves were boring. Henry got high marks in all of them, but only because he was so bright. The one he hated the most was history. Not that history couldn't be interesting. Henry had read all about the adventurous spies of World War II, the heroes of hand-to-hand combat in Korea, and the spectacular missions of the Special Forces in Vietnam. History *was* exciting. Mr. White was murdering it. He droned on and on in the most boring monologues. It sounded as though he was reading one perpetual run-on sentence that only stopped because the bell announcing the end of the period would ring. All the students were bored with the class. However, since Mr. White counted "attentiveness" in class as part of the final grade, everyone acted interested.

Mr. White not only demanded attention, but insisted that everyone take notes in a rigid outline form. Once a week he collected the notebooks and graded them. The hardest part of the class was looking at Mr. White. If he caught you glancing at another student, or even looking at the history book while he was talking, he would suddenly announce your name in such a tone that you felt like a defendant on trial for treason. There was simply no freedom in Mr. White's class.

Although Mr. White's classroom was on the second floor, Sergeant Tommy could slip into a tactical harness and rappel down from the roof until he got to the window. There he would establish a position on the ledge and watch for targets of opportunity. Sometimes he would slip into the classroom and creep up on a student whom Henry had targeted. All Henry had to do was stare at his target and Tommy would do the rest. When a student had the audacity to give Henry the finger, Henry glared at him until Sergeant Tommy was in position. Tommy clamped the boy's hand to the table, chopped off the offending finger with a machete, then shoved it into the boy's rectum. The sergeant was a real *mamzer*, a superlatively clever bastard.

One day Mr. White was repeating a lecture he had already given the class several days before. Nobody had the guts to tell him. Henry thought that if he could stare hard enough at Mr. White, maybe he could transmit the message nonverbally the way he did with Tommy. Suddenly the round red light of a ruby laser started dancing on Mr. White's forehead. It came to rest directly between his eyes. Henry turned to the window and saw Sergeant Tommy aiming a rifle equipped with a laser gun sight. Tommy looked up, saluted, and resumed his firing stance. Henry turned back to Mr. White.

"Yisgadal, vyiskadash," Henry said under his breath. They were the first two words of the mourner's prayer honoring the dead. Mr. White finally stopped repeating himself as his head exploded in a bright red cloud.

The next day Mr. White didn't show up at school. The principal said he was sick. Henry wondered if Sergeant Tommy had actually hurt him. A substitute teacher took over the class. The students went wild. They switched seats, passed notes, and talked among themselves. Spitballs flew across the room like missiles. The substitute teacher did his best to prevent a riot and cover the material assigned for the day.

Henry signaled for Sergeant Tommy to enter the room. Tommy crawled along the aisle until he got to Henry's seat.

"The whole works, Sergeant," he said. "The faster the better."

Then Henry opened his black leather briefcase. Inside the

top cover he had fashioned Velcro straps to hold a steel letter opener. He pulled the straps, removed the long spike, and handed it to Tommy. Sergeant Tommy ran up to the front of the classroom and buried all six inches of the letter opener in the substitute teacher's thigh. The point poked out the other side. Blood poured like a stream of syrup onto the classroom floor. The teacher screamed and pushed Henry to the floor. Henry sat in the pool of blood, horrified. He was still sitting there when the police arrived.

After months of interviews with Henry and his family, I understood how the frustration and anger that kept Sergeant Tommy alive had been released by the stabbing. Henry told me that Tommy ran away after the stabbing and never came back. With proper therapy, Tommy might never return. That's what I told the court that sentenced Henry to several years in a California Youth Authority camp.

Still, I remain troubled by my last meeting with Henry. I said goodbye. Henry smiled. Then he saluted.

PART FOUR

LIFE-THREATENING DANGER

14

THE
CAGE

The blade passed lightly over the back of his bowed head. Martin knew why they were doing this to him. It caused the muscles in his neck to automatically stiffen, and this would allow a good, clean chop. Decapitation was always messy but these gooks knew what they were doing. Although his hands were tied behind his back, and he was kneeling, Martin prepared to throw himself flat against the dirt as soon as the executioner started the final swing of the machete. He might survive. The light flickered through the corner of his blindfold. Martin sensed the blade rising above him. He threw himself into the ground so hard that he chipped his front teeth. The machete never came down. Martin started crying. His captors started laughing.

They never intended to kill Martin; they were warning him not to try to escape again. Since they had ambushed his patrol and taken him prisoner, he had tried to run away twice on the long hike through the zoo, a popular term for the jungles of Vietnam. Now they were yelling at him in Vietnamese not to try it again. The yells were punctuated with slaps across his face.

Martin whimpered that he would not attempt another escape. But he was determined to survive. The Clintons were survivors.

Martin Clinton was raised in Ilion, a small town in upstate New York. His family had been there for as long as anyone could remember. Martin's father worked in a local Remington Arms factory, and his mother was an active member of the Daughters of the American Revolution. The Clintons flew the flag on every national holiday, and Martin learned to play the drums so he could march in parades with the American Legion youth band. He was proud to be an American; even prouder to be a Clinton. A distant relative had fought fearlessly in the Revolution. He was wounded during a particularly bloody battle and lay on the ground, pretending to be dead. A Seneca Indian, who was fighting with the British, ran a scalping knife around his skull, tearing off the hair and skin from his head. He lived to tell the tale. Then, in World War I, a great uncle's legs were blown off just below the knees, yet he managed to hobble across a line of fire to safety. In World War II, Martin's father lost most of his hearing as a gunner on a naval warship in the Pacific. A Clinton fought in every war and always came home. That's why he told his parents not to worry when he volunteered for a second tour of duty in Vietnam. Besides, it was only toward the end of his first twelve-month tour that he felt he had attained maximum combat efficiency. Now he was really ready to fight.

He was walking point when his patrol was ambushed by part of a Viet Cong main force unit. Most of the men fell in cross fire from three sides. Martin may have been spared because he was wearing a captured North Vietnamese Army (NVA) floppy hat and carrying a captured AK-47 instead of the standard M16. These were tricks he had borrowed from the long-range reconnaissance boys. The gear confused the enemy and caused them to hesitate. Their moment of hesitation could be filled with a thirty-round burst from the AK-47. But Martin didn't get a chance to fire. When he heard the attack, he spun around instantly. A rifle butt smacked him in the face and he blacked out. When he came to, he found his hands tied with ropes behind his back. The VC were all over the place, stripping the bodies of weapons and ammo.

He saw Vernon's body, a short-timer who was scheduled to finish his tour in a few weeks. Vernon always wore his dog tags on his boots so he could be identified in case he was mutilated. Now Vernon's feet were gone, blown away by a mine. Martin desperately looked around for the tags. "Find his fuckin' tags, man! Find his tags!" he screamed to the VC. They ignored him. Martin noticed that some of the VC were wearing leather thongs around their wrists so they could be dragged away by their comrades if killed.

One of the VC pulled Chris into the clearing near Martin. Chris was his drag man, the last man in the patrol. He was still alive with a huge gut wound, the worst kind. There was nothing the primitive VC medicine could do for him. He needed a medevac chopper. A stone-faced VC officer examined Chris with the detachment of someone looking over meat in a market, then put a burst through his head.

"*Duma! Duma!* Fuck your mother, fuck your mother, you cocksuckers! *Duma!*" cried Martin until another rifle butt knocked him out.

When he recovered this time he was gagged and blindfolded, but alive. He was determined to keep it that way as his captors pushed and pulled him through the jungle. Every time there was the sound of aircraft, they pushed him flat to ground, then pulled him to his feet when the sounds faded. Martin took the pushing and pulling without protest. Eventually they reached a small village and took Martin into one of the huts, where they tied him securely to a wall of bamboo poles. They took off his blindfold and gag.

To Martin's surprise a NVA officer, a gnome of a man, was inside the hut. The officer nodded to Martin, then went to a cooking area in the center of the hut. He took a small bar from his pocket. Martin recognized the piece of C-4 plastic explosive. The officer held a lighter to the material, then dropped it just as it burst into a brilliant flame. He held a pot of water over the high-intensity fire. It started boiling in a few seconds. He made some tea and offered sips from a cup to Martin. They drank their tea in silence. Martin knew that he was being prepared for interrogation. He prepared himself to say as little as possible. After tea, the officer had his men tape a small piece of C-4 to Martin's left eye. He stood with a lighter directly in front of Martin's other eye. Martin could see the insignia of the United States Air Force on the lighter. This guy's been around, thought

Martin. He decided to answer every question. Martin was no hero, just a survivor.

After the interrogation, he was given a large bowl of rice and some water. Then he was thrown into a small bamboo tiger cage inside the hut. The cage was approximately five feet long, three feet wide, and five feet high. In the corner of the cage, Martin saw an empty bucket that smelled of shit. He marked the location in his mind just as they blindfolded him and tied his hands to the wall. His hands were tied in such a way that he could sit down or stand up and the ropes would slide along the bamboo poles. They locked him in the cage, then secured the hut.

Martin fell asleep for several hours. He woke up in the dark. For a moment he saw that the door to his bedroom was open. He could see down the hallway to his parents' room. Before his brain recognized that he was still blindfolded, it detected the humid smells of the jungle. A diarrhea attack brought him back to the reality of the cage. He tried to move the shit bucket closer with his feet but couldn't manage it. Then he ruined his shorts. He called to the VC guards but no one came.

Perhaps they had gone on a night raid against a base camp. Martin suspected that there was one nearby; otherwise they would have put the tiger cage outside. At the very least he figured he was still deep inside friendly territory. But the presence of the NVA interrogation officer puzzled him. Maybe they were going to take him over the border to North Vietnam. He didn't cherish the idea of spending years inside the so-called Hanoi Hilton, although a concrete bed would be an improvement over the cage. If the VC kept him, they would probably end up torturing and killing him once they felt he had told them everything he knew. And he had already told them everything they asked! What more could he say? Martin's heart started racing.

The stories he had heard about VC interrogations flashed through his mind. They used the usual bag of dirty tricks: beatings with well-placed kicks, water dunkings, and pencils hammered into the ears. One of their favorites was to tie the arms back so tightly as to cause the shoulders to dislocate with audible pops. Then they started on the legs. Those that survived to tell about it were almost always permanently crippled. If you screamed too much, they beat you even more. Sometimes they stuffed your mouth with rags soaked in some noxious substance and you vomited through your nose.

Martin knew that his captors were capable of far more brutal tortures if they planned on making an example of your body. Once his men found an elderly South Vietnamese man left alive by the VC. His testicles, nose, ears, and tongue had all been cut off. Bamboo splinters were stuck in his eyes. He wandered aimlessly in the street, unable to help himself because his fingers and thumbs had been cut off.

The sound of voices outside the hut caused Martin to freeze. He was as tense and vigilant as if he were walking point. His hearing seemed amazingly sharp. It sounded like someone was being beaten. After a few minutes, the VC voices drifted away but Martin could still hear a man whimpering. He was very close. Another prisoner? "Hey!" Martin whispered. There was no answer. "Hang on, buddy!" said Martin to the wall.

Martin had to fight back waves of his own fear. His body was all messed up. The diarrhea was dehydrating him badly. Now it seemed like he was swollen all over. His hands and feet felt like cardboard. He couldn't stop sweating. This wasn't dysentery, but something far worse. Maybe he had contracted some mysterious tropical disease. For the first time, Martin believed he was going to die.

Only a few weeks ago he had been on R&R in Saigon. He had gone to a drug parlor where the mamma-san gave him the sweetest, most dreamy opium in the world. Now Martin tried to smell the opium again and remember how it made everything feel wonderful. It didn't work. All he could smell was his own shit and fear.

The sun came up, but very little of it filtered through Martin's blindfold. Some bugs scurried over his legs. At first he thought they were ants, but ants the size of his fist? Then he worried about snakes. There are 133 species of snakes in the jungles of Vietnam. All but two are poisonous. The most common are the kraits, favorites among the VC, who tether them inside their tunnels to kill unsuspecting intruders. Had his captors unleashed a snake or two inside the hut? Martin started panicking again. He pulled his legs in and stood up as high as possible against the bamboo poles. The green bamboo viper is just as deadly. Martin freaked and started thrashing against the ropes. They cut into his wrists. He stopped when they started hitting bone.

He was dying of thirst and called out to his guards. There was no response. Mucus started flowing from his rectum. Martin was crying. He whispered two parched words never before muttered by a Clinton: *"Chu hoi"* (I surrender).

Sleep gave him some escape from the oppressive heat of the day. When he awoke again, his body felt inflated like some balloon. *Where the hell are the guards?* thought Martin. He started yelling out loud.

"Hey, buddy," said a hoarse voice on the other side of the wall.

"Yes, yes," answered Martin. His voice sounded just as hoarse.

"They're gone. We have to stay alive until help comes," said the voice.

"Yes, yes," agreed Martin.

"Be strong."

Martin had heard a gunship off in the distance and figured the VC were caught in a firefight. He knew the voice was right. Someone—either the VC or friendlies—would return. They wouldn't let him die. But, either way, if he could get out, find some weapons, then it would be payback time. Martin began to plot his revenge. This occupied him for most of the day until he fell asleep again.

He awoke looking into the sky at night. There were stars all over. Some appeared like diamonds throwing off rainbows of color. Martin felt detached, almost as if he were floating in space. He stretched out his arms to bask in the feeling. The ropes around his wrists yanked him back to the shit-soaked earth of his cage. Although his body was full of aches and pains, he forced himself back to sleep.

In the morning, after a dreamless sleep, Martin was starving. He called for food but there was no answer. By tilting his head, he could peek out through the corner of his blindfold. After considerable maneuvering, he managed to see the door to the hut. Through a crack in the door, he caught a glimpse of the elephant grass outside. The distinct smell of fried fish filled the air and transported Martin to another time.

Martin always liked these trips in the country with his old man. They parked their trailer near a favorite creek where they fished for trout. Then they would fry the fish over a campfire. It didn't matter that his father caught all the fish. Martin felt happy enough just to share the time with him. Now they were standing in the creek, poles in hand, watching for the telltale tugs on their lines. Martin loved so many things about this spot: the serenity, the elephant grass bending in the wind, even the way the channels snaked their way through the rice paddies. Suddenly, a river assault boat came around the bend in the channel and opened fire on them. His father caught the first rounds. Martin sank to the bottom of the cage.

Now I'm going crazy, thought Martin. He didn't understand why he was hallucinating and suspected the worst.

"Psst," he said to the voice on the other side of the wall. "Where are we?"

"In country," came the answer. It was the grunt expression for Vietnam. Martin started laughing hysterically.

The day passed with Martin trying to find something to eat. He managed to twist his head to the cage floor and lick up what he thought were small grains of rice. After swallowing as much dirt as rice, he began wishing those fist-sized bugs would wander back into reach. At least they could provide some protein.

Sometime later Martin opened his eyes and saw the open door of his bedroom again. He walked out into the hallway. The Christmas tree lights were still on. There was a white cross on the top of the tree. It was glowing.

Much later the wind outside the hut started picking up. Martin recognized the sounds of a helicopter assault. It was over very quickly. The village had been deserted. Martin was the only inhabitant. Somehow he was not surprised to learn that there was no prisoner on the other side of the wall of his hut. And his thirsty body was not swollen, just bruised and numb. Martin felt better when the officer in charge let him torch the village before dust-off to base camp.

When Martin finished telling me his story, I felt that I knew exactly what had happened to him. He was one of several ex-POWs I had recruited for study. Their reactions to imprisonment were very similar.

"Part of what you saw sounds like the prisoner's cinema," I said. I explained that prisoners in solitary confinement or dark dungeons often experience the same visual sensations brought about by isolation and sensory deprivation. It's almost like a movie, I told him, beginning with simple lights and patterns like the Christmas tree lights and diamonds in the night sky. Later on, the movie changes to dreamlike scenes. The movie mixes distant memories, like the fishing trip, with recent or current images such as the elephant grass.

"You're saying it was a goddamn movie?"

"No, no," I said, ignoring his threatening tone. I rushed to add that it's only a movie in the sense that there are common scenes and plots, but everybody's experience is slightly different. For example, many people think about escape or rescue. The more life-threatening the confinement, the more likely these thoughts will turn into vivid images, then hallucinations. This can happen to anyone in a traumatic situation. Even the little kids from Chowchilla, California, who were kidnapped and buried underground in 1976 saw hopeful hallucinations of the outside world. I told Martin the story of the mine disaster in Pennsylvania where two miners were trapped for fourteen days in a small shaft three hundred feet below the ground. One miner saw a door leading to a set of marble steps and freedom. The second miner saw an open door leading outside to a big garden. Both men, who had strong religious backgrounds, saw Pope John, dressed in papal garb, promising them rescue.

"Your vision of an open bedroom door leading to a hallway and your parents' room," I explained, "was a blend of childhood memories and wishful thinking about a rescue. You said you wanted to go home. You also wanted company so badly you started talking to yourself. These imaginal dialogues can sometimes fool prisoners into believing that the 'inner voice' of their consciousness is actually another prisoner. Most of the hallucinations in solitary confinement are voices like these, not visions."

I told Martin about Edgar Allan Poe's experience when he was thrown into Moyamensing Prison in Philadelphia for forging a check. Poe was comforted by a white female figure who spoke to him in whispers. "If I had not heard what she said," declared Poe to a friend, "it would have been the end of me." Martin's dialogue with the imaginary POW functioned in the same comforting way. Of course, some hallucinations, like the vision of Martin's father getting killed, are unwanted and terrifying. Poe had a similar experience: "To torture me and to wring my heart, they brought out my mother, Mrs. Clemm, to blast my sight by seeing them first saw off her feet to the ankles, then her legs to the knees, her thighs to the hips."

"It wasn't real!" screamed Martin. "I saw men get wasted like that."

"But anxiety and stress can make such hallucinations seem real," I insisted. "Many prisoners in solitary confinement during Poe's time went mad because they believed their hallucinations *were real*."

Then I told Martin about the experiments conducted in a special "watery tomb" designed to mimic the type of stress a POW might endure. The technique was to suspend subjects in a dark tank of water covered with a lightproof dome. In less than five hours everyone was hallucinating. Perhaps the most dramatic evidence that the stress of imprisonment could be duplicated by the watery tomb was obtained from a subject who had been a POW during the Korean War. When the researchers placed him in the tank, he reacted hysterically and began reliving the horrifying ordeal of being tortured by the Chinese Communists. He saw and heard the torture. He believed it was happening again.

"Bullshit!" yelled Martin. "I've had my share of flashbacks about it, but they're different." He leaned forward on the chair and put his nose within a hair of my own. "Ever get scared of the dark, buddy?" he snarled.

"Sure," I said. "Sometimes everyone gets frightened." I was feeling a little frightened by Martin's sudden aggression.

Martin moved back on his chair. "So I like to sleep with the lights on and a gun under my pillow. So what the fuck does that mean? That I'm still in the cage?" He was sneering.

"What do you think?" I asked him.

"Fuck no! I might still be rattled by Nam, but nothing, absolutely *nothing* is the same as being there in the cage."

Martin stood up and started pacing around my small office. "You act like some kind of holier-than-thou professor. You don't know diddly." He kicked the file cabinet, then turned around and pointed at the tape recorder. "You can listen to what happened to me, but you can't know what it felt like. Ever think you would die in a cage?" He yelled this last question into my ear.

"Martin, please sit down. You're making me nervous." I knew it was the wrong thing to say even as the words were still forming on my tongue.

"Nervous? You sit in a fuckin' cage!"

"Okay," I said as calmly as I could. Martin glared at me. "I'll try. . . . I'm serious," I added. I was.

Klüver had once told me to "become the fly" and participate in my own experiments in order to experience and understand hallucinations. I had done this before. Some of the studies involved long hours inside dark soundproofed rooms or floating in water tanks. I didn't think that sitting in a tiger cage for a few days would be too difficult. Besides, I had already spent the better part of a day cramped up inside a small monkey cage in my primate lab in order to better understand what the animals were experiencing. After that, a tiger cage should seem like the Taj Mahal.

I decided to set up a sensory isolation experiment. I wanted to see if the stress of imprisonment in a cage alone, minus the life-threatening conditions, would be sufficient to produce hallucinations. Martin agreed to act as both technical advisor and co-experimenter. He would supervise my imprisonment in a facsimile of the tiger cage.

I located an unused steel baboon cage of almost the exact same measurements as the bamboo cage used by the VC. We moved it into building 156, an isolated structure located on the grounds of the Brentwood Veterans Administration Hospital, where the Vietnam movie *Coming Home* was filmed. The building was once home to psychiatrically disturbed vets but had been turned into a dead storage area. The wards were now packed with file cabinets, boxes, empty animal cages, and discarded laboratory equipment. Some of my own equipment had been stored there for years.

We opened the basement door to 156 and started rolling the cage down a long corridor. The lights didn't work. There was no longer any electricity to the building. Small vent holes in the side rooms off the main corridor funneled in narrow beams of sunlight. The air seemed smoky and full of dancing dust particles. In this eerie light, I saw that our shoes left footprints in the thick dust that carpeted the floor. We found an empty room in the center of the basement floor. It had a concrete floor, thick concrete walls covered with plaster, and a concrete ceiling lined with disconnected water pipes and electrical lines. You could scream your head off in here and nobody would hear. When the door to the room was closed, it was so dark that a blindfold would be unnecessary. There was no ventilation in the room, and we were both sweating profusely. Martin said it was hotter than Nam. I knew this room was the perfect place for my cage.

We waited for the Thanksgiving holiday weekend to begin. It would be the only time when I could spare a "lost weekend" and the best time to avoid any intruders on our experiment. I entered the cage on Thursday, Thanksgiving day. My only meal of the day was a bowl of rice and all the water I could drink. Martin watched as I swallowed a handful of laxatives to simulate the diarrhea. Then he frisked me to make sure I had nothing other than my T-shirt, underpants, shorts, and sneakers. He handed me a plastic shit bucket and pushed me inside the cage.

There were two concessions to comfort and safety. One was to eliminate the ropes. Since the ropes had prevented Martin only from reaching the door to his bamboo cage without ever completely restricting his movements, I decided this would not be a critical factor in the production of hallucinations. Besides, the steel door to my cage was strong enough to withstand the pounding of any primate. The other concession was that Martin would return each day with a bowl of rice and water. He would also have a first aid kit with glucose and salt tablets, electrolyte fluids, and high-energy food bars—just in case. But he would not speak to me and would not open the cage until two and a half days had elapsed, no matter what. I kept reminding him to check on me every twelve hours and feed me every twenty-four.

Martin padlocked the cage door. "You're gonna have to be a magician to get out of here," he snickered. He closed the room door, then started taping up the cracks with duct tape. That wasn't in the game plan!

"Hey!" I yelled. "What are you doing?"

As the last flicker of light disappeared, he yelled back from the darkness: "Ever think you would die in a cage, buddy?"

I started screaming at Martin. The only ventilation was from the door and now he had sealed it! I was worried about getting enough air to breathe. Then, as my eyes adjusted to the darkness, I saw a hole where the doorknob and lock had been removed. Martin hadn't sealed it and some light was spilling through from the basement hallway. That meant I would get some air with the added bonus of knowing whether it was day or night.

Only sixty more hours to go, I thought.

The first thing I did was inspect my new home. I could sit easily enough, but it was impossible to stand up without hunching over. Lying down on the steel mesh floor was just as problematic unless I curled up in a fetal position. Since I was already sweating from the limited exploration of the cage, I removed my shorts and folded them into a little pillow. By resting my head on the pillow, and keeping my back on the cold steel floor with my knees raised, I was almost cool, but far from comfortable. I regretted not putting a mat and dirt on the cage floor to make it both softer and more realistic.

It was very quiet. I tried to lie perfectly still and listen. I thought I heard the muffled sound of a truck outside, but nothing else. I called out "hello." There was no echo; the cry just seemed to die out in the distance. I called again. Again the sound trailed off without finding a wall or other object to bounce it back. I felt that I was in the center of some vast, uncharted hollow.

Boredom was my first worry. Despite my planning for this experiment, I had neglected to bring along a mental plan of action to amuse myself. I knew that subjects in sensory deprivation experiments go through a predictable sequence of cognitive activities that are difficult to stop. At first they tend to think about the experiment. Then come the thoughts about personal problems. This is followed by reminiscences of recent memories. As times goes on, more distant childhood memories emerge. Some subjects have busied themselves with details of a particular movie, travel plans, or even solving mathematical puzzles in their heads. Eventually, concentration becomes too difficult and people let their minds wander. That's when the hallucinations start. Since there was nothing I could do to hasten events, I decided to play along with the naturally evolving program.

My most pressing personal problem was the experiment. Now that I was committed to it, it seemed overwhelmingly real. As I went over the details in my mind, I realized it had been designed in haste. I probably hadn't needed to make it so severe. I made a mental list of several items that could have improved my comfort without compromising the scientific value: a floor mat, an electric fan, maybe even some environmental tapes to provide background sounds of wind and birds. Even Martin could listen to such sounds outside his hut.

Then I started to think a lot about Martin. Although the VA psychiatrists had decided he was not suffering from post-traumatic stress disorder, he exhibited several characteristic symptoms. First, he admitted to having flashbacks about Vietnam, including the tiger cage. Despite his claim that he could handle these events, I remembered that he refused to enter the baboon cage and inspect it! Second, he admitted he was always on edge, especially at night, and didn't sleep well. Third, he had persistent outbursts of anger, as I had discovered. I recalled the venom in his voice when he spoke those haunting words: "Ever think you would die in a cage?" Martin may not have been certifiable, but he was *troubled*. The word made me uneasy. I had entrusted my safety to this man.

Martin was the only person in the world who knew I was here. I could die in here without him. What if he got in a car accident with that beat-up old van of his? He never wore seat belts. What if he ended up unconscious or dead? *I should have arranged some emergency back-up*, I thought. At the very least, I should have kept a key to the padlock. I sat up and pulled on the lock. Martin had chosen a hardened steel lock, pick-proof and saw-proof. I sat down and closed my eyes, telling myself that he would be back in a few hours to check on me. *Then I'll ask him for an emergency key*.

There wasn't a big difference between closing my eyes and keeping them open. The blue arcs and spots of phosphenes were not shy. They danced unabashedly around the periphery of my visual field. I noticed a number of checkerboards, one of the hallucinatory form constants discovered by Klüver, but a pattern I personally saw only on rare occasions. Perhaps the checkerboardlike mesh of the cage floor, which I had been silently cursing for hours, was impressing itself on more than my backside. Although I hadn't rigged a tape recorder for this experiment, I started describing the imagery out loud using the psychonaut code. This kept me busy for what seemed like a very long time. I stopped only when I realized my mouth was getting dry and I had to conserve my strength.

I glanced over to the door. The light was no longer visible

through the hole so I assumed it was night. I closed my eyes again and tried to sleep.

Sometime later I was startled by a rumbling. I snapped to attention only to discover the noise was coming from my intestines. The laxatives were plowing their way through. I tried to ignore it for a while, hoping the sensations would disappear. They didn't. Finally, I was forced to use the bucket, only to discover there was no toilet paper. I added it to my wish list.

I used the bucket several more times before the night was over. A cover for the bucket would have helped. I tried to ignore the smells by closing my eyes and concentrating on the visuals. I saw a dark tunnel that looked like a pit. Somehow I couldn't shake the idea that it was a latrine and the little specks of light dancing in the tunnel were latrine flies. Then they started to remind me of fireflies.

Fireflies were one of the things I missed in California. As a boy I used to spend endless hours watching them dart along the hedges in our backyard in Herkimer, New York. Sometimes I would catch a few and put them in a bottle. But I always felt sorry for them and let them go. It was more fun trying to figure out their flashing code. A male firefly would send out a rhythmic pattern of flashes when he was ready to mate. A receptive female, usually sitting on the hedges, would answer with the same pattern of flashes, only brighter. Then the male would fly to the female and touch her with his antennae. One night, I saw a male and female start to copulate. This wild sex scene was rudely interrupted by my mother, who called me into the house.

"Ronnie." My eyes popped open at the sound of my name. It was my mother's voice, but I didn't know if I had imagined it or heard it. My heart was beating hard. I realized where I was and suddenly felt trapped by the darkness, the heat, and the fear.

I've been here before. I was about ten years old and a member of the Club, a group of neighborhood boys who played together. We were good kids, nothing like the Snake Gang several blocks away. The Snake Gang threw their enemies into a pit filled with an unimaginable assortment of reptiles. One day, when we were feeling particularly brave—or stupid—we went searching for their pit. We found it. From the top of the pit we could see a lone garter snake. I inched forward to see if there were others. The grass at the edge of the pit was slippery and in I went, feet first.

I was trapped in the pit, which was a good six feet deep. I started crying hysterically. My friends kept saying that garter snakes won't hurt you. I didn't trust garter snakes and suspected that anyone who said they were harmless had never been in a grave-deep pit with one of them. I kept bawling until they found a man with a ladder who got me out.

Now in the darkness of the cage I watched red and yellow Day-Glo snakes twisting and curling on the ceiling of my vision. I chuckled. The snakes were funny. They nipped and licked at one another, then tied themselves into knots. The snakes drifted away and were replaced by rows of little yellow men wearing sailor hats. The sailors jumped into the water. Puddles of water flowed across the ceiling of the cage.

I was dying of thirst. I got up and looked at the door. The light was starting to come through the hole again. *Martin is sure to be here any minute. In fact, he should have been here at the twelve-hour mark, which would have been sometime during the night. What the hell happened? He probably called to me without opening the door and I was sleeping and didn't hear him. Of course, that's what happened.*

The light lifted my spirits and I started to sing. Then I tried to sleep some more.

I awoke in a panic. Martin had not shown up! I was getting worried. It had to be more than twenty-four hours. I yelled for him several times. No response. Then I screamed for help. Even if someone could hear me outside the building, a screaming man was nothing unusual on the grounds of the Brentwood VA. After all, this was the National Home for Men, the domicile of the worst psychiatric casualties from America's wars. And across the road from the VA was the National Cemetery, where there was no one to hear me.

Except the fly. A fly started buzzing near my shit bucket. I couldn't see it but I knew it was there. "Here, fly. Here, boy," I said. "Nice shit for you! Bring your friends. Have a picnic. Eat it all." The fly must have entered through the hole in the door. *Become the fly, Klüver had said. Ha! That's a laugh. If I could really become the fly, I'd fly out through that hole. Now I'm going to die in this shit hole with the fly.* I realized I had to plan an escape.

The fly and I formed an escape committee. I discussed all my options out loud with him. The wheels of the cage were locked with simple levers. If I could reach them through the bars, and manage to unlock them, the cage would be free to roll. By throwing my weight back and forth, and pushing with my hands against the walls of the room, I might be able to roll the cage to the door. Then, out the door, down the hall, and right up to the basement door. But the basement door could not be opened without the key! The fly rejected the plan.

Next, I suggested trying to remove the cage floor. The baboon cage was designed so that the mesh floor and stainless steel pan under it would slide out for cleaning. If I could slide them out, it would be a simple matter of tipping over the cage and crawling out the bottom to freedom. The only thing holding the floor and tray in place was a steel flange welded to the cage door. Somehow I had to break the flange. I couldn't reach the flange with my hand. But I might be able to make a hook from the wire handle of the shit bucket to do the trick. The fly didn't think it would be strong enough to break the weld. He was probably right.

I had to try something. So I got up off the floor by bracing myself between the bars and used my hands to slide the steel mesh floor toward the cage door. It moved about a half inch until the flange stopped it. I slid it back and tried again. The bucket made sloshing sounds, but I didn't think it would tip over. I began moving the floor back and forth, striking the flange as hard as I could. After about two hours of doing this, nothing happened. It might eventually weaken the weld, but the work was already taking a toll on my stamina. I assumed my supine position on the floor and fell asleep.

In my dream I was crawling on my belly through a maze of dry, dusty passages winding around and over and through one another like tunnels in an anthill. At some point I realized that I had crawled right back into the same spot where I started!

I woke up. The light was starting to fade again. It had to be way past twenty-four hours.

"Don't fuck with me, Martin," I yelled. "I know you're there." I rattled the cage door to get his attention. The fly was buzzing somewhere in the far end of the room.

"Go for the light," I said to the fly. If he didn't get out through the hole now, he might die in here.

I got up on the side of the cage wall again and started

working on the floor. It was exhausting, yet it kindled my competitive spirit. I was unwilling to accept defeat by the cage. The laxatives had finally stopped working and that made me feel relatively better. I pumped myself up with anger and continued banging as long as I could.

When I rested, I closed my eyes and concentrated on my imagery. There were the usual geometrics but little else. I tried to picture the grounds outside building 156. My car was still parked in the lot. I convinced myself that I would get in it and drive home as soon as the experiment ended in another day or so. The thought helped me sleep again.

I woke up with a terrific headache. The hole in the door told me it was the middle of the night. But I thought I saw a momentary flash of red light, like someone using a military flashlight with a night filter. Martin! There were rustling noises in the darkness.

"It's about time," I said.

There was no response. Of course he wouldn't answer; that was part of the agreement. No talking to the prisoner.

"I'd like some water," I asked.

Silence.

I realized he was not there. That's when I started planning my payback. I would discuss the details with the fly in the morning.

In the morning I heard the fly buzzing. The buzzing sounded like "fugazi," Namspeak for someone who goes mad. Call me fugazi but the revenge I planned against Martin was deserved. My idea was to set up a booby trap over the door to the room with my shit bucket. "Fuck 'im if he can't take a joke," I said to the fly, then laughed for the first time since I entered the cage. Of course, if Martin showed up right then with an ice-cold beer, I would have dropped the plan. For two beers and a chocolate bar I would have dropped the bucket on my own head.

I was too dizzy to work on the floor. Instead, I tried to watch my imagery but kept falling asleep. I was now trying to sleep as much as possible, hoping this would make the experiment go faster.

The fly died sometime after dark. I heard it buzzing around on the floor the way flies do at the end. There had been no more sounds from it for hours. *Become the fly and die, right, Klüver?*

I started calculating the time out loud. It was difficult to concentrate, but I finally decided that it was late Saturday night, close to the sixty-hour mark. If Martin didn't show up soon, I would have to go back to my escape plan.

A cramp in my foot woke me up. I took my sneakers off and massaged my feet. It felt good and I continued rubbing my legs, then my hands and arms. *What time is it?* I pushed the question out of my head, pretended that I wasn't there, and went back to sleep.

I woke up with my hands cupping my groin. I hadn't slept in that position since I was a little kid, frightened by a bad dream. The cold steel cage was all around me. This was no dream.

"Martin!" I yelled. It must have been more than seventy-two hours. The light was shining through the hole again.

"Martin! Is that you?"

"Yes, yes," he answered. "Hold on."

I heard the tape being ripped from the door. Martin came into the room.

"Jesus, it stinks in here," he said.

"Where were you?" I said as I eyed the emergency knapsack full of drinks and food.

"Went fishing. I wanted you to have a real experiment, so no food or water. And I waited an extra day. You okay, buddy?"

He opened the cage door. I stepped out on cardboard legs and grabbed a bottle of water.

"Yeah, I'm okay." I was too proud to tell him that I had thought about dying in the cage and too thankful to hit him.

POSTSCRIPT

Martin's symptoms have diminished over the years, and he no longer feels on edge. But he still has the occasional flashback whenever he sees an animal in a cage. I do, too.

15

DOPPELGANGER

Doppelganger. You may not recognize the word, but you would know one if you saw one. It is a ghostly double of yourself. Unlike ghosts of the dearly departed, a *doppelganger* is a hallucinatory duplicate of a living person, and that person is the only one who can see it. The effect is startling. Picture looking at yourself in a mirror—without the mirror. Or visualize bumping into an identical twin you never knew existed. Can you imagine the shock of running smack into an exact copy of yourself?

The fictional literature abounds with these doubles. Dostoevsky used the *doppelganger* motif in several novels, including *The Double*. His characters see their doubles at dusk or night, usually when they are alone in a bedroom. The doubles are gray or colorless and often behave in strange ways. While Dostoevsky understood that the double was a hallucination, his characters are not always so sure. Surrounded by chaos, darkness, and suffering, they see the figures as real.

But doubles are not just literary inventions. In the syndrome known as autoscopy, a person may have a hallucination of his own body image projected into external visual space. The syndrome is associated with a variety of organic conditions such as temporal-lobe epilepsy (the type of epilepsy known to have affected Dostoevsky). Autoscopic hallucinations can also be brought about by diseases that cause neurological damage. In *Le Horla*, Guy de Maupassant described the doubles he saw while suffering from advanced syphilis. Although he recognized the hallucinatory nature of the experience, it was still frightening.

A variety of psychological conditions can cause autoscopic hallucinations. Severe emotional stress, anxiety, depression, even physical exhaustion have all been known to bring on the syndrome. In order to cope with the inhuman conditions at Auschwitz, Nazi doctors gradually created doubles of themselves to carry out the diabolic killing. But fear of impending doom works fastest. Fear can literally scare the *doppelganger* out of someone. Edgar Allan Poe, himself a victim of periodic attacks of fear, described such a *doppelganger* in "William Wilson." In the story, the mentally troubled Wilson is tormented by visions of his double. He finally confronts the double in a small chamber and stabs him repeatedly through the bosom with a sword. As the double begins to totter, Wilson glances in a mirror and is horrified by what he sees: "But what human language can adequately portray *that* astonishment, *that* horror which possessed me at the spectacle then presented to view?" In the mirror Wilson sees that he is covered with blood and realizes he has murdered himself!

Poe's story came to life in 1964 when Mrs. F., a young woman who had recently moved from Okinawa, was shopping in Seattle, Washington. A woman who looked exactly like Mrs. F. walked past her. Mrs. F. became upset and rushed home. The next day, Mrs. F heard a knock on her apartment door. Before she had time to open it, the woman from the previous day was standing inside the door. The woman, speaking in a voice that sounded just like her own, told her to go outside. When Mrs. F. went to the closet to get her coat, the woman put a belt around her neck, then asked Mrs. F. to help hold it while she strangled her. Mrs. F. cried as the belt tightened, then passed out. When she recovered, the woman took a pair of scissors and proceeded to cut off the front portion of her tongue.

Mrs. F. opened the closet door and crawled to the kitchen, where she collapsed. Her husband found her and called the police. The police arrived and saw that the tiny closet was coated with blood. On the floor, they found a leather belt, a pair of bloody scissors, and a piece of tongue. There was no evidence of a struggle with another woman or anyone else. In fact, the closet barely had standing room for one small person. The police classified the incident as attempted suicide. A team of examining psychiatrists reported that Mrs. F. was suffering from severe depression. She felt friendless and anxious in her new country. It was this emotional distress that had liberated the aggressive double.

After reading about Mrs. F., I started looking for my own cases to study. In the Los Angeles County Jail I met a young man who had bumped into his double while on a PCP-assisted walk through a neighborhood park. The double chased the man back to his house, where he tried to grab a baseball bat from the closet. But the double got it first and repeatedly hit him over the head with it. Then, at the UCLA Hospital I saw a middle-aged woman who was recovering from the surgical amputation of a leg. Her double, who appeared with both legs intact, came out of a closet and attacked her with a pillow, attempting to suffocate her. The woman threw a pitcher of water on the double, causing it to dissolve.

I was beginning to believe that all *doppelganger*s found in books and closets were malcontents bent on doing harm to people. There didn't seem to be any friendly doubles until I met Agnes Hill, one of the sweetest grandmothers you'd ever want to meet. One night, in the unlikely location of her hall closet, Agnes Hill had the pleasure of meeting Agnes Hill.

Agnes Hill's hall closet measured two feet wide and six feet long. Inside were several light jackets, a red blouse she had stopped wearing years ago, and a raincoat that was totally unnecessary in the desert climate of Santa Ana, California. Agnes liked the climate, saying it was good for her arthritis and wonderful to be near her teenage grandson, Gary. They had always had a close relationship, and, since her husband died, Gary had been visiting her almost every day. Agnes let him use the extra bedroom whenever he wanted. He was always bringing in his young friends, sometimes at all hours of the night. But they were good children, never making noise and going so far as to talk in whispers so as not to disturb her. Having teenagers around the house made Agnes feel young. She started thinking about wearing the red blouse again.

The doorbell rang. Agnes looked at her watch. *Ten-thirty. It's probably Gary coming for the night,* she thought. She turned down the volume on the television, grabbed her cane, and went to the front door. The bell rang again before she could open the door. A tall, thin boy stood in the darkness.

"Is Gary here?" he asked.

"No dear, he's not," replied Agnes.

"He told me to wait if he wasn't here yet."

Normally, Agnes would have invited Gary's friends to wait inside. She'd offer them a glass of soda and some chocolate chip cookies she always kept on hand. But Agnes didn't recognize this boy. He seemed so much bigger and older than the rest of Gary's friends.

"Well dear, I don't—"

The boy lunged forward, cutting short Agnes's words and pushing her backward into the house. She slipped and fell on her hip. The shock took her breath away. In a split second the intruder was behind her, twisting her arms with a viselike grip.

"If you make a sound, *I'll kill you,*" he whispered. His breath had a medicinal smell. It wasn't alcohol, but more like the way Gary smelled after playing in his room with his friends. The intruder dragged her into the hall closet, then closed the door on her.

Agnes started to get up. It was difficult without the cane, but she knew that nothing had been broken in the fall. She braced herself against the walls of the closet and managed to get to her knees. The closet door flew open. The black silhouette of the intruder towered over her. He spun her around, then tied her hands behind her back with a length of telephone cord ripped from the wall. Agnes had only the one phone and wondered how she would call for help. But the question didn't seem to matter because now the boy was tying a gag around her mouth.

"Stay!" said the intruder. "Lie down! Stay!" He closed the closet door and left Agnes in darkness. She started crying.

She knew the noises of her house as well as her own body. After all, she had lived in both for more than sixty years. That's how she could tell that the intruder had gone into Gary's room and was busy opening drawers. What could he be looking for? There was nothing of value, except perhaps Gary's collection of pharmaceutical scales. After many minutes, she heard the intruder in the kitchen. Her silver was there! And her purse! Agnes started kicking her feet against the closet walls in frustration. The closet door flew open again. The black shape of the boy loomed in the doorway. He was holding something in his raised hand. Agnes recognized her favorite boning knife. She fainted.

When Agnes recovered, she was alone in the closet. The house was quiet. The hall light was still on, framing the edges of the closet door with a thin band of light. Agnes sat up and positioned herself in front of the keyhole. She had a good view of the hallway leading to the kitchen and bedrooms, as well as a direct view of the den. The boy was sitting on the couch eating something. The flickering glow in the room told her the television was on but without the sound. Agnes watched the boy for a while, then fell asleep.

The closet door opened and Agnes snapped awake. The boy said something about the bathroom. He helped her to her feet, then flashed the knife in front of her eyes. "Not a sound," he whispered. Agnes nodded her head. Then he untied her hands, removed the gag, and led her to the bathroom. Inside the bathroom, she noticed that her pill bottles had been disturbed and several were missing. But she found her calcium tablets and aspirin and took them with plenty of extra water. After she finished, he put her back in the closet.

Many hours later, Agnes had wiggled her hands free. She took the gag off and was starting to get up when the door opened again. Agnes saw the knife and threw her hands up in front of her face. The back of her left hand went into the knife. There was the sound of bone breaking. Agnes reached for her bleeding hand just as the knife came down into her right palm. She fell to the floor, covering her face with her arms. The knife came down again, this time knicking her forearm. The boy jumped on top of her, straddling her like a horse.

"Where's Gary's stash?" he yelled in her face. There was a slight quiver on his lips. "I found his pipe. Where's the base?"

Agnes was too scared to cry. She shook her head. She didn't

know what he was talking about. After all, she wouldn't recognize cocaine free base even if she smelled it. The boy retied her hands extra tight, put the gag back in her mouth, then left her in darkness again.

Sometime later Agnes felt like she was in a train tunnel. The closet door seemed hundreds of feet away. The light around the door started pulsating with flames of color. Each time a flame erupted, Agnes felt her hand throb with pain. The walls of the closet were covered with luminescent flowers and fancy lace patterns. Agnes tried to make them go away by blinking her eyes, but it only made them change colors.

She drifted in and out of sleep. At one point she thought she was dreaming when she saw the little cottage she used to rent for her vacations at Lake Arrowhead. She was still watching these scenes when she heard the boy start to tear the house apart. Agnes got to the keyhole—she felt like she was floating toward it—and looked out.

The hallway looked deserted. Then the black silhouette of the boy moved across the hall into the kitchen. Agnes watched helplessly. Suddenly she saw a little old woman appear in the hall. The woman had gray hair tied in a bun and was wearing a lavender dress identical to her own.

That's me, thought Agnes with remarkable acceptance.

Agnes watched through the keyhole as her double floated into the den—*without a cane!* Then the boy appeared in the hall carrying some tools. He entered the den, but somehow he didn't see the other Agnes. Agnes smiled at her double. The boy turned up the volume on the television, then went into Gary's bedroom. Despite the sounds from the television, Agnes could hear hammering noises. The boy was ripping up the hardwood floors. Agnes moaned.

The double waited until the boy came out of Gary's room and went into the kitchen. Then she went into Gary's room. Agnes knew she was inspecting the damage and straightening up as best she could. It would be all right for Agnes to sleep again.

Much later the door of the closet opened. He untied her hands, removed the gag, and gave her a bowl of food and a can of soda. Agnes recognized the leftover meatloaf and cold vegetables. Since he had not given her any utensils, and her hands hurt too much to hold the food, she was forced to eat with her mouth in the bowl. Agnes had always told Gary to eat slowly and act dignified at the table. Here she was wolfing down the food like an animal. She whimpered softly into her food. After eating everything, she wiped her face with the gag, then dabbed some soda on her cut hands. In a few minutes, the boy returned and retied the gag. Agnes could taste the meat loaf and dried blood on the cloth. She noticed that the cord around her hands was tied very loosely this time. *He has some goodness in him,* she thought.

During the night Agnes realized she had wet herself. She banged against the closet door until he opened it and took her to the bathroom again. The boy seemed especially nervous and irritable. Agnes didn't think he'd slept at all. On the way back to the closet, she was about to suggest he get some rest when she saw the duplicate Agnes standing in Gary's bedroom. She must have said something because the next thing she knew the boy bolted into Gary's room and began yelling for Gary to come out. The boy was frantic, running about the room, checking under the bed, even poking the knife into the drapes. Agnes stared at the damage already done to the room. The mattress and pillows had been ripped apart. Floorboards had been torn away. Even the covers over the air-conditioning vents had been pulled out of the walls. Every drawer was open, the contents strewn everywhere. Agnes bent down to pick up some of the clothes.

A hand grabbed her hair and yanked her to her feet. She saw his eyes. They were totally black, all pupils and no color. He looked as dead as the night. His other hand locked around her neck like a steel collar. He pulled her back to the closet. *Like a dog,* Agnes thought.

Agnes dreamed she was walking down a long aisle in a supermarket. Her cart was full of canned goods and produce. Without warning, a black man jumped in front of her cart, blocking her way. He started to take her groceries.

"Who are you?" asked Agnes.

"I am Night!" he answered. "I commit crimes."

.   .   .

Agnes woke up and stared into the emptiness of the closet. The pain in her hand was almost unbearable. From the kitchen she heard the refrigerator door open and the clinking of a bottle. She stayed awake listening and hurting until the morning when he came to take her to the bathroom.

On the way to the bathroom, Agnes noticed that the boy was no longer holding the knife. He was walking a few steps behind her as she passed her bedroom. Out of the corner of her eye she saw the double sitting on her bed. "Get help," she whispered.

The boy heard her, rushed into the bedroom, and started a frenzied search of the room. The double floated right past him and into the kitchen. Agnes followed herself into the kitchen and right out the back door of the house! She ran to a neighbor who telephoned the police.

When the police arrived, Agnes gave them a description of the boy. They arrested a transient wandering in the area who matched the description. The suspect claimed that they had the wrong person. "It must have been someone else," he said, "someone who looks exactly like me." Neither the police nor the jury believed him.

16

THE
SCREAM

I experienced the great, endless scream of nature.
—EDVARD MUNCH,
on *The Scream*

There's a torture that cannot be comprehended, a pain that goes on and on. The body is helpless to stop it. The mind cannot endure. So it journeys to another place, a side show where it is temporarily blinded by fantastic and wondrous scenes. The price of admission for one Phillip Frost, adventurer and petty criminal, was a simple scream.

Phillip Frost started his trip in Santa Cruz, a dusty, windswept town on the edge of the jungle in Bolivia. Although Santa Cruz had its share of modern tourist hotels and restaurants, part of the city had the look of a frontier town in the American West. There were roof-covered sidewalks, hot dust storms whirling across unpaved streets, and the sounds of raucous singing spilling from saloons. Phillip liked the saloons because he liked Pilsener, a local lager beer that he said was the best in Latin

America. He claimed there was nothing better than some *picante saleñas* (local meat stew and hot chili peppers wrapped in dough) washed down with Pilsener.

Of course, Phillip said a lot of things to make his contacts in Bolivia feel good. It was all part of developing deals for one of their other local products. Phillip was in the business of buying cocaine for shipment to the States. And cocaine was Bolivia's business.

It was also the business of Roberto Suarez, the kingpin of the Bolivian cocaine trade, who was determined to protect it. Suarez commissioned Klaus Barbie and Joachim Fiebelkorn to form a paramilitary unit to guard his operations. Barbie, the so-called "Butcher of Lyon," earned his reputation as the Nazi torturer of Jews in the German concentration camps. Joachim Fiebelkorn was little more than a Nazi wanna-be who swaggered around in an SS uniform, singing Nazi songs. The two organized a small band of ruthless thugs who engaged in death squad activity against political rivals and those opposed to Suarez's cocaine trade. They were called the Fiancés of Death.

In July 1980, while Phillip was drinking his Pilsener and trying to score a good coke deal, the one hundred and eighty-ninth coup in Bolivia's history was being planned. The Fiancés had stepped up their activity. Their ranks had grown in recent months, not with trained soldiers or disgruntled Bolivians, but with Italian and Argentinian mercenaries and paramilitaries. They operated as hooded gangs, increasingly arrogant and brutal. By the time the revolution started on July 17, they were kidnapping people off the streets. Barbie guided them on techniques of interrogation and torture.

Phillip was standing in the street that July day when it all started. He was exchanging dollars for pesos with a well-dressed Bolivian man. The official exchange rate was terrible, and Phillip, like many tourists, found it more economical to avoid banks and official exchange shops. Of course Phillip didn't need to do this—he had brought enough money into Bolivia to survive any exchange rate with comfort. But he always enjoyed the thrill of breaking the rules.

A car careened around the corner with tires squealing, then headed down the street. Phillip and the money man moved to the sidewalk and watched. The car stopped just beyond them. A gang of hooded men with automatic weapons got out and started trotting back to them. The money man turned to run but they caught him, beat him to a pulp, then emptied his pockets. Phillip was frozen in fear. The gang turned in his direction. He reached into his shirt, pulled out his money belt, and offered it to the first man who reached him. There was over five thousand dollars there, he said. The men took the money and beat him anyway. Then they hauled Phillip into the car and drove off.

Phillip woke up in a cement cell. He checked to see what time it was. Nine o'clock in the evening. They hadn't bothered to take his watch! Now he knew these were no ordinary thieves. But who were they? And where was he? The cell itself appeared to be part of a large complex of similar rooms. Perhaps it was a police jail or a military prison. Whatever it was, it was not designed for long-term occupancy. The corners of the cell were filled with puddles of excrement. Phillip curled up on the torn mattress and tried to sleep.

In the morning, two hooded men wearing civilian clothes escorted him out of the cell. He asked repeated questions in Spanish and English. They said nothing. He thought that they were after cocaine or money. He offered them tips on his cocaine contacts. He said he could get *muchos* dollars sent to them from the States. They still said nothing. Whatever they were going to do, Phillip at least knew they wouldn't kill him. They were still hiding their faces. Death would come if they took off their hoods.

They led him into a brightly lit room. A large rectangular wooden table stood in the middle. He was ordered to take off his clothes—all of them. Phillip removed his clothes, put his watch inside his shoe, then stood naked under the bright lights. They took him to the table and forced him to bend over one end so that his chest and upper body were flat against the table top. They strapped his wrists and arms to iron rings on the side of the table. Phillip started talking rapidly about his wealth, inflating the size of his cash assets by tens of thousands of dollars. His captors ignored his babbling as they spread his legs and strapped each one to a leg of the table. Phillip stopped talking. *What the hell are they going to do?* he asked himself.

He flashed on an incident from grade school, back in the days when teachers paddled students for unruly behavior. One of his friends was caught talking too much in study hall. He was ordered to come to the front of the class and bend over the teacher's desk. The teacher produced a wooden paddle, cut from a solid piece of pine in the school shop. Taking a stance like an angry batter, the teacher swung at the poor kid's behind with all his might. The first blow knocked the air out of the boy's lungs with an audible "whoompf." The second lifted his body slightly off the desk. The third turned his face carrot red. Phillip studied his friend as he walked back to his seat. The pain was etched on his face. Phillip never forgot that look.

Now Phillip believed he was going to get paddled or beaten, maybe whipped. Why else would they put him in this position? Since his capture, almost twenty-four hours ago, they hadn't asked him one question. What did they want?

A silver-haired man wearing a plastic apron walked into the room. He nodded to the two hooded men, and they grabbed Phillip's head, twisting it so that the man could see his face. He stared at Phillip with eyes magnified by thick glasses. The man had pockmarked skin and a tiny mustache that looked like it was drawn on his face with black pencil. He cupped his hand under Phillip's chin.

"Do you like sardines?" he asked. The accent sounded Mexican.

Phillip didn't know what to say. The question reminded him that he had not eaten and his stomach was growling.

"Yes," answered Phillip. "Please," he added, thinking he might get to eat.

The man gave a diabolic chuckle, then disappeared behind him. The two hooded men moved to the side of the room. Phillip heard some noises behind him but he couldn't identify them. He turned his head all the way to the side, but it was impossible to see what the man was doing.

Something very cold, an unknown liquid, was being rubbed over his rear. Phillip smelled ether. The man was washing him down with ether! Why? He felt a sharp needle pierce his flesh. The sharpness increased and spread. *Not a needle*, thought Phillip. *More like a razor!* It was cutting deep. He froze. His head snapped like an alarmed bird's and his eyes bulged. "Hey!" he yelled. Phillip gripped the table and pressed his body tight against it. He was afraid to move for fear of making the cut worse.

There was a second sharp pain, several inches to the side of the first one. It grew deeper and longer. Phillip felt a little blood running down his thighs. "Hey!" he yelled again. "Stop that!" He was drenched in sweat.

Everything happened quickly now. A third slice, this one on top, connected the other two. Phillip felt something pinch his skin, almost like a pair of pliers.

"Don't!"

Then another pinch.

"Please, don't! No!"

There were weights on the end of whatever was pinching him. It started to pull.

"No!"

His skin was coming up.

"What's going on, what's going on, what's going on, what's going on, what's going on?" wailed Phillip.

The pockmarked creature behind him didn't answer. He was concentrating on preparing the skin flap. First, he used a scalpel to cut down through the epidermis and into the dermis. He made the side cuts about four inches apart and four inches long. After joining them with the third cut, he attached hemostats to the corners and started to pull the skin away, trimming some of the fat lobules in order to free the ends of the flap. He could tell from the pattern of bleeding points that he was at the right depth. Once he had a good grip on the flap, he inserted another hemostat across the top and started rolling it down, much the way a metal key rolls the top off a sardine can. He started detaching the skin with slow, deliberate movements. As he ripped the skin from the underlying bed, stretching microscopic tendrils of tissue past their breaking points, the muscles tensed and stiffened. This acted to reduce the friction and actually made the skinning easier. The flap was going to be a good, thick, painful one.

Phillip uttered a cry of absolute terror. He didn't know if he actually made a sound, but his mouth was wide open. Veins pulsated against the surface of his neck, the muscles straining. The side of his face pressed into the table. He stared at the grain in the wood while his mind flashed on ancient images. A blistering sunburn when he was eight. The palms of his hands scraped raw when he fell off a bicycle at fourteen. And with every changing image, the pain grew. Phillip tried to talk to the man behind him. The creature's silence only added to the horror of his predicament.

Another turn of the hemostat. The pain sparked through his body. He rode the pain along nerves he never knew existed. His cry turned into a scream that vibrated through his body and echoed in his brain. He found he could adjust the frequency of the scream so that it resonated with the pain. He became the pain. This allowed him go ever deeper into his brain. Then, almost by accident, he hit just the right frequency, at just the right moment, and a door opened.

Phillip stepped through. There was no pain here. He turned around and caught a glimpse of his body wiggling in its torture like a frog on a dissecting tray. The body was still screaming. It had to. Otherwise, this sanctuary would cease to exist. But now he was in a place where no pain could touch him.

He was stretched out on the soft sand of a beach. A mist, warmed by the midday sun, sprayed over his body. He pressed himself into the beach, digging with his hands until he reached wet sand. He grabbed a handful. This is reality, he told himself. Everything else seemed ethereal, like a fading memory. The ocean started to seep into the area he had dug, forming a pool around his hand. Reality is here, not there, he told himself.

The air sparkled, fractured into tiny pieces of glass that rained down on him. He dug deeper into the wet sand. His fingers kept opening and closing on the reality of sand and ocean. He inhaled deeply and filled his lungs with the smell of salt water and a sweetish fragrance like gardenias.

It is really quiet here, he realized. You step through this door and enter another place. Then he saw that the place was empty. He decided to build himself a sand castle. When he finished, he crawled on his belly into the castle. It was cooler inside.

Here was the mystery of the universe. And he was lying on top of it. His body pressed into it, fucking it, trying to possess its secrets. The essence of time and space, of life and death, all condensed into a single idea, almost within his grasp. He must try harder to reach it. He almost had it when the foam of the ocean came in. It swept over his feet, around

his torso, and up into his mouth. Then it receded, pulling him out, past
the castle entrance and through the door.

Phillip stopped screaming. Foam dribbled from his mouth and nose. The hemostat turned again, then stopped. His body, convulsed with pain, sunk against the restraints. He felt the hemostats as they were removed, leaving a large flap of skin dangling from his rear like a bloody washcloth.

The hooded men removed his straps, then pulled him to his feet. Only the pain kept him from passing out. They let him lean on them as they guided him back to the cell. Phillip strained to look at his wound. The flap was still attached by the lower end. Carefully, he picked up the flap and put it back. He held it in place until he could crawl back to the mattress and lie on his stomach. A few minutes later, someone threw his clothes into the cell, then locked the door. *What kind of animals are these people?* he asked himself.

Later, a hooded man entered his cell and interrogated him. Phillip answered every question. He had never been so honest in his whole life.

Two days after that, they came for him again. He was weakened by lack of food and water and didn't protest when they strapped him onto the table. He had answered all their questions now and didn't know what else to say.

The man with the apron entered the room and cupped Phillip's chin again.

"Do you like sardines?" he asked.

Phillip started kissing his hand. The man gave one of his diabolic laughs, then pulled his hand away and went to work.

First, he inspected the flap. The process of adhesion had already begun with the growth of fibrin clots, causing the flap to stick to its bed of raw flesh. Soon capillary buds would start to grow into the fibrin layer. The fibrin would grow into fibrous tissue and complete the attachment process. The man took an edge of the flap in each hand and yanked it away.

Phillip bellowed curses.

Then the man started to prepare a new flap on the other side.

Phillip cursed, pleaded, confessed to impossible deeds, then cursed again. The incisions and clamping would not be interrupted. Phillip started screaming. He searched for the right frequency of scream. He had to find it quickly, before the man started to raise the new flap. By the time the hemostat was turning, Phillip was on the beach.

The sun was shining in a cloudless sky. Beads of perspiration ran down his face, dripping onto the sand. He watched as the sand sucked it up, leaving behind dark stains. He heard the ocean crashing against the rocks. Somewhere, seagulls were screaming.

He saw her standing there. She had slender hips and long hair. She was naked. She lay down next to him, inviting him to couple. He kissed her. Her lips felt sweaty. He embraced her, clutching her with all his strength, digging his fingers into her sides. Their legs locked around each other. He watched her face cry out, reflecting his own.

The seagulls screamed again. He looked up into the blue sky. The sky was inverted. It was ocean. Rocks were falling. Slivers of seashells and pellets of quartz sand rained down, stinging and burning him.

He found the castle and crawled in. The inside was aglow with luminescent sea creatures stuck to the walls. Here and there tiny insects scurried across the surface of fluorescent puddles. The light permitted him to see the shape of the room. It was a giant shell, a cathedral. The answer was here. The meaning of life, the secret of secrets. He inched forward. Then he realized he was still inside her, their bodies stuck together with sweat and sand. They pushed on as one, but they could not go very far. Up ahead, the answer. He tried to pull out of her. She wouldn't let him. She said it hurt too much.

Opposites are the same, he told her. Hot is cold. Pain is pleasure. We must go on. Just a little farther, a little longer. The answer to God, the universe, everything is waiting. He pushed away from her with a sudden backward thrust of his hips.

"My God! My God! My God!" she cried out.

The sea rushed into the castle. He was caught in a riptide and pulled away. He cried out as he left her wriggling in pain like a worm on a hook. He kept slipping backward. He saw the castle receding into the distance. Still he zoomed back. Now the beach was flying past him. He was moving backward across the ocean. Then he started to sink into its black depths. He gasped for air.

Phillip was hyperventilating now. The man had finished and was putting away the hemostats. When Phillip saw the flap he had prepared this time, he passed out.

Later, in his cell, they came and interrogated him again. They asked the same questions. He answered truthfully. Then the silver-haired man sprinkled sulfur powder into Phillip's wounds and attached some crude bandages.

That night they took him back to Santa Cruz and let him go.

POSTSCRIPT

The Fiancés of Death and their reign of terror ended in the spring of 1981.

Joachim Fiebelkorn fled to Brazil, where he was arrested carrying three kilos of cocaine and a collection of Nazi pamphlets and uniforms.

Klaus Barbie was extradited to France, where he was convicted of crimes against humanity and sentenced to life in prison. He was held in St. Joseph Prison at Lyon, just around the corner from the Hotel Terminus, where he had set up his first torture chamber. He died there in 1991.

Phillip Frost came to UCLA for reconstructive surgery. The plastic surgeon said that whoever did the original flaps must have been a butcher.

17

DEATH

I keep wondering if there is an afterlife, and if there is will they be able to break a twenty?

—WOODY ALLEN,
Without Feathers

Woody Allen worries a lot about death. The theme is found throughout his books, plays, and films. Despite the slapstick treatment, Allen's anguish over the end of life and his fear of nothingness after death are feelings shared by most people.

Death, in terms of its physical sequelae, is really no mystery. After death the body disintegrates and is reabsorbed into the environment. It seems logical that consciousness shares the same fate as the corpse. This, however, is not the prevalent view, and the majority of humankind rejects the notion of annihilation at death. Instead, people have formulated an assortment of beliefs about survival after death. Many of these beliefs center on the notion that the intact human personality survives in another dimension—an afterlife. While Woody Allen worries about whether rents are controlled in the afterlife, belief in life after death provides much comfort and security for the living. The uncertainty of dying is replaced by the certainty of immortality. The body dies, so goes the belief, but the soul lives on.

Some "scientists" who have tried to make a case for life after death use such absurd methods that they come across as characters from a Woody Allen play. Robert Crookall, a British geologist who became interested in parapsychology, believed that the soul, or spiritual body, is normally attached to the physical body by a silver cord. His evidence: an overwhelming number of "communications" from the dead as channeled through mediums. Jack Webber, a medium operating in London, once produced a cord from his mouth for the benefit of photographers. The award for best performance by a silver cord goes to Thomas Lynn, a young British miner, who produced his cord in front of the British College of Psychic Science in 1929. The cord, which emerged from Lynn's solar plexus, took the form of a luminous finger that proceeded to play a zither to everyone's delight!

According to Crookall and others, the silver cord snaps at death, thus freeing the soul to begin its posthumous journey. Duncan MacDougall, working at the Massachusetts General Hospital in the early part of the century, weighed bodies at the time of death. He determined that there was an immediate weight loss of approximately one ounce. According to MacDougall, that was the precise weight of the departing soul or spirit. Mediums could sometimes persuade these spirits to ring bells or tap on tables during seances, thereby verifying their existence. A committee to investigate mediums was formed in 1924 by *Scientific American* and included the magician Harry Houdini. They caught many mediums ringing the bells and tapping the tables themselves. However, no one was able to explain a seance described by Woody Allen in which "a table not only rose but excused itself and went upstairs to sleep."

Julius Weinberger solved the problem of untrustworthy mediums by using a more sensitive and reliable apparatus: the Venus flytrap. Julius would ask the plant a question, then read its answer on a graphic recorder displaying the plant's electrical signals. Others have bypassed mediums, both human and botanical, by recording the voices of the dead themselves. In 1959 Friedrich Jurgenson, while taping the songs of the Swedish finch in his backyard, recorded the voice of his deceased mother calling: "Friedel, my little Friedel. Can you hear me?"

The easiest way to hear the dead speak is to wait until they call. Writer Anthony Burgess claimed to have received a series of such phone calls from his deceased wife and used them as the basis for a novel. While no one knows what to make of these calls—even some parapsychologists consider them too bizarre to take seriously—one investigator claims that they are increasing in frequency.

And what do all these ghosts and spirits have to say? Their descriptions of life after death sound uncannily similar to Woody's speculation that the afterlife is not unlike Cleveland. One spirit claimed there are exactly fifty-seven mansions in the afterlife, all in separate parks, but many people are forced to live in one-room apartments. While that sounds a tad overcrowded, another spirit told his surviving wife that there were colorful flowers and "a lawn that would put any Earth golf club to shame." Fortunately there is no need to walk or bother with a golf cart; transportation is provided by golden chariots that fly in the sky. Despite such heavenly conveniences, the spirits warn about swimming in the local lake—it's filled with fire and brimstone, which certainly makes Cleveland sound like a better place to visit.

My opinion of these "scientific" reports was best illustrated by the location I assigned them on my bookshelves. I placed the books, with such titles as *Phone Calls from the Dead* and *Journeys Out of the Body*, next to my collection of Woody Allen. Far removed from these shelves was one of the few books in my library I never read. It was a highly technical text on microbiology by a friend whom I will call Horace Woods.

Professor Woods had volunteered to be a psychonaut in my experiments. As a young man he had spent time in the Middle East, where he tried hashish and had a number of profound hallucinatory experiences. Now he wanted to explore them as a subject in my studies. But the medical school committee that reviewed my research wouldn't let me use him because he was too old. Still, I liked him and cultivated his friendship. We discovered that we had many things in common including an appreciation for the work of Heinrich Klüver and the humor of

Woody Allen. Despite the difference in our ages, "Ace" and I became good friends.

Over the years we met for frequent lunches at the UCLA Faculty Center, where we swapped stories about the latest findings from our labs. When he handed me a signed copy of his textbook, I gave it a prominent position on my biology shelf. But there came a time when I thought about moving the book to the Woody Allen shelf. That was when Ace called to tell me he had just returned from the dead! "Come up to the house this weekend and I'll tell you all about it," he said. I could bring my tape recorder.

Ace lived in a cliffside house in Malibu. I drove past it twice until I realized that his house, which I remembered as gray, was now painted sky blue. As I approached the front door, I noticed where the painters had missed several patches of gray near the roof. The patches reminded me of storm clouds.

He greeted me at the door with the same bone-crushing handshake I always feared but never complained about. His eyes sparkled and there was a hint of a tan on his face. He was no zombie. But I was shocked to see him in a wheelchair. He wheeled around and led the way into the den before I had a chance to ask what had happened.

Ace poured a glass of chilled white wine for me. It was a little too early in the day to drink, so I just held the glass and went to work on a nearby plate of cheese. I believe he purposely waited until my mouth was full before he spoke.

"I'm paraplegic now," he said. "Never walk again. But I'm alive and the old noodle is as good as ever." Ace raised his glass and I raised mine. "To survivors," he said.

"L'chaim!" I said and touched my lips to the wine. Ace began telling me about his accident. As he talked, I forgot about the time of day and gradually drained my glass.

Ace had been painting his house when he fell off a ladder. As he fell backward, he felt his body was evaporating. He was floating. His mind was racing. Which way did the ladder fall? What happened to the paint can? Time slowed. Or was he falling over the cliff and that was why it was taking so long to hit? He considered where he would land. Now he was sorry he had cleared the chaparral from the top of the cliff. It could have cushioned his fall. But there were still thick clumps of brush on the lower slope. If he missed them, he would probably die. What if he hit at an angle parallel to the slope? Would he slide down the mountain? He didn't know. If he did survive, he must remember not to move right away. It would be best to lie still and call for help. Would anyone hear him? Then he thought about those he would leave behind if he didn't make it. His sons were grown and married, so they would be okay. His wife was strong enough to recover. He had always said she would outlive him. There was plenty of money in the bank. He hoped she would find his last paycheck, which was still in his desk at the university. Images from the family scrapbook flashed before him: his wedding, a birthday party, his mother and father. Everything was bathed in feelings of beauty and love. In the distance he heard a dull thud.

The fall was over. Ace was lying on his back looking at the sky. There was no pain. There was no sound. Nothing moved. It was like the calm before some great earthquake when all the birds are silent and the world stops for a moment. Suddenly a black figure dashed in front of him.

"I guess that's when I blacked out," said Ace.

When he regained consciousness, the paramedics were looming over him. They were hitting him. Then they put something in his ear that hurt. Ace noticed a clear tube running into his arm from a bag. He started to move. Something snapped. The black figure covered his eyes.

"That's when I died," he said, pausing to refill our glasses. "You're gonna love this next part."

I did. Ace described a classic near-death experience. It began with a series of high-pitched sounds, like sirens. Only the sirens were singing "Ave Maria."

"It was the most beautiful rendition you could ever imagine. It filled me with such peace. I could feel the music literally pick me up. It wasn't me, just a part of me." Ace was twisting his face as he searched for the right words. "You know what I mean."

"No," I lied. "Tell me."

"I guess I had one of those out-of-body experiences. My consciousness was floating over my chest—only a few inches, mind you, but separated from the rest of me. I still sensed the paramedics working on me, but I couldn't see them. I was looking up. There, in the sky, was something like a long subway tube or tunnel. It had smooth crystalline walls which glistened with a bright light coming from the end."

"You sure you weren't looking at the I.V. tube against the sun?" I asked.

"Perhaps. But since when do I.V. tubes sing? The music was coming from the tunnel, tugging right here." Ace patted his heart, close to the area where silver cords are known to materialize.

"The music pulled me into the tunnel," Ace continued, "but all the time I knew I was still only inches above my chest. Yet those inches seemed like light years. Inside the tunnel was a whole new world. I was entering the realm of some supreme force. I've never felt such peace and calm. It was . . . well, dammit, heavenly. Okay, it was *heavenly!*"

I could tell that Ace was embarrassed to say the word. He was a proud agnostic who shunned all religious metaphors. But he had been confronted by an ineffable experience and was searching for the most powerful language he could find. He had never spoken this way before and I was surprised by the new vocabulary. I was equally surprised by his increased drinking. Ace was now opening a second bottle of wine.

Before he refilled his glass, he excused himself to go to the bathroom. I took advantage of the break to talk to his wife, who was in the kitchen preparing dinner.

"Are you still vegetarian?" she asked. I could see she was making a chicken dish.

"Chicken's fine," I said. I didn't know I had been invited for dinner, and I wasn't about to be fussy.

Doris quietly asked me if I thought Ace was all right. Yes, I told her. He had had a very common hallucinatory experience, typical of falls and near-death accidents. Under the circumstances, his newfound love of wine was also to be expected. On the other hand, the tears in Doris's eyes suggested she was not adjusting very well to everything that had happened.

"Did he tell you about his brother?" she asked.

"I didn't know he had a brother."

"He died a long time ago, but Ace said he talked to him." A teardrop rolled slowly down her cheek. "Is that normal?"

I didn't answer.

"Ask him about Barbra Streisand. He heard her, too, and

she's not even dead," Doris said. "He can't even keep his hallucinations straight." She bit her lip, then switched gears. "Do you
like chicken?"

The question was for the benefit of Ace, who had just
wheeled into the kitchen to find me.

"Chicken's fine," I said.

We went back to the den, where Ace picked up his story.

"I was nearing the end of the tunnel when the sirens
stopped," Ace said excitedly. "There was nothing there. Yet it
wasn't dark as you might expect. It was light! Opaque, white
light. I couldn't see anything. I sensed that there were many
other presences."

"Presences?" I asked.

"Presences, spirits, souls, whatever. They were part of the
light."

"And the light?" I was egging him on.

"Okay, force the atheist to say it—God. The light was God.
You happy now? Anyway, these presences were trying to communicate with me. They talked in whispers which trailed off in
the light before I could make sense out of them. But I heard
my brother."

"Say what?"

"I don't know. At least I don't remember. All I know is that
at the time I was certain it was his voice. I turned and saw him
waving to me. I knew he was dead so it had to be his spirit."

I made a face.

"You've got to understand that at the time I thought I was
dead and I was willing to believe everything in those terms."

"Did you think you might be having a lucid dream?" I asked.
In lucid dreams consciousness is awakened so that the dreamer
becomes aware of the dream. The dreamer can actually take a
semblance of control over the dream itself, like choosing to turn
right instead of left at a dreamscape crossroads.

"It was much too real, and almost psychedelic. I had the
feeling that I was about to be given the key to understanding
the nature of God and the universe. I've had those experiences
with hashish, but never in a dream."

Ace had discussed his hashish experiences with me many
times. Hashish intoxications are replete with elements of near-
death experiences including auditory sensations, feelings of

peace and well-being, body separation, tunnels of light, encounters with others, as well as visions and thoughts of great knowledge. Ancient Arabians used hashish to allow the spiritual body to separate from the physical body and thereby ascend to "heavenly understanding." As a young man, Ace experienced similar ecstasies complete with tunnels filled with simple and complex imagery, bright lights, and a sense of transcendence. I asked him how this fall-induced experience was any different. After all, sometimes drug users have "high dreams," or flashbacks in the dream state to one of their drug trips.

"It wasn't that different. Except that I wasn't intoxicated, and there were none of the stuporous effects, so it all seemed very very real. The sense of sacredness was more profound than I remember with hashish. I could have stayed there forever."

"Why didn't you?" I asked. The obvious answer was that he didn't die. But, by definition, no one who reports these experiences ever died. Many report that the voice of God tells them it's not time. Some hear a deceased relative telling them to go back. Others are rescued by a supernatural force. Still others are pulled back by their silver cord, which sometimes functions like a bungee rope.

"Barbra Streisand brought me back," exclaimed Ace with a straight face. "I heard her singing that song about people who need people, and the next thing I know I'm vomiting in the emergency room of the hospital." Ace shook his head at the absurdity of what he had just said and gulped from his glass.

I poured another glass of wine for myself.

"You know, I never even liked her singing," he continued. "Now I play her tapes all the time."

I've heard of people returning from near-death experiences with changed attitudes and beliefs. But I really expected something more erudite from the professor. Perhaps a renewed interest in religious studies, or a desire to read the works of Emanuel Swedenborg or Elisabeth Kübler-Ross. But Barbra Streisand recordings?

Our subsequent drinking was finally interrupted by Doris's announcement that dinner was ready. Ace allowed me to wheel him into the dining room. I was glad to have the wheelchair to steady myself. Doris served a marvelous meal of free range chicken, homemade pasta, and fresh vegetables from her garden.

There were two different wines, and we all drank more than we should have. The conversation centered on the similarity of near-death experiences to other hallucinatory experiences.

I explained that there are many triggers for these experiences, including drugs, stress, fever, loneliness, isolation, and fear. Given an infinite variety of triggers, the brain responds with a finite number of responses, hence the similarity of Ace's near-death visions and his hashish experiences. The deathbed is another place where such experiences are reported. People on their deathbeds face a very real threat to their bodies. This triggers fantasies, including the memories and fantasies of childhood. In this sense, an individual turns away from his or her sick or disabled body, minimizes its presence in the perceptual field, and enters a state where the threat does not exist. The feelings of floating out-of-the-body, of dissociation, of depersonalization—all are part of these defensive reactions.

The precise physiological mechanisms of action for these events is largely unknown, although we do know something about how drugs work as triggers. Visionary drugs like hashish cause cerebral excitation that enables thoughts and memories to become transformed into sensory impressions. Drugs that anesthetize the body and kill pain act to block awareness of sensory impressions, thus allowing the mind to focus on the same internal imagery of thoughts and memories. Some researchers think that the emotional or physiological processes in dying or in near-fatal accidents work in similar ways. Indeed, one study of alpine climbers who survived near-fatal falls found that they had the same reactions Ace experienced: a sense of detachment, flashes of past memories, and a mystical state of consciousness including visions of an afterlife. And, like Ace, they all reported dozens of thoughts and images in the space of only a few seconds.

I offered Ace and Doris an analogy to illustrate the process. I asked them to picture a man in his living room, standing at a closed window opposite the fireplace and looking out at the sunset. He is absorbed by the view of the outside world and does not visualize the interior of the room. As darkness falls outside, however, the images of the objects in the room behind him can be seen reflected dimly in the window. With deepening darkness the fire in the fireplace illuminates the room, and the man now sees a vivid reflection of the room, which appears to be outside the window. As the analogy is applied to the near-death experience, the daylight (sensory input) is reduced while the interior illumination (the general level of arousal in the brain) remains bright, so that images originating within the rooms of the brain may be perceived as though they came from outside the windows of the senses. Thus, when the Book of John tells us, "In my Father's house there are many mansions," or when Ace tells us that there are many spirits in the light, there are probably no more mansions and spirits than there are images of those structures in our own brains.

"It sounds like a dream," said Doris, glancing at Ace for signs of his reaction.

"It's really a waking dream," I said, "jarred loose by the shock of the accident and organized by the nervous system in such a way to keep the personality of the victim intact. Just as physiological shock helps keep the body together, the near-death experience keeps potentially disorganizing emotion in check. It's an adaptive way for us to survive a life-threatening situation."

"Don't dismiss it too readily," warned Ace. He spoke with professorial authority. "Maybe everybody sees the same vision of the afterlife because it's really there."

"Of course it's really there," I said. "But it's in mental not physical space. We know that because you people it with your own images. In a million near-death visions, I could never meet your brother unless I knew what he looked like or sounded like in the first place. And you could never see or hear my deceased father."

"He told me to tell you not to marry the *shiksa*," replied Ace with a wink.

"Horace!" said Doris loudly. She was clearing the table and had missed the wink.

"You're forgetting the most important part," said Ace. "It was the most solemn and beautiful experience of my life. Inside the light, I felt I was lying in the open hand of God. I'd like to believe that when it's time, he'll close his hand and take me to him."

"It's a beautiful image, Ace," I said. There was no reason why he shouldn't hang on to it. When all is said and done, finding that Ace's experience was a hallucination was not the same as finding proof against life after death. Ace's belief in the afterlife was not likely to disappear with my analysis. "Since death is a precondition for entry into the afterlife," I continued, "I suppose we the living may never know the answer."

"Would the living like some drop-dead dessert," quipped Doris as she presented us with bowls of berries and whipped cream. Then came the steaming cups of café au lait.

The conversation over coffee drifted to my research with animals. Ace and Doris were always fascinated by my stories of drunk, stoned, and otherwise intoxicated animals who behaved just like their human counterparts. One intriguing story involved a sober animal, but it seemed most appropriate tonight.

I described how a team of psychologists taught a gorilla to communicate with American Sign Language. Once he acquired a basic vocabulary, the gorilla showed that he had sophisticated thoughts about life and death. There was great wisdom in his signs, especially when asked "What is death?"

I signed the answer he gave. My palms were turned up, fingers pointing away from my body. Then I moved my hands together so they touched, rotated them inward, and moved them apart until the palms faced downward.

The sign meant *finished, the end.*

AFTERWORD

These have been the stories of brave men, women, and children who confronted the fires in the brain. They were my research patients and subjects, but they were also my teachers. They allowed me to enter their lives and minds, to explore the fascination and horror of their perceptions. Together we marveled at the sights and sounds. We were amused. And we were frightened.

Somehow I always found my way out. Afterward, I could look back and laugh at myself, at what I had seen and done. I discovered it was often the best way to fight the fires and put them out for good. Many of my patients learned the same lesson. They laughed because they finally realized that they were not crazy. It was the visions that were out of their minds. It's a good lesson and advisory for all travelers to the hinterland of the mind.

BIBLIOGRAPHY

GENERAL REFERENCES

ASAAD, G. 1990. *Hallucinations in Clinical Psychiatry*. New York: Brunner/Mazel.

BRIERRE DE BOISMONT, A. 1853. *Hallucinations: or, the Rational History of Apparitions, Visions, Dreams, Ecstasy, Magnetism, and Somnambulism*. Philadelphia: Lindsay and Blakiston.

CAUGHEY, J. L. 1984. *Imaginary Social Worlds*. Lincoln: University of Nebraska Press.

CLARKE, E. H. 1878. *Visions: A Study of False Sight*. Boston: Houghton, Osgood.

EVANS, H. 1984. *Visions, Apparitions, Alien Visitors*. Wellingborough: The Aquarian Press.

———. 1987. *Gods, Spirits, Cosmic Guardians*. Wellingborough: The Aquarian Press.

EY, H. 1973. *Traité des Hallucinations.* Vols. 1 and 2. Paris: Masson et Cie.

GREEN C., and McGREERY, C. 1975. *Apparitions.* London: Hamish Hamilton.

HOROWITZ, M. J. 1970. *Image Formation and Cognition.* New York: Appleton-Century-Crofts.

IRELAND, W. W. 1893. *The Blot Upon the Brain: Studies in History and Psychology.* New York: G. P. Putnam's Sons.

JOHNSON, F. H. 1978. *The Anatomy of Hallucinations.* Chicago: Nelson-Hall.

KEUP, W., ed. 1970. *Origin and Mechanisms of Hallucinations.* New York: Plenum.

KLÜVER, H. 1926. "Mescal Visions and Eidetic Vision." *American Journal of Psychology* 37: 502–15.

———. 1928. *Mescal: The 'Divine' Plant and Its Psychological Effects.* London: Kegan Paul, Trench, Trubner & Co.

———. 1965. "Neurobiology of Normal and Abnormal Perception." In *Psychopathology of Perception,* ed. P. H. Hoch and J. Zubin, 1–40. New York: Grune & Stratton.

———. 1966. *Mescal and Mechanisms of Hallucinations.* Chicago: University of Chicago Press.

MAUDSLEY, H. 1887. *Natural Causes and Supernatural Seemings.* London: Kegan Paul, Trench & Co.

McKELLAR, P. 1957. *Imagination and Thinking: A Psychological Analysis.* New York: Basic Books.

MOREAU. J.–J. [1845] 1973. *Hashish and Mental Illness,* trans. G. J. Barnett. New York: Raven Press.

PARISH, E. 1897. *Hallucinations and Illusions: A Study of the Fallacies of Perception.* London/New York: Walter Scott/Charles Scribner's Sons.

RAWCLIFFE, D. H. 1952. *The Psychology of the Occult.* London: Derricke Ridgway.

RICHARDSON, A. 1969. *Mental Imagery.* New York: Springer Publishing.

SARBIN, T. R., and JUHASZ, J. B. 1978. "The Social Psychology of Hallucinations." *Journal of Mental Imagery* 2: 117–44.

SEGAL, S. J., ed. 1971. *Imagery: Current Cognitive Approaches.* New York: Academic Press.

SHEEHAN, P. W. ed. 1972. *The Function and Nature of Imagery.* New York: Academic Press.

SIEGEL, R. K. 1977. "Hallucinations." *Scientific American* 237: 132–40.

———. 1977. "Normal Hallucinations of Imaginary Companions." *McLean Hospital Journal* 2: 66–80.

———. 1978. "Cocaine Hallucinations." *American Journal of Psychiatry* 135: 309–14.

———. 1979. "Experimental Analysis and Modification of Hallucinations." In *Modification of Pathological Behavior,* ed. R. S. Davidson, 69–108. New York: Gardner Press.

———. 1980. "The Psychology of Life After Death." *American Psychologist* 35: 911–31.

———. 1984. "Hostage Hallucinations: Visual Imagery Induced by Isolation and Life-Threatening Stress." *The Journal of Nervous and Mental Disease* 172: 264–72.

———, and WEST, L. J., eds. 1975. *Hallucinations: Behavior, Experience, and Theory.* New York: John Wiley & Sons.

SLADE, P. D., and BENTALL, R. P. 1988. *Sensory Deception: A Scientific Analysis of Hallucination.* London: Croom Helm.

SMYTHIES, J. R. 1956. *Analysis of Perception.* London: Routledge and Kegan Paul.

SULLY, J. 1887. *Illusions: A Psychological Study.* London: Kegan Paul, Trench & Co.

TYRRELL, G. N. M. 1953. *Apparitions.* London: The Society for Psychical Research.

WATKINS, M. 1976. *Waking Dreams.* New York: Harper & Row.

———. 1986. *Invisible Guests: The Development of Imaginal Dialogues.* Hillsdale: The Analytic Press.

WEST, L. J., ed. 1962. *Hallucinations.* New York: Grune & Stratton.

ZUBEK, J. P., ed. 1969. *Sensory Deprivation: Fifteen Years of Research.* New York: Appleton-Century-Crofts.

CHAPTER REFERENCES

INTRODUCTION

LILLY, J. C. 1977. *The Deep Self.* New York: Simon and Schuster.

———. 1978. *The Scientist.* Philadelphia: J. B. Lippincott.

McKELLAR, P. 1957. *Imagination and Thinking: A Psychological Analysis.* New York: Basic Books.

SIEGEL, R. K. December 1988. "Altered Stats." *Omni*: 89.

SIDGEWICK, H. A., et al. 1894. "Report of the Census of Hallucinations." *Proceedings of the Society for Psychical Research* 26: 25–422.

WEST, D. J. 1990. "A Pilot Census of Hallucinations." *Proceedings of the Society for Psychical Research* 57: 163–207.

1. THE PSYCHONAUT AND THE SHAMAN

BERRIN, K., ed. 1978. *Art of the Huichol Indians.* New York: Harry N. Abrams.

BURROUGHS, W., and GINSBERG, A. 1963. *The Yage Letters.* San Francisco: City Lights Books.

EICHMEIER, J., and HÖFER, O. 1974. *Endogene Bildmuster.* Munich: Urban & Schwarzenberg.

HUXLEY, A. 1956. "Mescaline and the 'Other World'." In *Lysergic Acid Diethylamide and Mescaline in Experimental Psychiatry*, ed. L. Cholden, 46–50. New York: Grune & Stratton.

JUNG, C. G. [1934–50] 1969. *The Archetypes and the Collective Unconscious.* In *The Collected Works of C. G. Jung*, trans. R. F. C. Hull, vol. 9(1). Princeton: Princeton University Press.

———. ed. 1968. *Man and His Symbols.* New York: Doubleday.

LUMHOLTZ, C. May 1900. "Symbolism of the Huichol Indians." *Memoirs of the American Museum of Natural History*, vol. 3.

MOSS, T. 1974. *The Probability of the Impossible: Scientific Discoveries and Explorations of the Psychic World.* Los Angeles: J. P. Tarcher.

OSTER, G. February 1970. "Phosphenes." *Scientific American* 222(2): 83–87.

OTT, J. 1986. "Carved 'Disembodied Eyes' of Teotihuacan." In *Persephone's Quest: Entheogens and the Origins of Religion*, R.

G. Wasson, S. Kramrisch, J. Ott, and C. A. P. Ruck, 141–48. New Haven and London: Yale University Press.

POE, E. A. [1842] 1843. "The Pit and the Pendulum." In *The Gift, a Christmas and New Years Present*, 133–51. Philadelphia: Carey and Hart.

WASSON, R. G. 13 May 1957. "Seeking the Magic Mushrooms." *Life* 100–120.

2. CONVERSATIONS WITH GOD IN C-SHARP MINOR

BIRCHWOOD, M. 1986. "Control of Auditory Hallucinations through Occlusion of Monaural Auditory Input." *British Journal of Psychiatry* 149: 104–7.

CRITCHLEY, M, and HENSON, R. A., eds. 1977. *Music and the Brain: Studies in the Neurology of Music.* London: William Heinemann.

FEDER, R. 1982. "Auditory Hallucinations Treated by Radio Headphones." *American Journal of Psychiatry* 139: 1188–90.

GROSS, M. M., HALPERT, E., SABOT, L., and POLIZOS, P. 1963. "Hearing Disturbances and Auditory Hallucinations in the Acute Alcoholic Psychoses. I: Tinnitus: Incidence and Significance." *Journal of Nervous and Mental Disease* 137: 453–65.

HAMMEKE, T. A., MCQUILLEN, M. P., and COHEN, B. A. 1983. "Musical Hallucinations Associated with Acquired Deafness." *Journal of Neurology, Neurosurgery, and Psychiatry* 46: 570–72.

JAMES, D. A. E. 1983. "The Experimental Treatment of Two Cases of Auditory Hallucinations." *British Journal of Psychiatry* 143: 515–16.

KAPLAN, J., MANDEL, L. R., STILLMAN, R., WALKER, R. W., VAN DEN HEUVEL, W. J. A., GILLIN, J. C., and WYATT, R. J. 1974. "Blood and Urine Levels of N,N,-Dimethyltryptamine Following Administration of Psychoactive Dosages to Human Subjects." *Psychopharmacologia* 38: 239–45.

LEARY, T. 1966. "Programmed Communication During Experiences with DMT (Dimethyltryptamine)." *Psychedelic Review*, no. 8, 83–95.

MASTERS, R. E. L., and HOUSTON, J. 1966. *The Varieties of Psychedelic Experience.* New York: Holt, Rinehart and Winston.

McKENNA, T. K. 1984. *True Hallucinations.* Berkeley: Lux Natura.

————, and McKENNA, D. J. 1975. *The Invisible Landscape. Mind, Hallucinogens, and the I Ching*. New York: The Seabury Press.

MILLER, T. C., and CROSBY, T. W. 1979. "Musical Hallucinations in a Deaf Elderly Patient." *Annals of Neurology* 5: 301–2.

MORLEY, S. 1987. "Modification of Auditory Hallucinations: Experimental Studies of Headphones and Earplugs." *Behavioural Psychotherapy* 15: 240–51.

MYERS, F. W. H. [1903] 1975. *Human Personality and Its Survival of Bodily Death*, vol. 2. New York: Arno Press.

RICHARDSON, A. 1969. *Mental Imagery*. New York: Springer.

ROSS, E. D. 1978. "Musical Hallucinations in Deafness Revisited." *Journal of the American Medical Association* 240: 1716.

————, JOSSMAN, P. B., BELL, B., SABIN, T., and GESCHWIND, N. 1975. "Musical Hallucinations in Deafness." *Journal of the American Medical Association* 231: 620–22.

SARAVAY, S. M., and PARDES, H. 1970. "Auditory 'Elementary Hallucinations' in Alcohol Withdrawal Psychoses." In *Origin and Mechanisms of Hallucinations*, ed. W. Keup, 237–44. New York: Plenum Press.

SCHULTES, R. E., and HOFMANN, A. 1979. *Plants of the Gods*. Maidenhead, Eng.: McGraw-Hill.

SCOTT, M. 1979. "Musical Hallucinations from Meningioma." *Journal of the American Medical Association* 241: 1683.

SEMRAD, E. V. 1938. "Study of the Auditory Apparatus in Patients Experiencing Auditory Hallucinations." *American Journal of Psychiatry* 95: 53–63.

STAFFORD, P. 1983. *Psychedelics Encyclopedia*. Los Angeles: J. P. Tarcher.

SZARA, S. 1956. "Dimethyltryptamine—Its Metabolism in Man; The Relation of Its Psychotic Effect to the Serotonin Metabolism." *Experientia* 12: 441–42.

————. 1961. "Hallucinogenic Effects and Metabolism of Tryptamine Derivatives in Man." *Federation Proceedings* 20: 885–88.

3. RAPE IN A DALI LANDSCAPE

COLLIER, B. B. 1972. "Ketamine and the Conscious Mind." *Anaesthesia* 27: 120–34.

CYTOWIC, R. E. 1989. *Synthesthesia: A Union of the Senses*. New York: Springer-Verlag.

"Dart Soothes Game, Paints Pictures." July 1971. *The Cap-Chur News* [Douglasville, Georgia]: 8.

FINE, J., and FINESTONE, S. C. 1973. "Sensory Disturbances Following Ketamine Anesthesia: Recurrent Hallucinations." *Anesthesia and Analgesia: Current Researches* 52: 428–30.

HANSEN, G., JENSEN. S. B., CHANDRESH, L., and HILDEN, T. 1988. "The Psychotropic Effect of Ketamine." *Journal of Psychoactive Drugs* 20: 419–25.

KHORRAMZADEH, E., and LOFTY, A. P. 1973. "The Use of Ketamine in Psychiatry." *Psychosomatics* 14: 344–46.

KREUSCHER, H., ed. 1969. *Ketamine*. Berlin: Springer-Verlag.

MEYERS, E. F., and CHARLES, P. 1978. "Prolonged Adverse Reactions to Ketamine in Children." *Anesthesiology* 49: 39–40.

MICHAUX, H. [1961] 1963. *Light Through Darkness*, trans. H. Chevalier. New York: The Orion Press.

MOORE, M., and ALTOUNIAN, H. 1978. *Journeys into the Bright World*. Rockport, Mass.: Para Research.

PEREL, A., and DAVIDSON, J. T. 1976. "Recurrent Hallucinations Following Ketamine." *Anaesthesia* 31: 1081–83.

ROGO, D. S. 1984. "Ketamine and the Near-Death Experience." *Anabiosis* 4: 87–96.

SIEGEL, R. K. 1978. "Phencyclidine and Ketamine Intoxication: A Study of Four Populations of Recreational Users." In *Phencyclidine (PCP) Abuse: An Appraisal*, ed. R. C. Petersen and R. C. Stillman 119–47. National Institute on Drug Abuse Research Monograph 21. DHHS Publication no. (ADM) 78-728. Washington, D.C.: Superintendent of Documents, U.S. Government Printing Office.

SMUTS, G. L., BRYDEN, B. R., DE VOS, V., and YOUNG, E. 18 March 1973. "Some practical advantages of CI-581 (Ketamine) for the field immobilization of larger wild felines, with comparative notes on baboons and impala." *The Lammergeyer*: 1–14.

"Women at His Mercy." 5 February 1987. ABC News "20/20." Producer B. Lange, correspondent S. Phillips.

4. FLASHBACK AND DEADBALL

FISCHER, R. 1976. "Hypnotic Recall and Flashback: The Remembrance of Things Present." *Confinia Psychiatrica* 19: 149–73.

FREEDMAN, S. J., and MARKS, P. A. 1965. "Visual Imagery Produced by Rhythmic Photic Stimulation: Personality Correlates and Phenomenology." *British Journal of Psychology* 56: 95–112.

HOLSTEN, F. 1976. "Flashbacks: A Personal Follow-up." *Archiv Fur Psychiatrie und Nervenkrankheiten* 222: 293–304.

KNOLL, M., KUGLER, J., EICHMEIER, J., and HÖFER, O. 1962. "Note on the Spectroscopy of Subjective Light Patterns." *Journal of Analytical Psychology* 7: 55–69.

MATEFY, R. E., HAYES, C., and HIRSCH, J. 1978. "Psychedelic Drug Flashbacks: Subjective Reports and Biographical Data." *Addictive Behaviors* 3: 165–78.

———, and KRALL, R. 1975. "Psychedelic Drug Flashbacks: Psychotic Manifestation or Imaginative Role Playing." *Journal of Consulting and Clinical Psychology* 43: 434.

McGEE, R. 1984. "Flashbacks and Memory Phenomena: A Comment on 'Flashback Phenomena—Clinical and Diagnostic Dilemmas.'" *The Journal of Nervous and Mental Disease* 172: 273–78.

SHICK, J. F. E., and SMITH, D. E. 1970. "Analysis of the LSD Flashback." *Journal of Psychedelic Drugs* 3: 13–19.

SMYTHIES, J. R. 1959. "The Stroboscopic Patterns. I. The Dark Phase." *British Journal of Psychology* 50: 106–16.

———. 1959. "The Stroboscopic Patterns. II. The Phenomenology of the Bright Phase and After-Images." *British Journal of Psychology* 50: 305–24.

———. 1960. "The Stroboscopic Patterns. III. Further Experiments and Discussion." *British Journal of Psychology* 51: 247–55.

WESSON, D. R., and SMITH, D. E. 1976. "An Analysis of Psychedelic Drug Flashbacks." *American Journal of Drug and Alcohol Abuse* 3: 425–38.

5. THE SUCCUBUS

ALLEN, T. E., and AGUS, B. 1968. "Hyperventilation Leading to Hallucinations." *American Journal of Psychiatry* 125: 84–89.

CRICK, F., and MITCHISON, G. 1983. "The Function of Dream Sleep." *Nature* 304: 111–14.

DEMENT, W., HALPER, C., PIVIK, T., FERGUSON, J., COHEN, H., HENRIKSEN, S., MCGARR, K., GONDA, W., HOYT, G., RYAN., L., MITCHELL, G., BARCHAS, J., and ZARCONE, V. 1970. "Hal-

lucinations and Dreams." In *Perception and Its Disorders,* ed.
D. Hamburg, 335–59. Baltimore: Williams & Wilkins.

FISHER, C., KAHN, E., EDWARDS, A., and DAVIS, D. M. 1973. "A
Psychophysiological Study of Nightmares and Night Terrors." *The Journal of Nervous and Mental Disease* 157: 75–98.

GOOCH, S. 1984. *Creatures from Inner Space.* London: Rider.

HARTMANN, E. 1975. "Dreams and Other Hallucinations: An
Approach to the Underlying Mechanism." In *Hallucinations:
Behavior, Experience, and Theory,* ed. R. K. Siegel and L. J.
West, 71–79. New York: John Wiley & Sons.

HUFFORD, D. J. 1982. *The Terror That Comes in the Night.* Philadelphia: University of Pennsylvania Press.

JONES, E. 1951. *On the Nightmare.* London: Liveright.

JUNG, C. G. [1958] 1970. "Flying Saucers: A Modern Myth of
Things Seen in the Skies." In *The Collected Works of C. G.
Jung,* trans. R. F. C. Hall, vol. 10, 307–433. Princeton:
Princeton University Press.

MELVILLE, H. 1851. *Moby Dick: Or, The Whale.* New York: Harper
& Bros.

WALLER, J. 1816. *A Treatise on the Incubus, or Night-Mare, Disturbed
Sleep, Terrific Dreams, and Nocturnal Visions. With the Means of
Removing These Distressing Complaints.* London: E. Cox and Son.

6. UFO

AGGERNAES, A., and NYEBORG, O. 1972. "The Reliability of Different Aspects of the Experienced Reality of Hallucinations
in Clear States of Consciousness." *Acta Psychiatrica Scandinav-
ica* 48: 239–52.

BAKER, R. A. 1989. "Q: Are UFO Abduction Experiences for
Real? A: No, No, A Thousand Times No!" *Journal of UFO
Studies* 1: 104–10.

EICHMEIER, J. and HÖFER, O. 1974. *Endogene Bildmuster.* Munich:
Urban & Schwarzenberg.

EVANS, H. 1980. "Abducted by an Archetype." *Fortean Times* 33:
6–10.

GREENLER, R. 1989. *Rainbows, Halos, and Glories.* Cambridge:
Cambridge University Press.

ISAKOWER, O. 1938. "A Contribution to the Patho-Psychology
of Phenomena Associated with Falling Asleep." *International
Journal of Psychoanalysis* 19: 331–45.

KEEL, J. A. 1970. *Strange Creatures from Time and Space*. Greenwich: Fawcett Publications.

―――. 1988. "Seeing Things. Hallucinations, UFOs and Fortean Investigations." *Strange* 3: 14–17, 58–59.

KLASS, P. J. 1988. *UFO-Abductions. A Dangerous Game*. Buffalo: Prometheus Books.

LAWSON, A. H. 1979. "Hypnosis of Imaginary UFO 'Abductees.' " *UFO Phenomena International Annual Review* 3: 219–71.

LORENZEN, C., and LORENZEN, J. 1976. *Encounters with UFO Occupants*. New York: Berkley Medallion Books.

ROGO, D. S., ed. 1980. *UFO Abductions*. New York: Signet.

SCHACTER, D. L. 1976. "The Hypnagogic State: A Critical Review of the Literature." *Psychological Bulletin* 83: 452–81.

TYNAN, P., and SEKULER, R. 1975. "Moving Visual Phantoms: A New Contour Completion Effect." *Science* 188: 951–52.

7. DAYMARE

BRADBURY, R. [1948] 1987. *Fever Dream*. New York: St. Martin's Press.

HARTMANN, E. 1984. *The Nightmare: The Psychology and Biology of Terrifying Dreams*. New York: Basic Books.

MACNISH, R. 1834. *The Philosophy of Sleep*. New York: D. Appleton & Co.

Spectral Visitants, or Journal of a Fever: By a Convalescent. 1845. Boston: S. H. Colesworthy.

STILL, G. F. 3 February 1900. "Day-Terrors (Pavor Dirunus) in Children." *The Lancet* 292–94.

WOLFF, H. G., and CURRAN, D. 1935. "Nature of Delirium and Allied States." *Archives of Neurology and Psychiatry* 33: 1175–1215.

8. SHEILA AND THE SWASTIKAS

BABKOFF, H., SING, H. C., THORNE, D. R., GENSER, S. G., and HEGGE, F. W. 1989. "Perceptual Distortions and Hallucinations Reported During the Course of Sleep Deprivation." *Perceptual and Motor Skills* 68: 787–98.

BELENKY, G. L. 1979. "Unusual Visual Experiences Reported by Subjects in the British Army Study of Sustained Operations, Exercise Early Call." *Military Medicine* 144: 695–96.

BLISS, E. L., CLARK, L. D. and WEST, C. D. 1959. "Studies of Sleep

Deprivation—Relationship to Schizophrenia." *A.M.A. Archives of Neurology and Psychiatry* 81: 348–59.

BRAUCHI, J. T., and WEST, L. J. 1959. "Sleep Deprivation." *Journal of the American Medical Association* 171: 11–14.

FREED, S. A., and FREED, R. S. January 1980. "Origin of the Swastika." *Natural History*: 68–74.

GILBERT, R. M. 1976. "Caffeine as a Drug of Abuse." In *Research Advances in Alcohol and Drug Problems, Volume Three*, ed. R. J. Gibbins, Y. Israel, H. Kalant, R. E. Popham, W. Schmidt, and R. G. Smart, 49–176. New York: John Wiley & Sons.

GOWERS, W. R. 1904. *Subjective Sensations of Sight and Sound, Abiotrophy, and Other Lectures.* Philadelphia: P. Blakiston's Son & Co.

GUILLEMINAULT, C., BILLARD, M., MONTPLAISIR, J., and DEMENT, W. C. 1975. "Altered States of Consciousness in Disorders of Daytime Sleepiness." *Journal of Neurological Sciences* 26: 377–93.

KASS, W., PREISER, G., and JENKINS, A. H. 1970. "Inter-Relationship of Hallucinations and Dreams in Spontaneously Hallucinating Patients." *The Psychiatric Quarterly* 44: 488–99.

KATZ, S. E., and LANDIS, C. 1935. "Psychologic and Physiologic Phenomena During a Prolonged Vigil." *Archives of Neurology and Psychiatry*: 307–17.

KLEITMAN, N. 1927. "Studies on the Physiology of Sleep. V. Some Experiments on Puppies." *American Journal of Physiology* 84: 386–95.

KOLLAR, E. J., PASNAU, R. O., RUBIN, R. T., NAITOH, P., SLATER, G. G., and KALES, A. 1969. "Psychological, Psychophysiological, and Biochemical Correlates of Prolonged Sleep Deprivation." *American Journal of Psychiatry* 126: 488–97.

"Leonardo's Secret: Cat Naps." 1990. *Science* 249: 244.

NICHOLSON, A. N., PASCOE, P. A., and STONE, B. M. 1990. "The Sleep-Wakefulness Continuum: Interactions with Drugs Which Increase Wakefulness and Enhance Alertness." *Alcohol, Drugs and Driving* 5–6: 287–301.

WEST, L. J., JANSZEN, H. H., LESTER, B. K., and CORNELISON, F. S. 1962. "The Psychosis of Sleep Deprivation." *Annals of the New York Academy of Sciences* 96: 66–70.

WILSON, T. 1896. *The Swastika.* Washington, D.C.: Government Printing Office/U.S. National Museum.

9. THE GIRL WITH DRAGON EYES

AMES, L. B., and LEARNED, J. 1946. "Imaginary Companions and Related Phenomena." *The Journal of Genetic Psychology* 69: 147–67.

AUG, R. G., and ABLES, B. S. 1971. "Hallucinations in Nonpsychotic Children." *Child Psychiatry and Human Development* 1: 152–67.

BENDER, L., and VOGEL, B. F. 1941. "Imaginary Companions of Children." *American Journal of Orthopsychiatry* 11: 56–65.

BYRD, R. E. 1938. *Alone.* New York: G. P. Putnam's Sons.

HARVEY, N. A. 1918. *Imaginary Playmates and Other Mental Phenomena of Children.* Ypsilanti: State Normal College.

MANOSEVITZ, M., PRENTICE, N. M., and WILSON, F. 1973. "Individual and Family Correlates of Imaginary Companions in Preschool Children." *Developmental Psychology* 8: 72–79.

NAGERA, H. 1969. "The Imaginary Companion: Its Significance for Ego Development and Conflict Solution." *The Psychoanalytic Study of the Child* 24: 164–96.

PERKY, C. W. 1910. "An Experimental Study of Imagination." *American Journal of Psychology* 21: 422–52.

RITTER, C. 1954. *A Woman in the Polar Night.* New York: E. P. Dutton.

SCHATZMAN, M. 1980. *The Story of Ruth.* New York: G. P. Putnam's Sons.

SINGER, J. L., and STREINER, B. F. 1966. "Imaginative Content in the Dreams and Fantasy Play of Blind and Sighted Children." *Perceptual and Motor Skills* 22: 475–82.

STEVENSON, R. L. 1913. *Across the Plains with Other Memories and Essays.* London: Chatto & Windus.

———. 1923. *The Complete Poems of Robert Louis Stevenson.* New York: Charles Scribner's Sons.

SVENDSEN, M. 1934. "Children's Imaginary Companions." *Archives of Neurology and Psychiatry* 32: 985–99.

VOSTROVSKY, C. 1895. "A Study of Imaginary Companions." *Education* 15: 393–98.

WALTER, W. G. 1960. *The Neurophysiological Aspects of Hallucinations and Illusory Experience.* London: Society for Psychical Research.

10. CHANNELING

GOODMAN, L. S. 1968. *Sun Signs*. New York: Taplinger Publishing Co.

HAVENS, L. 1962. "The Placement and Movement of Hallucinations in Space: Phenomenology and Theory." *International Journal of Psychoanalysis* 43: 426–35.

KLIMO, J. 1987. *Channeling: Investigations on Receiving Information from Paranormal Sources*. Los Angeles: J. P. Tarcher.

O'MAHONY, M., SHULMAN, K., and SILVER, D. 1984. "Roses in December: Imaginary Companions in the Elderly." *Canadian Journal of Psychiatry* 29: 151–54.

REES, W. D. 1975. "The Bereaved and Their Hallucinations." In *Bereavement: Its Psychosocial Aspects*, ed. B. Schoenberg, I. Gerber, A. Wiener, A. H. Kutscher, D. Peretz, and A. C. Carr, 66–71. New York: Columbia University Press.

ROGO, D. S., and BAYLESS, R. 1979. *Phone Calls from the Dead*. Englewood Cliffs: Prentice-Hall.

TANOUS, A., and DONNELLY, K. F. 1979. *Is Your Child Psychic?* New York: Macmillan Publishing Co.

TOMPKINS, P., and BIRD, C. 1973. *The Secret Life of Plants*. New York: Harper & Row.

11. ALONE

CALLAHAN, S. 1986. *Adrift: Seventy-Six Days Lost at Sea*. Boston: Houghton Mifflin.

GIBSON, W. 1953. *The Boat*. Boston: Houghton Mifflin.

KUSCHE, L. D. 1975. *The Bermuda Triangle Mystery—Solved*. New York: Harper & Row.

LINDEMANN, H. 1958. *Alone at Sea*. New York: Random House.

SLOCUM, J. 1900. *Sailing Alone Around the World*. New York: Century.

12. TAKE A PICTURE

BENDER, L., and LIPKOWITZ, H. H. 1940. "Hallucinations in Children." *American Journal of Orthopsychiatry* 10: 471–90.

DRUFFEL, A., and ROGO, D. S. 1989. *The Tujunga Canyon Contacts*. New York: Signet/New American Library.

HAVENS, L. L. 1962. "The Placement and Movement of Hallucinations in Space: Phenomenology and Theory." *International Journal of Psychoanalysis* 43: 426–35.

KLÜVER, H. 1931. "The Eidetic Child." In *A Handbook of Child Psychology*, ed. C. Murchison, 643–68. Worcester: Clark University Press.

LUKIANOWICZ, N. 1960. "Imaginary Sexual Partner." *Archives of General Psychiatry* 3: 429–49.

———. 1969. "Hallucinations in Non-psychotic Children." *Psychiatric Clinica* 2: 321–37.

SAGER, M. 15 June 1989. "The Devil and John Holmes." *Rolling Stone*: 50–61, 150, 152.

SIMONDS, J. F. 1975. "Hallucinations in Nonpsychotic Children." *Journal of Youth and Adolescence* 4: 171–82.

13. SERGEANT TOMMY

GOLDMAN, A. 1988. *The Lives of John Lennon*. New York: William Morrow.

HARRIMAN, P. L. 1937. "Some Imaginary Companions of Older Subjects." *American Journal of Orthopsychiatry* 7: 368–70.

HUNT, U. 1914. *Una Mary: The Inner Life of a Child*. New York: Charles Scribner's Sons.

HUYGHE, P. 1985. "Imaginary Companions." In *Glowing Birds: Stories from the Edge of Science*, 13–21. Boston: Faber and Faber.

SCHAEFER, C. E. 1969. "Imaginary Companions and Creative Adolescents." *Developmental Psychology* 1: 747–49.

SIZEMORE, C. C., and PITILLO, E. S. 1977. *I'm Eve*. Garden City: Doubleday.

WICKES, F. G. 1988. *The Inner World of Childhood*. Boston: Sigo Press.

14. THE CAGE

COMER, N. L., MADOW, L., and DIXON, J. J. 1967. "Observations of Sensory Deprivation in a Life-Threatening Situation." *American Journal of Psychiatry* 124: 68–73.

HERON, W. 1957. "The Pathology of Boredom." *Scientific American* 196: 52–56.

HESLOP, J. M., and VAN ORDEN, D. R. 1973. *From the Shadow of Death: Stories of POWs*. Salt Lake City: Deseret Book Company.

NOYES, R., and KLETTI, R. 1976. "Depersonalization in the Face of Life-Threatening Danger: A Description." *Psychiatry* 39: 19–27.

ROBERTSON, J. W. 1923. *Edgar A. Poe: A Psychopathic Study.* New York: G. P. Putnam's Sons.

TERR, L. 1990. *Too Scared to Cry: Psychic Trauma in Childhood.* New York: Harper & Row.

VAN DER KOLK, B. A., ed. 1984. *Post-Traumatic Stress Disorder: Psychological and Biological Sequelae.* Washington, D. C.: American Psychiatric Press.

VERNON, J. A. 1963. *Inside the Black Room.* New York: Clarkson N. Potter.

ZUCKERMAN, M., and COHEN, N. 1964. "Sources of Reports of Visual and Auditory Sensations in Perceptual-Isolation Experiments." *Psychological Bulletin* 62: 1–20.

15. DOPPELGANGER

BAKKER, C. B., and MURPHY, S. E. 1964. "An Unusual Case of Autoscopic Hallucinations." *Journal of Abnormal and Social Psychology* 69: 646–49.

DEWHURST, K., and PEARSON, J. 1955. "Visual Hallucinations of the Self in Organic Disease." *Journal of Neurology, Neurosurgery and Psychiatry* 18: 53–57.

KOHLBERG, L. Spring 1963. "Psychological Analysis and Literary Form: A Study of the Doubles in Dostoevsky." *Daedalus* 345–62.

LIFTON, R. J. 1986. *The Nazi Doctors: Medical Killing and the Psychology of Genocide.* New York: Basic Books.

LUKIANOWICZ, N. 1958. "Autoscopic Phenomena." *A.M.A. Archives of Neurology and Psychiatry* 80: 199–220.

ROSENFIELD, C. Spring 1963. "The Shadow Within: The Conscious and Unconscious Use of the Double." *Daedalus* 327–44.

TODD, J., and DEWHURST, K. 1955. "The Double: Its Psycho-Pathology and Psycho-Physiology." *Journal of Nervous and Mental Disease* 122: 47–55.

16. THE SCREAM

BØE, A. 1989. *Edvard Munch*, trans. R. Ferguson. New York: Rizzoli.

LINKLATER, M., HILTON, I., and ASCHERSON, N. 1984. *The Nazi Legacy: Klaus Barbie and the International Fascist Connection.* New York: Holt, Rinehart and Winston.

17. DEATH

ALLEN, W. 1971. *Getting Even.* New York: Random House.

————. 1976. *Without Feathers.* New York: Warner Books.

BENAYOUN, R. 1985. *The Films of Woody Allen,* trans. A. Walker. New York: Harmony Books.

BURGESS, A. 1976. *Beard's Roman Women.* London: Hutchinson.

CROOKALL, R. 1961. *The Supreme Adventure: Analyses of Psychic Communication.* London: James Clarke.

GIBBS, J. C. 1987. "Moody's Versus Siegel's Interpretation of the Near-Death Experience: An Evaluation Based on Recent Research." *Anabiosis* 5: 67–82.

KÜBLER-ROSS, E. 1969. *On Death and Dying.* New York: Macmillan.

LABERGE, S. 1985. *Lucid Dreaming.* Los Angeles: J. P. Tarcher.

NOYES, R., and KLETTI, R. 1972. "The Experience of Dying from Falls." *Omega* 3: 45–52.

RICKARD, R., and KELLY, R. 1980. *Photographs of the Unknown.* London: New English Library.

RING, K. 1980. *Life at Death: A Scientific Investigation of the Near-Death Experience.* New York: Coward, McCann & Geoghegan.

ROGO, D. S. 1986. *Life After Death: The Case for Survival of Bodily Death.* Wellingborough, Eng.: The Aquarian Press.

————, and BAYLESS, R. 1979. *Phone Calls from the Dead.* Englewood Cliffs: Prentice-Hall.

SIEGEL, R. K. 1980. "The Psychology of Life After Death." *American Psychologist* 35: 911–31.

————, and HIRSCHMAN, A. E. 1984. "Hashish Near-Death Experiences." *Anabiosis* 4: 69–86.

SWEDENBORG, E. 1778. *A Treatise Concerning Heaven and Hell.* London: James Phillips.

TART, C. T. 1969. The 'High' Dream: A New State of Consciousness. In *Altered States of Consciousness,* ed. C. T. Tart, 169–74. New York: John Wiley & Sons.

WEINBERGER, J. 1977. "Apparatus Communication with Discarnate Persons." In *Future Science: Life Energies and the Physics of Paranormal Phenomena,* ed. J. White and S. Krippner, 465–86. Garden City: Doubleday.

ACKNOWLEDGMENTS

My thanks are first due the late Heinrich Klüver for the inspiration of his teachings. Portions of letters to and from Klüver are reprinted with permission of Henry Schwenk.

I am indebted to Bethany Muhl, who assisted with library research and provided many helpful and critical comments on the manuscript. I also want to thank Reid Boates, my literary agent, for his encouragement and advice throughout the writing.

For helpful discussions along the way, I thank the late Sidney Cohen, M.D.; Frank Ervin, M.D.; the late Henri Ey; Roland Fischer, Ph.D.; Allen Ginsberg; Eric Halgren, Ph.D.; John Hanley, M.D.; Ernest Hartmann, M.D.; Mardi J. Horowitz, M.D.; Oscar Janiger, M.D.; Murray E. Jarvik. M.D., Ph.D.; Joseph B. Juhasz, Ph.D.; Weston La Barre, Ph.D.; Martin H. Lebowitz, M.D.; John Lilly, M.D.; the late D. Scott Rogo; Theodore R. Sarbin, Ph.D.; C. Wage Savage, Ph.D.; Jan Silverton, M.D.; the late R. Gordon Wasson; Louis Jolyon West, M.D.; and Wallace D. Winters, M.D., Ph.D.

I extend my appreciation to the nurses, residents, and staff members at the UCLA Center for Health Sciences, who provided support services for many of the clinical cases. Some names and identifying or circumstantial details have been changed.

Some Yiddish words in chapter 13 are transliterated phonetically according to *A Dictionary of Yiddish Slang & Idioms* by Fred Kogos (Citadel Press, 1967) and *The Yiddish Dictionary Sourcebook* by Herman Galvin and Stan Tamarkin (Ktar Publishing House, Inc., 1986).

I wish to extend my gratitude and love to Jane, Katherine, Emily, and Christopher for the many ways in which they provided support for my writing.

1853